Visualize Complex Processes with Microsoft Visio

A guide to visually creating, communicating, and collaborating business processes efficiently

David J Parker

Šenaj Lelić

BIRMINGHAM—MUMBAI

Visualize Complex Processes with Microsoft Visio

Group Product Manager: Alok Dhuri
Publishing Product Manager: Akshay Dani
Senior Editor: Nithya Sadanandan
Technical Editor: Jubit Pincy
Copy Editor: Safis Editing
Project Coordinator: Deeksha Thakkar
Proofreader: Safis Editing
Indexer: Subalakshmi Govindhan
Production Designer: Ponraj Dhandapani
Developer Relations Marketing Executive: Deepak Kumar and Mayank Singh
Business Development Executive: Puneet Kaur

First published: May 2023

Production reference: 1270423

Published by Packt Publishing Ltd.
Livery Place
35 Livery Street
Birmingham
B3 2PB, UK.

ISBN 978-1-83763-192-6

www.packtpub.com

To my wife, Beena, for letting me explore my passion for data visualization, to the Visio team for providing the paint brush and canvas; and to my fellow Visio MVPs over the years (John Goldsmith, Chris Roth, Michel Laplane, Scott Helmers, and my co-author Šenaj Lelić) for continuing to inspire me, thank you.

-David J Parker

To the fabulous Visio product team, Prateek Sharma, Ankur Vashishta, Karan Malik and all the others who supported me and made the product what it is today. Also, to my co-MVPs and especially my long-term friend and co-MVP, David Parker, who is with me on this Visio-journey from the beginning of time.

-Šenaj Lelić

Contributors

About the authors

David J Parker is an experienced data-visualizer who loves to create stunning and informative graphics with Visio. He has a rich background in architecture and database design, which gives him an edge in understanding complex data and presenting it in a clear and engaging way. He has been using Visio since the mid-90s, and has become an expert in linking it to external data sources. He runs his own company, bVisual.net, where he creates Visio-based solutions for clients worldwide. He also shares his knowledge and passion for Visio through his blog, books, and presentations. He has been a Microsoft MVP for many years, and a respected member of the Visio community. David and wife have two grown up kids, and lives in Reading, UK.

We want to thank John Marshall for checking each chapter, and the technical reviewers, Vijay Shekhar Shukla and Barry Allyn. We would also like to thank the editors and the team at Packt for their help and support throughout the process.

Šenaj Lelić has worked in IT since 1991. He and studied economy at the university of Munich (special studies: strategic management and software-based Business Process management). Starting with BORLAND, he went on to work with Visio Corporation in 1996. Since then, he has worked on many visualization solutions for different customers. When Visio was acquired by Microsoft in 2000 his focus shifted to Microsoft.NET and SharePoint, extending to support technologies such as SQL Server and Microsoft Teams.

One consistent activity has been the creation and planning/architecture of BPM solutions and technologies - always using Visio as the graphical engine, but extending with SQL Server and SharePoint to create powerful but easy to use BPM solutions.

About the reviewers

Vijay Shukla has been a practicing IT Business Analyst for the last 2 decades. He has started his career with **NTT Data FA Insurance Systems** (**NDFS**) in the Insurance vertical in Tokyo, Japan. He has also worked with HCL Perot systems (now part of Dell) in the same role. He later worked as Product Manager in the ed-tech space for a successful higher education, assessment, and e-learning solution in India. Since last 10 years Vijay has been working as a Director, Principal Consultant and Trainer at QBI Institute (www.qbi.in) where he has trained many batches professionals in Business Analysis, Product Management and Scrum. etc. Vijay has been a corporate trainer and consultant to reputable companies including Xceedance, S&P IHS Markit, Reliance Jio, and Net Prophets. Vijay has been a speaker, coach, and a community participant for multiple global products including MS Visio, JIRA, Balsamiq, and Bizagi Business Modeller. An engineer from IIT Roorkee (1994) and Masters in Management from IIT Bombay (1997), Vijay got introduced to MS Visio in his first job assignment in 1997. He remains a Visio learner, enthusiast, trainer, and consultant since then. Microsoft has called Vijay a 'trainer extraordinaire' in Visio.

Vijay lives in Noida (NCR-Delhi), India, he spends his free time learning Japanese language and Japanese culture. Vijay can be reached at director@qbi.in.

Barry Allyn has worked as a professional software engineer for over 30 years, specializing in Windows client application architecture, user interface design, graphics, and performance. He graduated from Penn State University in 1992 with a computer science and math degree. Barry is currently a Principal Architect on the Microsoft Office Security team. He joined Microsoft through the Visio acquisition, where he thoroughly enjoyed working on the Visio diagramming engine, performance, and various UI features. Later, he spent time on the Visual C++, Office User Experience, Excel Charting, and Office Performance teams.

Table of Contents

3

Learning to Manually Create Process Flow Diagrams   43

4

Using Visio for Desktop with BPMN   79

5

Utilizing Data Sources to Create and Enrich Business Process Diagrams   109

6

Learn How to Diagram Efficiently   133

7

Preparing Diagrams for Presentation and Collaboration   155

8

Securing and Providing Access to Diagrams   179

9

Integrating Visio with Other Microsoft Apps   205

10

Customizing Master Shapes and Templates   233

11

Improving the Provided Flowchart Shapes   251

Preface

Every business has process flows, but not all of them are fully described or verified for accuracy with each stakeholder. This not only presents a risk for business continuity, but also removes the ability to make insightful improvements. To make these complex interactions easy to grasp, it's important to describe these processes visually using symbology that everybody understands. Different parts of these flows should be collaboratively developed and stored securely as commercial collateral.

Visualize Complex Processes with Microsoft Visio helps you understand why it is crucial to use a common, systematic approach to document the steps needed to meet each business requirement. This book explores the various process flow templates available in each edition of Microsoft Visio, including BPMN. It also shows you how to use them effectively with the help of tips, techniques, and examples to reduce the time required for creating them, as well as how you can improve their integration and presentation.

By the end of this book, you'll have mastered the skills needed to create data-integrated business flowcharts with Microsoft Visio, learned how to effectively use these diagrams collaboratively yet securely, and understood how to integrate them with other M365 apps, including Excel, Word, PowerPoint, and Power Automate.

Who this book is for

If you're a manager, analyst, or designer of business processes, then this book will help you create professional process diagrams effectively and consistently to improve the accuracy of communication and facilitate impactful insights. It is also useful for beginners or power users who are seeking tips and techniques to capture process flows from context and customize diagrams to meet academic as well as corporate standards.

What this book covers

Chapter 1, Choosing the Correct Business Process Diagram Type, describes four basic process flowchart diagram types that are required to start analyzing an organization's business processes, from an overview to a detailed level, and uses them to introduce the features and capabilities of the web and desktop editions of Microsoft Visio

Chapter 2, Choosing the Best Visio Edition for Our Needs, covers which editions can be used to create the four most common types of business process diagrams and provide an explanation of the differences between the Visio editions and their user interfaces.

Chapter 3, Learning to Manually Create Process Flow Diagrams, provides an understanding of adding more shapes and connecting shapes together, and labeling them. You will also learn about special container shapes, such as swimlanes, and how we can link flowcharts across multiple pages.

Chapter 4, Using Visio for Desktop with BPMN, focuses on one specific diagram type and template – the BPMN template. Here, you will learn how to not only use the BPMN template and stencil, but also the very specifics of how to use the more hidden features, allowing you to create full BPMN 2.0-compliant diagrams.

Chapter 5, Utilizing Data Sources to Create and Enrich Business Process Diagrams, will review the no-code techniques available to us. Some business process steps may be stored within a data source, such as Microsoft Excel. Visio can be used to create process diagrams automatically from such data and can even keep the data and diagram steps and relationships synchronised..

Chapter 6, Learn How to Diagram Efficiently, will go through some skills to make our lives easier. You will learn how to make some useful hidden commands visible and some shortcut keys and keys combined with mouse actions that can speed up diagramming. You will also learn how to select a group of shapes and align or distribute them.

Chapter 7, Preparing Diagrams for Presentation and Collaboration, covers how to control the navigation, dictated text and color contrast for accessibility, and consider how to present the diagrams in multiple languages.

Chapter 8, Securing and Providing Access to Diagrams, covers how to make Visio diagrams available to others through Microsoft SharePoint, Microsoft OneDrive, and Microsoft Teams, while ensuring that the file and content are kept safe.

Chapter 9, Integrating Visio with Other Microsoft Apps, covers various features that helps to integrate Vision with other Microsoft apps such as Excel, One Drive and so on and teaches to use them effectively.

Chapter 10, Customizing Master Shapes and Templates, introduces the basics of custom shapes. The concepts are easy to comprehend for anyone who has dabbled with cell formulas in Excel.

Chapter 11, Improving the Provided Flowchart Shapes, covers how to display both the function and phase of shapes within cross-functional flowcharts and the label of the built-in container shapes.

To get the most out of this book

This book is about using Visio for the web and Visio for the Windows desktop. A Visio Plan 2 license will cover every aspect of the content, but other Visio users will find relevant content in some chapters.

Software/hardware covered in the book	Operating system requirements
Microsoft 365 (optional)	Any
Microsoft Visio for the Web (some chapters)	Any
Microsoft Visio for the Desktop (every chapter)	Windows
Microsoft Teams (optional)	Any

Visio for the web is evolving quickly, so some content and screenshots may differ from what is available at the time of reading.

If you are using the digital version of this book, we advise you to type the code yourself or access the code from the book's GitHub repository (a link is available in the next section). Doing so will help you avoid any potential errors related to the copying and pasting of code.

For those readers who wish to learn more about customizing Visio, and writing code to automate processes, there are several other Visio books available by David Parker from Packt at `https://subscription.packtpub.com/search?query=David+Parker+Visio`.

Download the example code files

You can download the example code files for this book from GitHub at `https://github.com/PacktPublishing/Visualize-complex-processes-with-Microsoft-Visio`. If there's an update to the code, it will be updated in the GitHub repository.

We also have other code bundles from our rich catalog of books and videos available at `https://github.com/PacktPublishing/`. Check them out!

Download the color images

We also provide a PDF file that has color images of the screenshots and diagrams used in this book. You can download it here: `https://packt.link/vVvaH`.

Conventions used

There are a number of text conventions used throughout this book.

`Code in text`: Indicates code words in text, database table names, folder names, filenames, file extensions, pathnames, dummy URLs, user input, and Twitter handles. Here is an example: "Note that Visio desktop has a **My Shapes** category that can include any stencils that we add to the `<Documents>/My Shapes` folder locally."

Bold: Indicates a new term, an important word, or words that you see onscreen. For instance, words in menus or dialog boxes appear in **bold**. Here is an example: "All line pattern values are numbers that color by Owner:assigningcan be read from the **Dash type** drop-down menu on the **Format Shape** panel."

> **Tips or important notes**
> Appear like this.

Get in touch

Feedback from our readers is always welcome.

General feedback: If you have questions about any aspect of this book, email us at `customercare@packtpub.com` and mention the book title in the subject of your message.

Errata: Although we have taken every care to ensure the accuracy of our content, mistakes do happen. If you have found a mistake in this book, we would be grateful if you would report this to us. Please visit `www.packtpub.com/support/errata` and fill in the form.

Piracy: If you come across any illegal copies of our works in any form on the internet, we would be grateful if you would provide us with the location address or website name. Please contact us at `copyright@packt.com` with a link to the material.

If you are interested in becoming an author: If there is a topic that you have expertise in and you are interested in either writing or contributing to a book, please visit `authors.packtpub.com`.

Share Your Thoughts

Once you've read *Visualize complex processes with Microsoft Visio*, we'd love to hear your thoughts! Scan the QR code below to go straight to the Amazon review page for this book and share your feedback.

https://packt.link/r/1837631921

Your review is important to us and the tech community and will help us make sure we're delivering excellent quality content.

Download a free PDF copy of this book

Thanks for purchasing this book!

Do you like to read on the go but are unable to carry your print books everywhere?

Is your eBook purchase not compatible with the device of your choice?

Don't worry, now with every Packt book you get a DRM-free PDF version of that book at no cost.

Read anywhere, any place, on any device. Search, copy, and paste code from your favorite technical books directly into your application.

The perks don't stop there, you can get exclusive access to discounts, newsletters, and great free content in your inbox daily

Follow these simple steps to get the benefits:

1. Scan the QR code or visit the link below

https://packt.link/free-ebook/9781837631926

2. Submit your proof of purchase

3. That's it! We'll send your free PDF and other benefits to your email directly

1
Choosing the Correct Business Process Diagram Type

It is critical for a business that its processes are clearly understood by all of those involved for each step to run smoothly. Too many processes are not documented properly, and this presents a risk to business continuity. Writing down each step can be long and laborious, and it can still fail to describe the flow of a process and the interaction between different stakeholders or departments. However, a clear diagram can show what the process steps are, who is responsible, when a decision has to be made, and how one process relates to another.

These flow diagrams represent a model of an organization's processes to achieve a desired outcome and demonstrate how various stakeholders, or actors, interact with each other along the way.

It is essential that some diagramming and symbology standard is adopted; otherwise, there are bound to be misunderstandings and ambiguity when interpreting these diagrams. Diagrams should be validated by all of the stakeholders involved in each part of every process and kept accurate and up to date. They need to be accessible to all those that need to see them, collaborate on them, and comment on them.

Microsoft Visio has been the most popular flowchart diagramming application since the early 1990s and has recently added Visio web editions to its Windows desktop editions. This has vastly increased the number of Visio users worldwide, and each edition has something to offer to create process flowcharts, but some editions offer more than others. Visio is a smart vector data-diagramming application with some powerful features for flowcharting, both manually and automatically.

This chapter describes four basic process flowchart diagram types that are required to start analyzing an organization's business processes, from an overview to a detailed level, and uses them to introduce the features and capabilities of the web and desktop editions of **Microsoft Visio**.

In this chapter, we will cover the following topics:

- Setting the scope with *context diagrams*
- Determining who and what with a *functional flow diagram*
- Capturing the interactions with a *cross-functional flow diagram*
- Defining the detail with a *flowchart diagram*

Technical requirements

These are the Microsoft apps that are utilized in this chapter, and we should have access to at least one of the Visio subscriptions, but Visio Plan 2 subscribers will be able to use all of the features described:

- **Teams** – desktop or web app
- **Visio Reading View** – web-only app
- **Visio in Microsoft 365** – web-only app
- **Visio Plan 1** – web-only subscription app
- **Visio Plan 2** – desktop and web subscription apps
- **Visio Professional 20xx** – Windows one-time purchase only
- **Visio Standard 20xx** – Windows one-time purchase only

The term *Visio for Web* is often used to describe the online Visio edition for Visio Plan 1 and Visio Plan 2 license holders. Visio in Microsoft 365 is also online, so the terms online Visio or Visio web editions are used interchangeably throughout this book.

Setting the scope with context diagrams

A **context diagram** sets a helicopter view of an organization with the external entities and actors involved in a process. It should not be too complex but provide the main interactions between the actors and the organization. It is normal for the central organization to be represented by a circle, surrounded by the external actors as rectangles, but often, the simple circles and rectangles are replaced by suitable symbols. The main interactions are merely labels on arrows depicting the direction of flow. Multiple interactions can be labeled on each arrow, rather than extra arrows being added.

For example, the following diagram shows the context of this book:

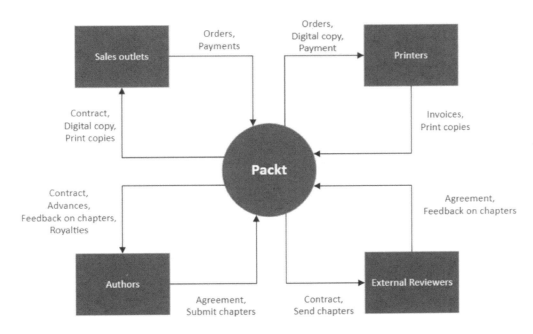

Figure 1.1 – A typical context diagram

This diagram type is often created during a workshop, which is increasingly taking the form of a hybrid meeting, so the ability of Visio to co-author and collaborate in **Microsoft Teams** is a great advantage, but Visio web editions can all collaborate without Teams too.

In Visio, connectors, such as the directional arrows in the preceding example, can be glued to shapes at either end. They can be glued to a specific connection point on the shape, where it will remain fixed, or just to the shape only, which allows it to re-route itself dynamically. Automatic routing of connectors can be a great time-saver, and the appearance of many connectors in Visio can be switched between right-angular, curved, and straight.

Another tip is that all Visio shapes can be supplemented with text because they have an integrated text block, so it is not necessary to create a separate one, and this text moves with its shape or connector.

We will learn some techniques to efficiently create these diagrams in the next chapter, but first, we need to know how to start creating diagrams from each Visio interface.

Starting a context diagram in Microsoft Teams

The simplest way to create a context diagram in **Microsoft Teams** is as follows:

1. Navigate to the required **Teams** channel.

2. Select the **Files** tab.

3. Select **Visio drawing** from the **New** drop-down menu:

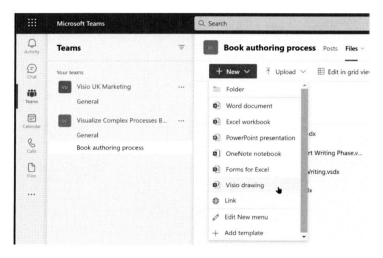

Figure 1.2 – Starting a new Visio drawing in Teams

4. We will then be prompted to enter the name of the drawing.

Figure 1.3 – Naming a new Visio drawing in Teams

5. A blank **Visio** drawing will then open with two stencils, **Basic Shapes** and **Arrow Shapes**, ready for us to drag and drop master shapes from the stencil onto the blank page.

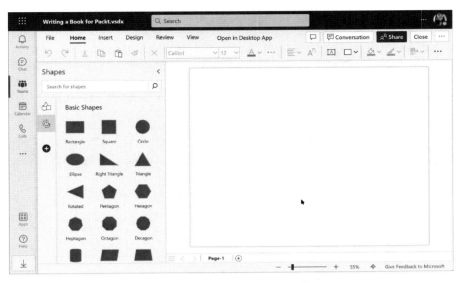

Figure 1.4 – A new Visio drawing in Teams

These stencils contain all of the shapes and connectors that are required to draw a context diagram in Visio. Any of the shapes displayed in the stencils window, called *master shapes*, such as **Ellipse**, can be simply dragged from the stencil onto the page, and then positioned, labeled, resized, rotated, and formatted to suit. We will go through these steps in the next few chapters.

The Visio document is automatically saved back into the **Teams** channel | **Files** tab, which you can return to by clicking on the **Teams** icon on the left sidebar. The Visio document can be opened by all members of the **Teams** channel.

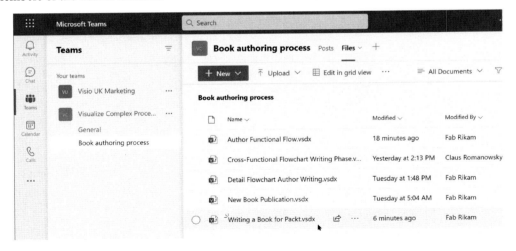

Figure 1.5 – A Visio document in Teams

Opening a Visio document in Microsoft Teams

This Visio document is immediately available to all members of the **Teams** channel, and if they then click on the document in the **Files** tab, they will open the Visio document in reading view mode. The user will have the **Edit in Teams** or **Open in Browser** options from the **Edit Diagram** drop-down menu. The **Open in Desktop App** option will only be enabled if a desktop edition of Visio is installed on the active Windows device.

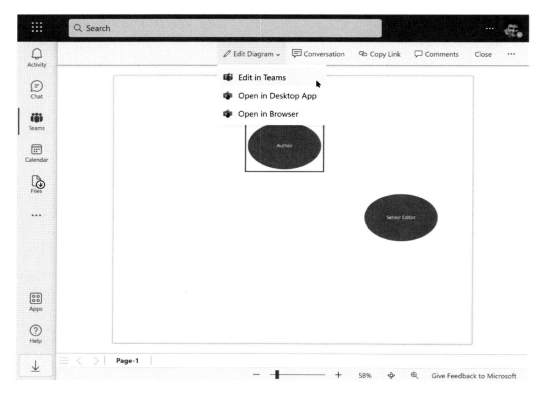

Figure 1.6 – Opening a Visio document in Teams

If the **Edit in Teams** option is chosen, then the diagram is open in edit mode, and any co-authors who have the document open in this mode are shown in the header.

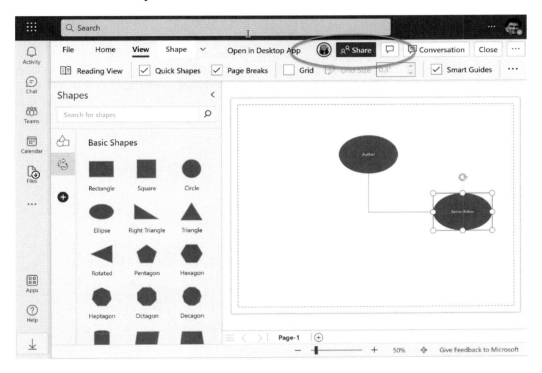

Figure 1.7 – Editing a Visio document in Teams

We will go through the co-authoring and collaborating features in *Chapter 8*.

> **Important note**
>
> The reading view of a Visio document can display any Visio files that are stored in Teams, **SharePoint Online**, or **OneDrive**. This is true for legacy Visio files too, which were saved in an older format with a `.vsd` extension (the current Visio file format has a `.vsdx` or `.vsdm` extension). This viewer has a read-only programming interface that can be utilized by Teams and SharePoint app developers.

Now that we have identified the main entities and their interactions in the overall context, we can move on to a particular phase of the process to capture the relationships between the different actors throughout the steps.

Determining who and what with a functional flow diagram

This phase examines each of the interactions between the external actors, such as the author, and simply shows what happens between the external and internal actors during the logical flows labeled in the *context diagram*. This should be validated by the stakeholders before proceeding to a more detailed analysis of the interactions between all of the actors. In this example, the chapters for this book pass through the **preliminary draft** between the **author** and **senior editor**, and then the **final draft** stage through the **project coordinator** and **technical reviewers**. The latter phase is analyzed in the following diagram:

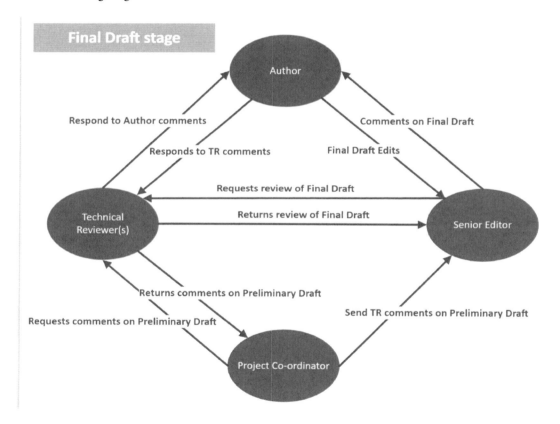

Figure 1.8 – A typical functional flow diagram

Each actor is a labeled ellipse, and the interactions are directional, labeled arrows. Multiple actions between the same actors, in the same direction, can be added to the label of a single arrow, rather than adding more arrows.

Again, this can easily be drawn and labeled during a hybrid workshop using Microsoft Teams or Visio online, and it can also be co-authored and collaborated on.

Starting a functional flow diagram in Visio for Web

A *functional flow diagram* can be created within Microsoft Teams; however, we can also start a **Visio** diagram from Office.com:

1. Click the **Apps** button from the sidebar if **Visio** is not shown there; if it is still not visible, click the **All apps** button.
2. Click the **Visio** button to open Visio in the same frame.
3. Alternatively, right-click the **Visio** button and select **Open in new tab**.

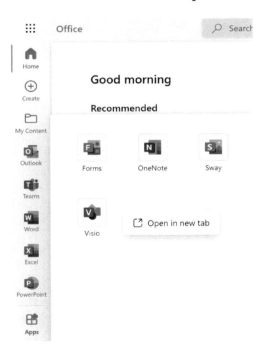

Figure 1.9 – Creating a Visio document from Office.com

We will then be presented with a choice of templates to create a diagram with, or the option to open previously created **Visio** documents. The functional flow diagram type only requires the new blank drawing to be clicked:

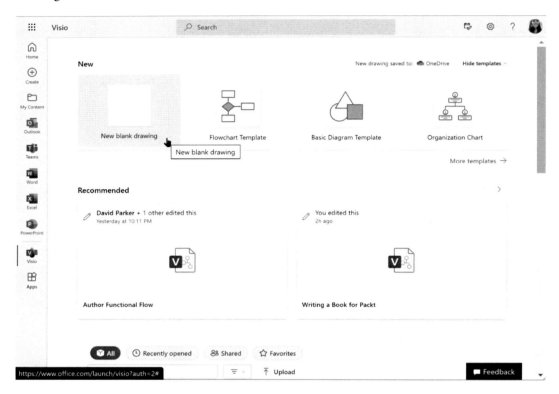

Figure 1.10 – Creating a new blank drawing in Visio online

The Visio online editor will then open, and the document will be automatically assigned a temporary name and saved automatically to **OneDrive for Business**. It is good practice to rename this document immediately by clicking on the document name in the header – in this case, Drawing5.

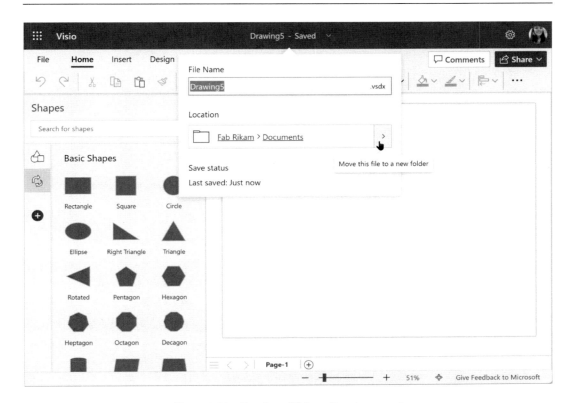

Figure 1.11 – Naming a Visio online document

Note that this document will be automatically saved to the default location in OneDrive unless we change the location by clicking the arrow button on the right of the **Location** editing area. This will allow us to move the document to another folder in My files or SharePoint, or to select a Teams channel, as shown here:

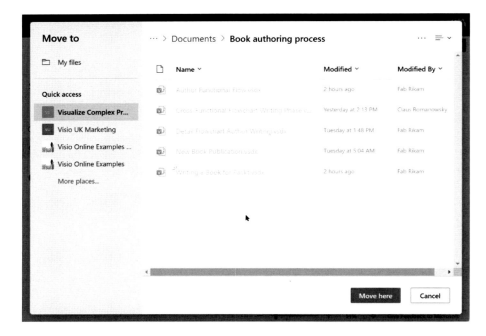

Figure 1.12 – Naming a Visio for web document

The Visio document will then be available to all members of the Teams channel. If the document is left in OneDrive, then it can be shared with others, but it will be stored in a personal area, rather than an organization's collaborative area, and could be lost if an individual leaves the organization.

We will go through the different process flow templates offered in each edition of Visio later, in the *Comparing templates and features in Visio editions* section in *Chapter 2*.

Next, we will analyze the sequence of process steps and interactions across the *final draft stage*.

Capturing interactions with a cross-functional diagram

Once the relationships between the actors of a process are agreed to, then it is time to define exactly what happens between them, and when. This is best depicted in a **cross-functional flowchart diagram**, which is sometimes called a **swimlane diagram**. In this type of diagram, the actors, or organizational teams, are shown as horizontal or vertical bands, and the steps that must be done are linked together in the sequence that they follow. The following example shows the process steps and flow of responsibility for actions, from the start to the end, of the *final draft stage* of this book.

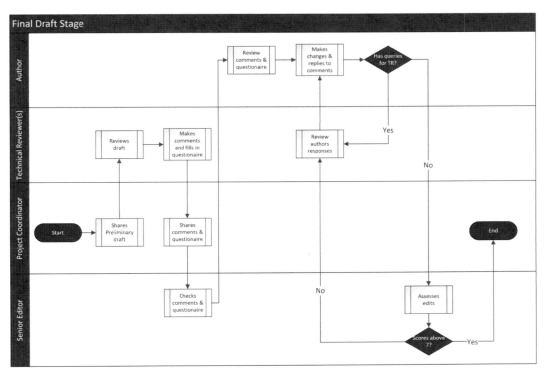

Figure 1.13 – An example of a cross-functional flowchart diagram

In the preceding example, each step has been shown as a sub-process to indicate that there is a further breakdown of each step in another diagram. Other cross-functional flowcharts could be a mixture of process and sub-process shapes.

Flowcharts should not be too large that they are difficult to understand or follow, but they should define clearly the steps required between the start and end of the process phase.

There are several diagram templates in Visio that can be used to create a cross-functional flowchart. This chapter deals with perhaps the simplest form, but we will also be introduced to the *business process modeling notation* alternative in *Chapter 4*.

> **Important note**
>
> The cross-functional flowchart is one of the diagram types that cannot be created from templates available for Visio in Microsoft 365 users. Moreover, it cannot be edited by Visio in Microsoft 365 users either.

This template opens the **Basic Flowchart Shapes** and the **Cross-Functional Flowchart Shapes** stencils (see *Figure 1.16* and *Figure 1.17*), which should provide all of the shapes we need to capture the sequential flows and interactions across the process. The basic guidelines for their use are as follows.

Starting and ending with rounded terminator shapes

There should be a specific entry point, a start, and maybe one or more endpoints. These are normally shown as circles or rounded rectangles (as shown in *Figure 1.13*). Each of the flows should be traceable from start to finish, by following the direction of the arrow-headed connectors; this is normally from left to right/top to bottom, but not necessarily so.

Defining process steps with rectangular shapes

Each of the steps, which are normally shown as rectangles, which may have rounded corners, should be labeled with the action that happens. In the preceding example, *Figure 1.13*, these process steps are shown as rectangles with extra vertical lines on the left and right. This denotes a process that contains more than one process and should be detailed on another diagram, which could be another page in the same document. They are referred to as **sub-processes**, and the desktop apps, **Visio Plan 2** and **Visio Professional**, have some specific capabilities to create new ones on another page or link to an existing one on another page or document. We will explore this more in *Chapter 3*.

Highlighting decisions with diamond shapes

There are parts of the process that require a decision to be made, and the answer will determine the flow of the process. For example, each chapter needs to be scored higher than 7 out of 10 before it is accepted as complete, so a diamond shape is labeled as a question that elicits a *yes* or *no* response, and the flows out of this shape should be clearly labeled so.

Labeling swimlanes for each actor

There should be a separate swimlane for each actor, and the swimlane should only contain steps performed by the labeled actor.

> **Important note**
>
> **Visio Professional** and **Visio Plan 2** can check whether flowcharts are well-formed with a feature called **validation rules**, which is found on the **Process** tab in the **Diagram Validation** group.

Starting a cross-functional diagram in desktop Visio Plan 2

A *cross-functional flowchart diagram* can also be created by a Visio online subscriber; however, I will use desktop Visio in this example to create a diagram from a template:

1. Open desktop Visio.
2. Click the **More templates** button, or the **New** button if it is not a recent template.
3. Click the **Cross-Functional Flowchart** button.

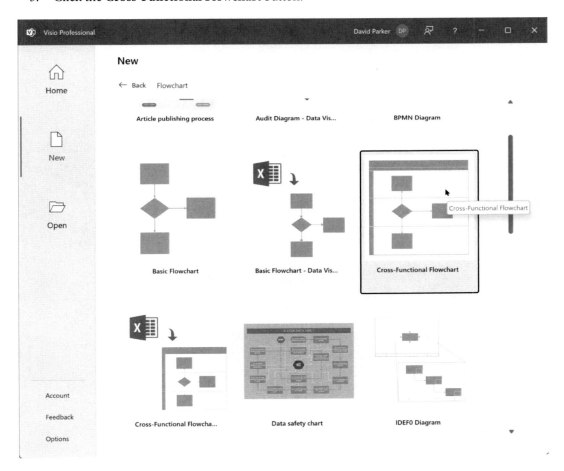

Figure 1.14 – Selecting a cross-functional flowchart template in desktop Visio

4. Ensure that the blank diagram is selected.
5. Click the **Create** button.

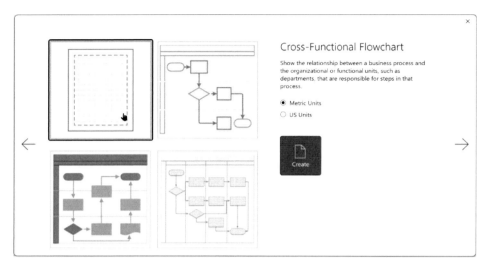

Figure 1.15 – Starting a blank cross-functional flowchart in desktop Visio

Visio will then open a cross-functional diagram with two empty swimlanes, and two stencils open on the left-hand side. The active one in *Figure 1.16* is **Cross-Functional Flowchart Shapes**, and the second is the **Basic Flowchart Shapes** stencil.

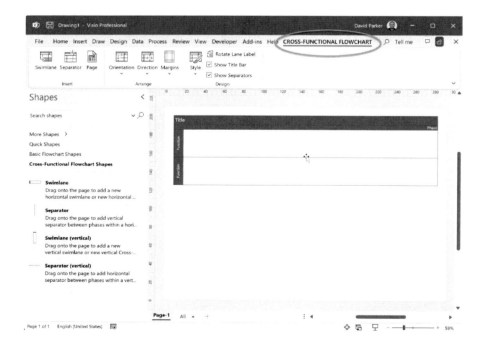

Figure 1.16 – A blank cross-functional flowchart in desktop Visio

Note that there is an extra ribbon tab on the top next to **Help**, **CROSS-FUNCTIONAL FLOWCHART**, which appears when this type of document is open. This indicates that there are some extra, specific features available for this diagram type.

The default diagram also has a *title bar*, which can be hidden by unticking the **Show Title Bar** checkbox under **CROSS-FUNCTIONAL FLOWCHART | Design**.

There is also a single **Separator** shape, labeled **Phase**, which can also be hidden with **Design | Show Separators**. More **Separator** shapes can be added to the diagram by dragging and dropping from the stencil. These separators are fixed at right angles to the swimlanes and should be labeled with the phase or stage name.

> **Important note**
>
> You may have noticed that there is a second template labeled **Cross-Functional Flowchart** in the new choices in desktop Visio Plan 2, but with an **Excel** symbol in the top-left corner. In fact, there are several templates with the **Excel** icon, and they use a feature called **Data Visualizer** that allows a Visio flowchart diagram and an Excel table to synchronize. This will be explained in *Chapter 5*.

Starting a cross-functional diagram in Visio Plan 1

The same type of diagram can be created and edited in Visio Plan 1, although it currently has slightly fewer options available in the **Cross Functional Flowchart** tab.

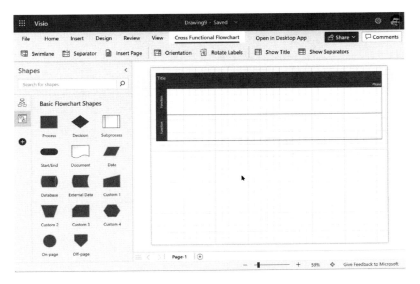

Figure 1.17 – A blank cross-functional flowchart in Visio for the web

Specifically, it does not have the following capabilities:

- Switching the flow direction with the **Arrange | Direction** menu

- Changing the margin size with the **Arrange | Margins** menu

- Changing the title and swimlane appearance with the **Design | Style** menu

If we want to use these features, then the diagram can be opened in Visio Plan 2, edited, saved, and still be editable by a Visio Plan 1 user.

Saving a desktop Visio document to a Teams channel

When we create a new Visio document in desktop Visio, it will not automatically save the document anywhere, so we will need to select **File | Save As**, then **SharePoint Sites**, and then navigate to our Microsoft Teams channel.

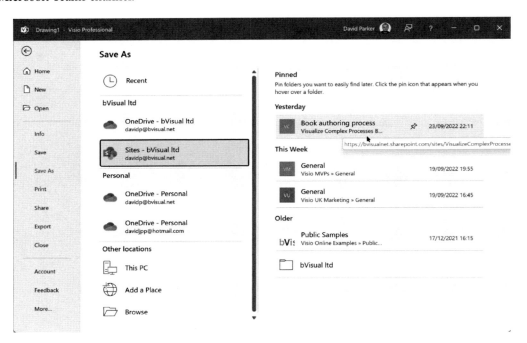

Figure 1.18 – Saving a document from desktop Visio

This is not currently as simple as it should be, so we will return to the Microsoft Teams channel and click on the **Files** tab, and click either **Add a shortcut to OneDrive** or **Open in SharePoint** from the three-dots button menu.

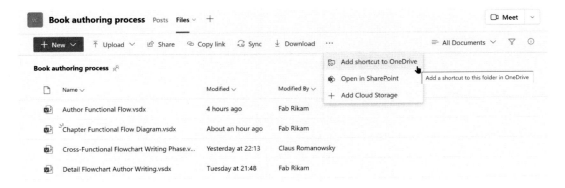

Figure 1.19 – Getting the network location of a Microsoft Teams channel

If we open the SharePoint site, then copy the address; however, we will need to delete all the text after `Shared%20Documents` before pasting it into File Explorer back in desktop Visio. We will then need to select the channel to be in the correct folder.

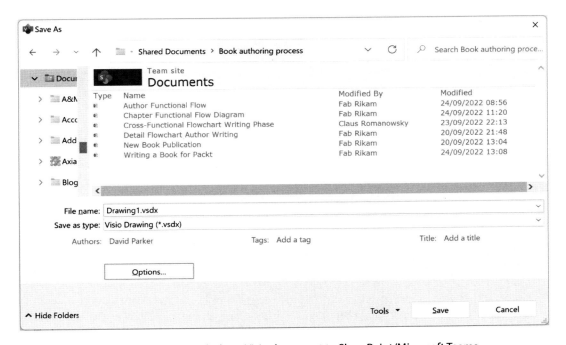

Figure 1.20 – Saving a desktop Visio document to SharePoint/Microsoft Teams

We can also go to **File | Options | Save** and enable the setting for **Save AutoRecover information every xx minutes** for desktop Visio so that we do not lose our work if something goes wrong.

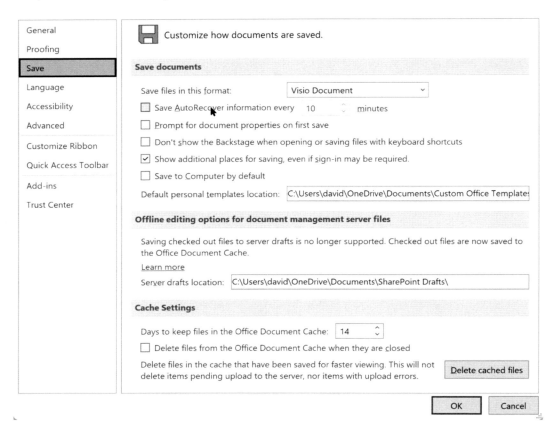

Figure 1.21 – Setting the time for auto-recovery in desktop Visio

Now that we have defined the sequential interactions between the different actors across the process flow, we can drill down to the steps taken by a single actor for one of those processes.

Defining the detail with a flowchart diagram

Each of the process steps in the cross-functional flowchart in the previous section (see *Figure 1.13*) had subprocesses within them. Some of these subprocesses may involve interaction with other actors, but some do not. For example, the writing of this chapter does not involve others until it is ready for the senior editor to review. There are many subprocesses within the chapter writing process, such as research and testing, and a specific specification for inserted images must be followed. So, any process that does not involve more than one actor can be defined with a *flowchart diagram*.

A flowchart diagram can be created by any of the Visio editions, either by using the **Basic Flowchart** template or by starting with a blank diagram and opening the **Basic Flowchart Shapes** stencil.

The following example explains the process required for an author to insert an image into the preliminary draft chapter. It uses only the *Start/End*, *Process*, and *Decision* shapes, sequentially linked together with directional arrow lines, which is actually the *Dynamic connector* shape. All of the flowchart shapes are uniquely labeled, and the connectors out from the *Decision* shapes are labeled to indicate the **Yes** or **No** direction of flow.

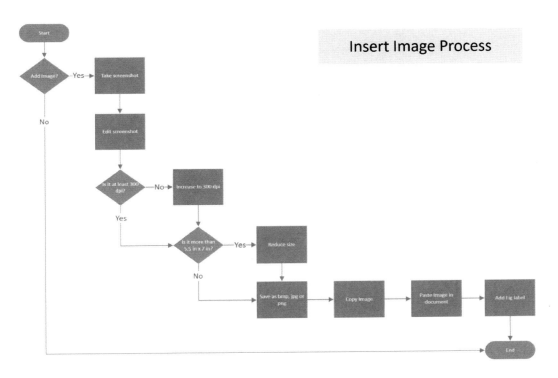

Figure 1.22 – A detailed flowchart diagram example

Knowing when to use the flowchart shapes

The flowchart diagram uses the same shapes as those in the cross-functional flowchart diagrams, except for the swimlane and separator ones, because it is important to have consistency within an organization. In this case, I am using those on the **Basic Flowchart Shapes** stencil; however, I rarely use them in order to avoid adding complexity.

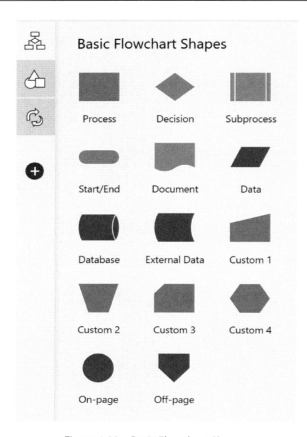

Figure 1.23 – Basic Flowchart Shapes

A **Subprocess** shape should be used to indicate that there is another page with a more detailed breakdown of that particular process. There is a section, *Creating subprocesses*, in *Chapter 6*, but we can add a hyperlink to this shape after we have created the page with that subprocess on it.

If a process interacts with a **Document**, **Data**, **Database**, or **External Data** shape, then certainly use these shapes with suitable directional arrows.

Use the **Custom** numbered shapes if we want the shape to be different from some process or artifact that does not fit with the other shapes.

The **On-page** shape, labeled as **On-page reference** in desktop Visio, is simply used with a label to visually link two areas of a diagram together, without the need for a connecting arrow.

The **Off-page** shape warrants a fuller description in the next section.

Using the Off-page (reference) shape

The **Off-page** shape, labeled as **Off-page reference** in desktop Visio, is used to indicate that there is a hyperlink to another page or document. In Visio online, this hyperlink must be added manually.

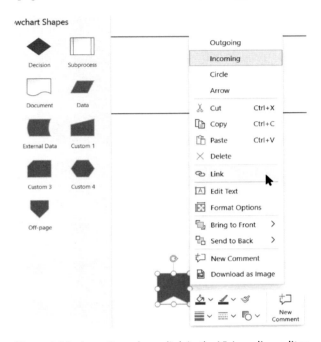

Figure 1.24 – Inserting a hyperlink in the Visio online editor

In fact, we can add a hyperlink to any shape in the online edition of Visio using the right-click menu **Link** command.

Figure 1.25 – Inserting a hyperlink in Visio for web

However, the hyperlink dialog in desktop Visio is a little different because it allows multiple hyperlinks per shape. These hyperlinks can be useful to open supporting documentation for a particular step in a process, or for emailing someone. The following screenshot shows the **Hyperlinks** dialog that can be opened from **Insert** | **Links** | **Link** (or *Ctrl + K*).

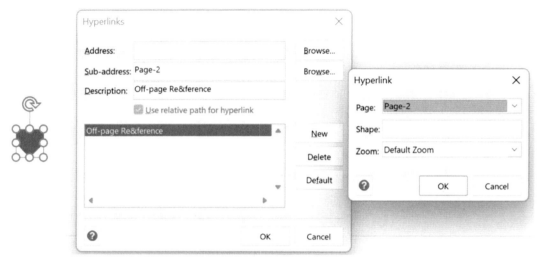

Figure 1.26 – Inserting a hyperlink in Visio for desktop

Note that the **Address** field can contain an internet protocol address, such as `https://` or even `mailto:`, but it should be left blank if the **Sub-address** field contains the name of a page within the same Visio document. The **Description** field is the display name of the hyperlink.

Also, the Off-page reference shape behaves differently when dropped onto a page in the desktop edition, because it runs an add-on that displays a dialog to create a twinned copy with hyperlinks pointing back to each other.

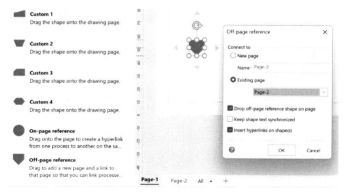

Figure 1.27 – The Off-page reference add-on dialog

In fact, this add-on also adds a double-click action to the shapes in the desktop edition, which will automatically turn to the target page. Add-ons do not run in the online editions of Visio, so double-clicking the same shape on the web will just enter text edit mode, if you are not in reading view mode. We will also learn a little more about customizing this shape in the last chapter of this book, *Improving the Provided Process Shapes*.

Summary

In this chapter, we have seen how we can drill down from a broad overview of the context of a process, through the steps involving each stakeholder, and down to a detailed flowchart. We have also learned that we can manually create and edit most key types of business process diagrams with any of the Visio editions, apart from cross-functional flowcharts, which can only be created and edited in the paid-for editions of Visio, so not Visio in Microsoft 365.

In the next chapter, we will learn about the key differences between the features and capabilities of the different editions of Visio so that we can be sure we are using the right edition for our particular needs.

2
Choosing the Best Visio Edition for Our Needs

Microsoft Visio is the most popular business diagramming application when coupled with **Microsoft Teams** and **SharePoint**. It provides organizations with a familiar toolset that can create process diagrams to several visual standards that can be easily created, co-authored, collaborated with, commented on, and yet be securely stored with suitably assigned access permissions.

Meetings or workshops are often required to analyze and document processes, and now that many of these meetings are hybrid gatherings, it is important to use an application within Microsoft Teams that allows both physical and virtual attendees to participate.

All business users of **Microsoft 365** now have Visio in Microsoft 365 included, and this provides everyone with an entry-level professional diagramming application. There are also subscription plans and one-time purchase licenses for Microsoft Visio available for the web and for desktop users who need more diagram types and functionality. Each edition has its own list of features and capabilities, which can become confusing. This chapter demystifies those differences and provides the knowledge to select the right edition for our specific needs and the type of diagram required.

> **Important note**
> Business process analysts are more likely to need Visio Plan 2, or at least Visio Professional, but others may be happy to use Visio in Microsoft 365 for occasional diagramming, or Visio Plan 1 for creating basic flowcharts.

All editions of Microsoft Visio include basic flowchart diagram types, whereas cross-functional (swimlane) diagrams can only be created with a subscription and one-time purchase editions. We will learn which editions can be used to create the four most common types of business process diagrams and provide an explanation of the differences between the Visio editions and their user interfaces:

- Understanding the different Visio editions
- Getting to know the Visio user interface

Technical requirements

These are the Microsoft apps that are utilized in this chapter, and we should have access to at least one of the Visio edition subscriptions, but Visio Plan 2 subscribers will be able to use all of the features described:

- **Teams**: The desktop or web app

- **Visio Reading View**: The web-only app

- **Visio in Microsoft 365**: The web-only app (not in personal editions of Microsoft 365)

- **Visio Plan 1**: The web-only subscription app

- **Visio Plan 2**: The desktop and web subscription apps

- **Visio Professional 20xx**: Windows one-time purchase only

- **Visio Standard 20xx**: Windows one-time purchase only

Understanding the different Microsoft Visio editions

Every Microsoft 365 business user (*A, E,* and *F* plans) gets Visio in Microsoft 365 for free, providing easy access to 11 diagram templates and a blank diagram. Visio in Microsoft 365 is a web-only edition and is therefore available in all modern browsers on all modern devices, including Apple Macintosh.

There are also two subscription editions of Visio and two one-time purchase editions for Microsoft Windows. The latter, sometimes referred to as perpetual licenses, are Visio Standard and Visio Professional, which are issued on a circa three-year cycle. The current editions are Visio 2021 Standard and Visio 2021 Professional. The Visio subscriptions, Visio Plan 1 and Visio Plan 2, are the recommended editions for Microsoft 365 users because their Microsoft 365 login controls them:

- A Visio Plan 1 subscription provides Visio online with a greater number of templates and master shapes than Visio in Microsoft 365.

- A Visio Plan 2 subscription provides Visio Plan 1 online and desktop Visio, delivered via the web and installed on Microsoft Windows. Visio Plan 2 includes everything that is in Visio Professional, plus some extra features, templates, and master shapes.

- In a similar way, Visio Professional includes everything that is in Visio Standard, plus more features, templates, and master shapes.

The following diagram illustrates that documents created in the lower editions are always compatible and editable in higher editions. However, documents edited in higher editions may include features that are not available in lower editions, which may render them non-editable, but we can always view them in Reading View.

Figure 2.1 – The compatibility and editability of the Visio editions

For example, the **BPMN Diagram** template is not available to Visio in Microsoft 365 users or Visio Plan 1-only subscribers. It is available online to Visio Plan 1 to Visio Plan 2 subscribers, meaning that the web edition has slightly more features if we have a Visio Plan 2 license.

We can discover which Visio online edition we have by clicking **File | About | License**. We can tell which desktop edition we have by looking at the **Product Information** panel displayed at **File | Account**. It is odd that the header bar of Visio Plan 2 currently displays **Visio Professional**, even with the Visio Plan 2 license.

Using Visio documents anywhere

Microsoft provides a web-only Reading View service that can be used to display any Visio file that is stored on **Microsoft SharePoint** or **Microsoft OneDrive** if the relevant permission is assigned.

The following diagram illustrates how each Visio edition can interact with Visio documents that are stored in Microsoft Teams, SharePoint, and OneDrive.

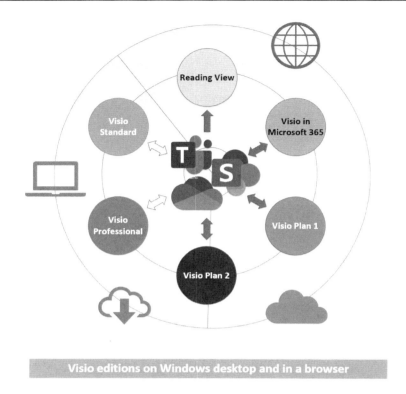

Figure 2.2 – The compatibility and editability of the Visio editions

The hollow arrows between Visio Standard and Professional editions and the online services indicate that access to these services is unavailable to older versions, and even the latest version will cease to have connectivity in 2026.

Visio Plan 2 straddles the web and desktop because it is delivered via the web, and some of its contents are only available when online.

The down arrow within the cloud indicates that the documents are brought down from the web to be edited locally.

The subscription editions are updated monthly or half-yearly via the web, but IT departments of organizations can choose when deployment is made to their end devices.

Although Visio in Microsoft 365 users can share Visio diagrams and add comments to pages and shapes, Visio Plan 1 and Visio Plan 2 subscribers can additionally participate in a conversation in Microsoft Teams.

Comparing templates and features of Visio editions

Visio Plan 1 users with Visio Plan 2 licenses also have extra stencils (currently the *BPMN diagram*) and access to **Shapes in the Document**. The importance of this latter feature will become clearer in later chapters. The following screenshot shows the list of templates currently available to Visio in M365 users:

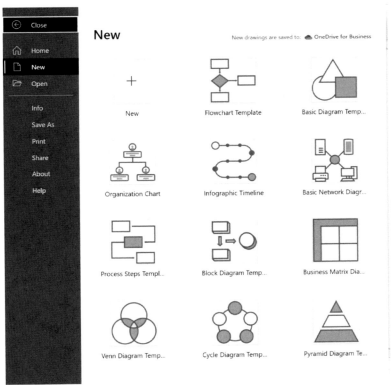

Figure 2.3 – Creating a new Visio in M365 drawing from Office.live.com

The list of available templates is longer for Visio Plan 1 subscribers in the browser and even longer for Visio Plan 2 subscribers in the browser or desktop. See the Microsoft support page *Featured Visio templates and diagrams* at `https://support.microsoft.com/en-us/office/featured-visio-templates-and-diagrams-27d4274b-5fc2-4f5c-8190-35ff1db34aa5` for more information about the current list of templates available in the subscription editions of Visio.

The following table indicates which editions of Visio can create and edit which type of process-related diagrams.

		Browser			Desktop		
	Reading View	Visio in M365	Visio Plan 1	Visio Plan 2	Visio Standard	Visio Professional	Visio Plan 2
Basic Diagrams		●	●	●	●	●	●
Basic Flowcharts		●	●	●	●	●	●
Cross-functional Flowcharts			●	●	●	●	●
BPMN Diagrams				●		●	●
SDL Diagrams			●	●		●	●
UML Diagrams			●	●		●	●
ITIL Diagrams						●	●
Six Sigma Diagrams						●	●
Value-stream maps						●	●
Data Visualizer Diagrams							●

Figure 2.4 – Comparison of process templates in Visio endpoints

The latest information about which types of diagrams are supported in each edition of Visio is available in the article *Types of diagrams that are supported in Visio in Microsoft 365* at `https://support.microsoft.com/en-us/office/types-of-diagrams-that-are-supported-in-visio-in-microsoft-365-877c30a8-0951-4b7a-a53b-daa3d81bea03`.

The hollow circles in the following table of features available indicate partial support in the different editions of Visio:

	Browser				Desktop		
	Reading View	Visio in M365	Visio Plan 1	Visio Plan 2	Visio Standard	Visio Professional	Visio Plan 2
Commenting	●	●	●	●	●	●	●
Co-authoring		●	●	●		●	●
Hyperlinks	○	○	○	○	●	●	●
Shape Data	○				●	●	●
Shape Reports					●	●	●
Data Linking & Data Graphics	○				○	●	●
Subprocesses & Validation Rules						●	●
Data Visualizer						●	●
Export to Word & PowerPoint							●
Access to Document Stencil				●	●	●	●

Figure 2.5 – Comparison of process features in Visio endpoints

Notice that Visio online in Reading View does allow comments to be viewed and added but only allows viewing of **Shape Data**, although it can display multiple hyperlinks per shape. It can also be refreshed to display the latest values of a suitable data source that has been linked in desktop Visio Professional or desktop Visio Plan 2.

Important note

There is an old Windows-only **Visio Viewer** component currently used by desktop **Outlook** to display a preview of Visio documents. There is also an iOS **Microsoft Visio Viewer** app that can display Visio documents on iPhones and iPads. These are not considered in this book.

Getting to know the Visio user interface

A template is a predefined page size and orientation, along with a predefined number of stencils open by default. Each stencil has a number of master shapes that can be dragged and dropped onto the page. More stencils can be opened to provide more master shapes, either by searching for a published master shape or by adding a stencil to the user interface.

Creating a new Visio drawing within a **Microsoft Teams channel** will create a blank drawing with two open stencils, **Basic Shapes**, and **Arrow Shapes**, although more stencils can be added with the + button.

All of the different user interfaces have a ribbon along the top and a status area along the bottom. The bottom - right edge of the Visio app has the following elements in all of the editions:

- A **Zoom out** button
- A **Zoom** slider, which allows us to increment or decrement the zoom level
- A **Zoom in** button
- A **Fit page to current window** button, which zooms to display the whole page

There is a zoom level status message and a **Give Feedback to Microsoft** button too.

Understanding the desktop Visio user interface

This is the most feature-rich user interface of all Visio editions and has no fewer than four anchor windows that can be moved, anchored, or docked around the screen. These are the top four items displayed in the **View | Show | Task Panes** drop-down menu and are as follows:

- **Shapes**: This displays the stencils in our workspace, a **Search shapes** input box, and a **More Shapes** button
- **Shape Data**: This is an edit window for data within each selected shape or page
- **Pan & Zoom**: This is a window that always displays the whole page and the currently visible area as a red rectangle and can be used to pan and zoom around the page
- **Size & Position**: This is an editable window for the position, size, and angle of the selected shapes

The last one on the **Task Panes** menu is **Navigation**, which is a pane that always positions itself fixed on the far-right edge of the application windows, labeled as **Diagram Navigation**. This window allows us to re-order the tabbing order of diagram elements, which is especially important for increasing accessibility.

The **Format Shape** pane is opened from the menu displayed if you right mouse click on a selected shape and is also positioned to the right. It will be to the left of the **Diagram Navigation** pane if that is also open:

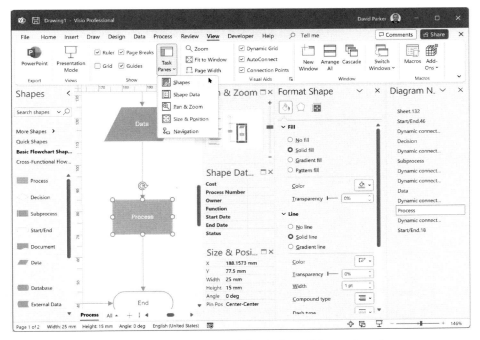

Figure 2.6 – The components of the desktop Visio user interface

There are some more task panes, such as **Comments**, that can be opened from ribbon tabs and will be introduced in later chapters.

Visio also allows us to draw primitive shapes, such as **Rectangle**, **Ellipse**, and **Line** or more complex shapes with the **Freeform**, **Arc**, and **Pencil** tools. These can be drawn by selecting an option from the **Home | Tools** group, where we can also find the **Text** and **Connector** tools:

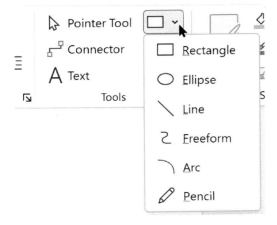

Figure 2.7 – Drawing a shape in desktop Visio

In desktop Visio, we can hold down the *Shift* key with the **Rectangle** and **Ellipse** tools to draw a *square* and *circle* respectively.

Pictures and **Icons** can be inserted from the **Insert | Pictures** ribbon group:

Figure 2.8 – Inserting an image in desktop Visio

The **Insert | Diagram Parts** ribbon group allows us to enclose shapes together within **Container**, associate a **Callout** shape with a target shape, or link shapes together with **Connector**. We cannot create the **Container** and **Callout** shapes currently in **Visio for Web**, and the **Connector** tool is also not available in **Visio for Web**. However, connector shapes can be created with the auto-connect arrows and by dragging and dropping connector shapes from a few stencils. For example, we can search for connector in the **Shapes** panel.

> **Important note**
> There is a particularly significant difference between shapes that are created by dragging and dropping a master shape from a stencil and those created by drawing, grouping, and inserting images. The ones from a stencil are all linked to a master shape in the document's own, normally hidden stencil. The last two chapters, *Chapter 10*, and *Chapter 11*, will show us how to take advantage of this to increase productivity.

Understanding the Visio online editor user interface

This interface for Visio is the same online or within Microsoft Teams and has far fewer components than the desktop interface. There are only three task panes:

- **Shapes**: This is fixed to the left edge of the Visio app

- **Format Options**: This is opened from the menu that appears when you right-click a shape and it is fixed to the right edge of the Visio app and shares this position with **Comments**

- **Comments**: This can be opened from a button present in the right corner of the header bar

The **Search for shapes** textbox allows us to search for more shapes to add the stencil that the found shape is on:

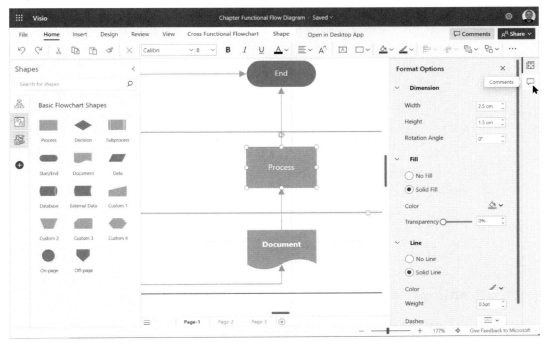

Figure 2.9 – The components of the Visio editor user interface

The left bar of the **Shapes** pane has a button for each open stencil, with a + sign button to add another stencil.

> **Important note**
> A Visio Plan 2 subscriber has an additional **Shapes in the document** button above the + button. This will show the master of each master shape instance that exists in the document. This is equivalent to **More Shapes | Show Document Stencil** in the desktop version of Visio.

The shapes that are not instances of a master shape are created with the **Insert** ribbon. These can be images from several sources, or a primitive shape, such as **Rectangle**, **Line**, or **Ellipse**.

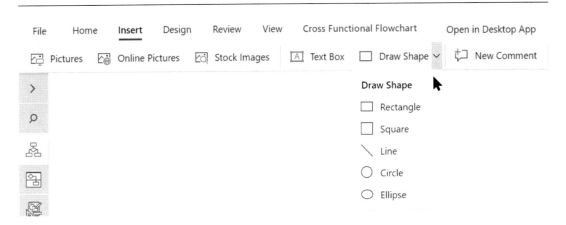

Figure 2.10 – Inserting images and drawing shapes in the Visio online editor

Square is just **Rectangle** where the width is equal to the height, and similarly, **Circle** is just **Ellipse**, as far as Visio is concerned. Notice that there is currently no option to create the desktop Visio **Freeform** or **Arc** shapes or to use the **Pencil** tool.

Understanding the Visio Reading View user interface

This is the same as selecting **View** | **Reading View** in the Visio online editor. It has the following options:

- **Pan & Zoom**: This is an anchored window that can be opened from a button on the bottom right of the status bar

- **Shape Info**: This is a task pane, fixed to the right edge, which displays **Hyperlinks** and **Shape Data** of the currently selected shape

- **Comments**: This is a pane that allows you to view and add threaded comments and @mentions

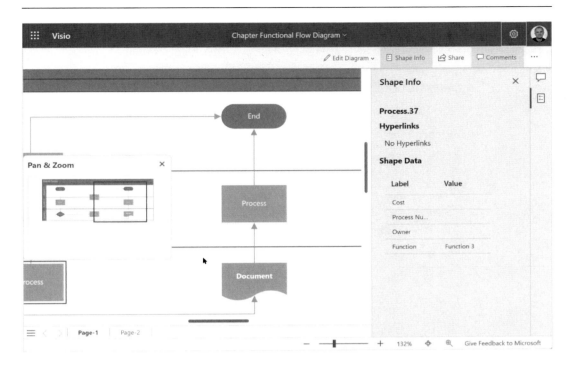

Figure 2.11 – The components of the Visio Reading View user interface

We can switch to editing the current diagram if we have a suitable license. Within the Microsoft Teams context, we will get the options **Edit in Teams**, **Open in Desktop App** (if we have desktop Visio installed), or **Open In Browser**:

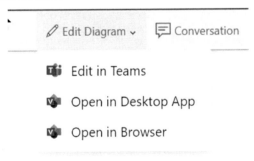

Figure 2.12 – The Visio file viewer Edit Diagram menu in Microsoft Teams

If you are viewing the Visio document in the browser, then the options are **Edit in Browser** or **Edit in Desktop** App (if Visio for Desktop is installed). The last option, **View in legacy Visio service**, is no longer available and can be ignored.

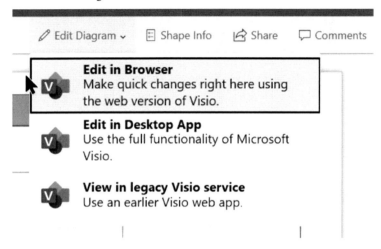

Figure 2.13 – The Visio online Edit Diagram menu options

We now have a better understanding of the Visio user interface in the online and desktop editions; however, we may want to use more than the master shapes on the stencils opened by the template defaults.

Adding stencils to the workspace

The template will usually open one or more default stencils, but we can add more stencils to our workspace to give us additional master shapes to drag and drop onto our page.

In **Visio** online, we can use the **Add Shapes** button at the bottom of the **Stencils** tab on the left of the **Shapes** pane, as shown in the left section of the following screenshot.

In the Visio desktop version, there is a **More Shapes** > button below the **Search for shapes** input box. This button will list the categories of stencils that are installed locally on our PC:

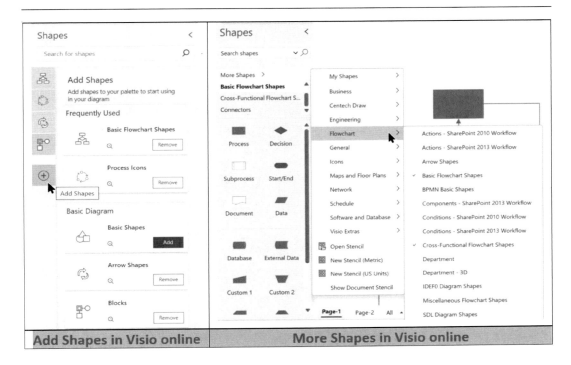

Figure 2.14 – Adding stencils in Visio online and desktop

Note that Visio desktop has a **My Shapes** category that can include any stencils that we add to the `<Documents>/My Shapes` folder locally.

We may also see categories that are not provided by Microsoft but are from a third party and have been installed locally, such as the **Centech Draw** category in the previous example.

The menu opened by the **More Shapes** > button also has the following commands at the bottom:

- **Open Stencil**: This opens Windows File Manager to select a Visio stencil (`*.vssx` or `*.vssm`) from our network folders

- **New Stencil (Metric)**: This creates a new stencil with *Metric* units

- **New Stencil (US Units)**: This creates a new stencil with *US Units*

- **Show Document Stencil**: This displays **Document Stencil** for the active document

Searching for shapes

In Visio online, we can use the plus button at the bottom of the **Stencils** tab on the left of the **Shapes** pane or enter a search term in the **Search for shapes** input box.

When the search shows results, which are grouped by the stencil that they are from, we can either drag and drop from the **Results** pane onto the page, or we can choose to click the small plus sign in a magnifier glass to the right of the stencil name. This will add the stencil to our workspace.

In the Visio desktop version, the **Shapes** search feature will check the locally installed and the Microsoft online stencils. We can drag and drop directly from the **Local** results tab, but we must download the online stencil to add it to our workspace before dragging and dropping a master shape:

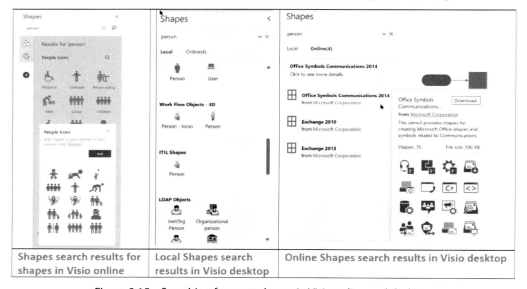

Figure 2.15 – Searching for more shapes in Visio online and desktop

We have learned how to add more stencils to our workspace in Visio online and Visio desktop, and we have seen how we can search for more Microsoft-provided master shapes.

Visio desktop users have the additional capability of adding more stencils from third-party or internal developers. They can also create their own custom master shapes, add them to a custom stencil or template, and distribute them to others. These custom templates and stencils can be installed so that they are available in the Visio desktop user interface.

Summary

In this chapter, we learned about the different editions of Visio and their key differences and capabilities. We saw that Visio diagrams created in online editions can always be edited in desktop editions, but not all documents created on the desktop can be edited online, although they can always be viewed. We also learned how we can add more Microsoft-provided stencils and shapes to the workspace, and how third-party shapes can be added to the Visio desktop workspace. In the next chapter, we will review the skills and techniques required to draw and annotate these business process diagrams quickly and efficiently.

3

Learning to Manually Create Process Flow Diagrams

We learned how to create a **Visio** diagram in *Chapter 1*, using each of the available Visio edition applications. In this chapter, we will learn how to efficiently and manually create flowchart diagrams. These skills will give us the confidence to quickly and efficiently work with many types of diagrams. This chapter will provide us with an understanding of adding more shapes and connecting shapes together, and labeling them. We will also learn about special container shapes, such as swimlanes, and how we can link flowcharts across multiple pages. The following are the specific topics that will be covered in this chapter:

- Setting the page size and orientation
- Adding basic flowchart shapes
- Relating shapes to each other
- Labeling shapes and relationships
- Adding more detailed information to shapes
- Creating sub-processes
- Validating the structure of these diagrams

Technical requirements

These are the Microsoft apps that are utilized in this chapter, and we should have access to at least one of the licensed **Visio** editions, but **Visio Plan 2 subscribers** will be able to use all of the features described:

- **Teams**: Desktop or web app
- **Visio Reading View**: Web-only app
- **Visio in Microsoft 365**: Web-only app

- **Visio Plan 1**: Web-only subscription app

- **Visio Plan 2**: Windows desktop and web subscription apps

- **Visio Professional 20xx**: Windows desktop one-time purchase only

- **Visio Standard 20xx**: Windows desktop one-time purchase only

Setting the page size and orientation

Visio documents can consist of multiple pages, each with a different size and orientation. A Visio page can be of a predefined size, for example, **Letter** or **A4**, or it can be allowed to grow and shrink as a multiple of the default size as you add, delete, or move shapes around.

Interestingly, the default orientation in the browser editions for the **Flowchart Template** is **Portrait**, but it is **Landscape** for the **Basic Flowchart** template on the desktop. However, we can change the orientation from the **Design** tab, as shown in the following screenshot:

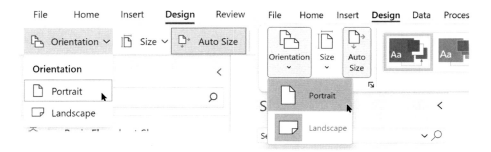

Figure 3.1 – Page orientation in Visio for web and desktop

Similarly, the default page size can be changed from the **Design** ribbon tab, but the desktop edition offers many more default page sizes. The next screenshot shows how the desktop editions have more options for the larger sheets that architects and engineers may use:

Figure 3.2 – Page Size in Visio for web and desktop

The desktop edition also supports the scaling of pages, which is necessary for engineering or architectural-type drawings, but not really for flowcharting. However, Visio online does not currently support scaled drawings.

Both the browser and desktop editions can toggle **Auto Size on** or **off** from the **Design** tab. The desktop edition has a **Page Setup** dialog that can be opened from the dialog launcher button in the bottom right corner of the **Design | Page Setup** ribbon group, from the right-click menu of the page tab at the bottom of the window, or even with the *Shift + F5* keys. The **Auto Size** option is labeled **Let Visio expand the page size as needed** here, as shown in the following screenshot:

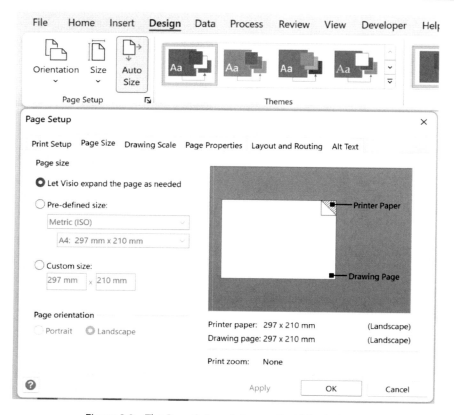

Figure 3.3 – The Page Setup dialog on the Visio desktop

Visio utilizes two types of measurement units, **Metric** and **US Units**, which are presented as the default for the Visio application user. The preceding screenshot is for a **Metric** user, so the page size and the measurement units, and the size of any master shape from a stencil will default to **Metric**. It is difficult to switch a document over once started, so it is best to choose the right option initially.

If the predefined page sizes are still not providing the exact size we need, then both editions allow us to enter a custom page size.

> **Important note**
>
> Visio defaults to using inches for dimensions unless we enter a unit of measure. We can enter any internationally recognized unit or its abbreviation, such as ft, in, m, cm, and mm. We can also enter the dimensions as calculations, such as 2 * 210 mm.

If we intend to print our Visio pages to paper, then it is usually best, but not essential, to have each page the same orientation and, if not the same size, then a multiple of the same page size. Visio pages can be printed in actual size, reduced size, or even enlarged, and there can be multiple printed pages of selected paper size to cover a single Visio page. For example, an **A3 Landscape** Visio page can be printed exactly on 2 * **A4 Portrait** printed pages.

We will now learn about adding, aligning, and connecting shapes on the page.

Adding basic flowchart shapes

Most process flowchart diagrams are created by dragging and dropping master shapes from a stencil onto a page. The shapes on the page are instances of the master shape, and not simple copies of it. These shapes are then usually connected with a connector, which is itself an instance of a *dynamic connector* master shape. This dynamic connector can re-route itself around other shapes and reposition its endpoints on the shapes to match.

Master shapes can simply be dragged and dropped from the stencil window, or existing selected shapes on a page can be duplicated (*Ctrl* + *D* or *Ctrl* + left mouse button drag) or copied and pasted (*Ctrl* + *C* then *Ctrl* + *V*). Although **Copy** and **Paste** appear on the right-mouse menu and on the **Home** ribbon, duplicating is actually more efficient when we need to copy shapes within our Visio document because it does not need to use the clipboard. This means that any existing contents of the clipboard are left intact.

The speed of drawing Visio flowchart diagrams can be increased by using the **Quick Shapes** and **AutoConnect** features that can eliminate the dragging and dropping of shapes from a stencil and connect them, as we will now learn.

Using Quick Shapes and AutoConnect

Visio can display suggested next shapes to drop via connectors on every side of a shape that a mouse cursor hovers over. This is called the **AutoConnect** and **Quick Shapes** menu and behaves slightly differently in the browser and desktop Visio editions.

The **AutoConnect** feature is always on in Visio for the web, but the **Quick Shapes** menu can be toggled on or off from the **View** ribbon tab. The **AutoConnect** setting is saved with the document in desktop Visio and will be off by default for some drawing types that are not normally required. The **Quick Shapes** menu displays the top five master shapes in the active stencil in the browser edition but only four in the Visio desktop editions, as shown in the following screenshot:

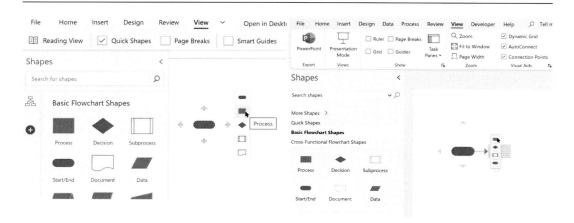

Figure 3.4 – Using the Quick Shapes option in Visio for web and desktop

Clicking one of the master shapes on the **Quick Menu** will drop it at the default distance away from the existing shape and connect it with the default connector, *a dynamic connector*.

The **AutoConnect** feature on the desktop can be toggled off from the **View** | **Visual Aids** ribbon group, which will also toggle the **Quick Shapes** menu visibility.

Desktop Visio has another useful feature that can speed up drawing because a master shape can be moved into a temporary position in the stencil window. The top four entries in a stencil window are displayed in order on the **Quick Shapes** menu:

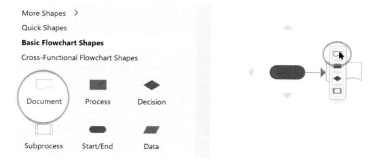

Figure 3.5 – Updating the Quick Shapes menu on the Visio desktop

Another useful feature of the desktop edition is the ability to drag a master shape off a stencil and drop it onto one of the *Quick Connect* arrows used by **AutoConnect** for an existing shape. This will automatically place the new shape at the default spacing away from the existing shape and connect it automatically with the indicated direction. The next screenshot shows how we can use the mouse to drag and drop a shape from a stencil or elsewhere on the page over the *Quick Connect* arrow of an existing shape:

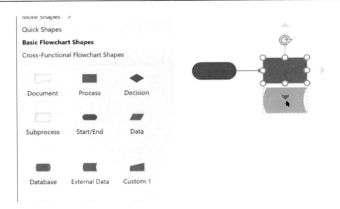

Figure 3.6 – Dropping a master onto a Quick Connect arrow

The dropped shape will then be placed automatically at the default spacing away from the existing shape and connected to it. We will now learn how Visio provides useful assistance for aligning and spacing shapes, even after adding them to the page.

Aligning shapes with Smart Guides and Dynamic Grid

The experience of placing shapes adjacent to existing ones is similar in both editions, but the feature is called **Smart Guides** on the **View** ribbon tab online, but called **Dynamic Grid** in the **View | Visual Aids** ribbon tab on the desktop edition. In either case, we are prompted with green alignment lines and spacing arrows to drop the new shape either horizontally or vertically and at the same spacing as the adjacent shapes:

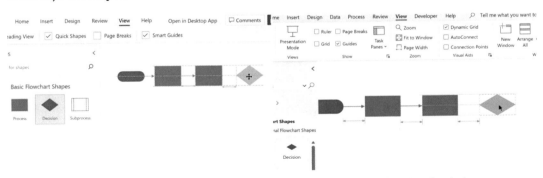

Figure 3.7 – Using Smart Guides in Visio for web and Dynamic Grid in Visio for desktop

The aspect ratio of the shapes and the default spacing between them is slightly different in the preceding screenshot because the online Visio user is using **US units**, but the desktop user is using **metric** units. If the desktop user edits the document that is in **US units** started by the online user, then it will stay as **US units**, and vice versa.

Desktop Visio has the extra capability of providing us with the option to change the default spacing of space between shapes from the **Layout and Routing Spacing** dialog that is opened from the **Spacing...** button on the **Layout and Routing** tab of the **Page Setup** dialog:

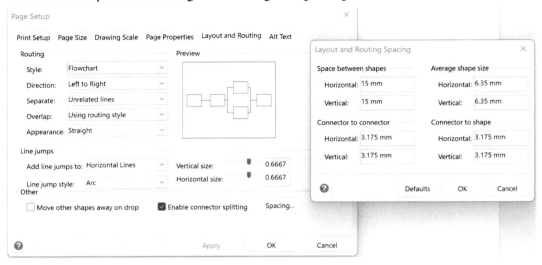

Figure 3.8 – Editing the default spacing in Visio desktop

Many other options in these dialogs provide the desktop Visio user with a finer control of the layout and routing, but many of them are set by the layout options in the **Design | Diagram Layout** feature that is discussed in the following *Automatically changing the diagram layout* section.

Process diagrams are all about connecting shapes to create a flow between them that can be followed visually or via automation, so we now need to understand how to create these connections correctly.

Relating shapes to each other

There is a **Line** option in the **Insert** or **Home | Draw Shape** drop-down menus in the browser edition. Although this can be used to glue to shapes and connection points, the line does not have the same capabilities as the connector line drawn by the **AutoConnect** arrow because it does not have any automatic routing capabilities, nor does its text box have a control handle to reposition it. The text rotates with the line rather than staying horizontal. For these reasons, it is always best to use the **AutoConnect** arrow to make connections between flowchart shapes because it will create an instance of the *dynamic connector* master shape. We can also use the **Home | Tools | Connector** or **Insert | Diagram Parts | Connector** commands in Visio desktop to create a connector between two shapes, which also uses the *dynamic connector* master:

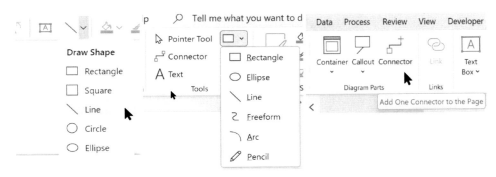

Figure 3.9 – The Visio web Draw Shape menu and the Visio desktop Tools and Diagram Parts groups

So far, we have been using the **AutoConnect** feature to connect process flowchart shapes, and they have been following the direction indicated by the ending arrow. This direction of flow is important for the diagram auto-layout feature to work correctly and for any data that might be exported from the diagram.

> **Important note**
>
> The **AutoConnect** arrow and the desktop **Connector** command use a special **one-dimensional (1D)** shape called **Dynamic connector** by default. This master shape is built into the flowchart templates and is preformatted with an arrow at the end of it. Be aware that other templates could contain a different format for the **Dynamic connector** master shape.

The **AutoConnect** arrow is suitable in most cases, but there are times when we do need to glue a connector end to a specific position on a shape or to reverse the direction of flow of a connector.

Now, we will learn how to use the **AutoConnect** arrow instead of the **Quick Shapes** menu.

Dragging the AutoConnect arrow

The **AutoConnect** arrow does more than just indicate the direction of the **Quick Shape** to drop and connect because it can also be dragged to glue to an existing shape without dropping a new one. The next screenshot shows the sequence of hovering over the **AutoConnect** arrow, then clicking and dragging the arrowhead to another shape in order to create a connection:

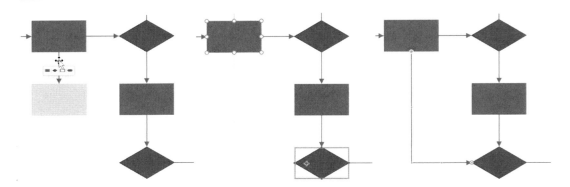

Figure 3.10 – Grabbing, dragging, and connecting the AutoConnect arrow

The **AutoConnect** arrow has another capability in the desktop edition because if there is another connectable shape within approximately twice the default spacing in the direction of the arrow, then clicking on the arrow will shoot it down to the target shape and glue it to it!

The **AutoConnect** feature will always create *dynamic* glue, which means that the location where the connector appears to be glued may reposition itself if the shapes are moved around. We will now learn about **static glue**, which means that the location of the glue remains constant when the shapes are moved around.

Gluing connectors to a specific position

There will be times when the connector just won't either begin or end where we want it to. This is often when connectors begin at a decision diamond because we really want to have them exit the diamond at different vertices. In the following example, the connector from the lower *Decision* shape is automatically attached to the right side of the *Process* shape above and to the left. This makes it appear that there is a bi-directional arrow between that *Process* shape and the *Decision* shape to its right. Therefore, we may want to ensure that the connector from the lower *Decision* shape glues to the bottom of the *Process* shape, as follows:

1.   Move the mouse to the end of the connector line until we see the **Move Endpoint** tooltip.

2.   Click the left mouse button down and drag the endpoint towards the center of the edge where we want to glue it.

3.   Release the left mouse button when the connection point shows a small green rectangle (or circle online) around it or the **Glue to Connection Point** tooltip appears:

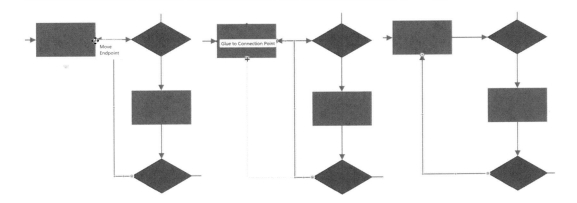

Figure 3.11 – Grabbing, moving, and gluing the connector endpoint

Each of the process flowchart shapes has a connection point at the center of its edges or the tip of the vertices of the diamond. If we connect to these points, it is called static glue because the connector will stay there even if we move the flowchart shapes around.

Many shapes have predefined connection points already, though we can add more with the **Home | Tools | Connection Point** button in desktop Visio. They can also be deleted or moved. However, we mostly want to have dynamic glue on these shapes because they will automatically move the end of the connector to the appropriate edge when shapes are moved, and the connectors are re-routed.

To change the connection back to dynamic glue, follow these steps:

1.   Move the mouse to the end of the connector line until we see the **Move Endpoint** tooltip.
2.   Click the left mouse button down and drag it toward the center of the shape.
3.   Release the left mouse button when the shape shows a green rectangle around it or the **Glue to Shape** tooltip appears.

The connector shape often includes an end arrow to denote the direction of the flow, but sometimes we get the direction wrong and need to swap it around. So, what should we do?

Reversing the direction of flow

We should not merely edit or format the connector by removing the arrow at the end of the line and adding one at the beginning. This may look like it has reversed the flow graphically, but it has not reversed the logical flow direction of the connector line. This could cause any validation, export to a data source, or automation tools to misinterpret the diagram. Instead, we should either delete the incorrect connector and redraw one in the correct direction or manually move the ends of the connector line from one end to the other using the instructions in the previous sections.

However, Visio desktop users have an extra option because there is a command, **Reverse Ends**, that can reverse the direction of an existing connector easily. This command can be made available by adding it to **Quick Access Toolbar** (**QAT**) or by customizing the ribbon. This can be done as follows:

1. Go to **File** | **Options** | **Quick Access Toolbar**.

2. Select **Commands Not in the Ribbon** from the **Choose commands from** drop-down list.

3. Scroll down to the **Reverse Ends** command.

4. Click the **Add>>** button.

5. Ensure **Show Quick Access Toolbar** is ticked.

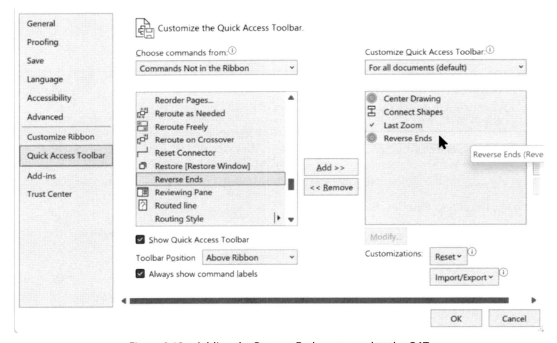

Figure 3.12 – Adding the Reverse Ends command to the QAT

Using the **Reverse Ends** command could not be simpler. In the following screenshot, an incorrect connector is selected, then the **Reverse Ends** button is pressed, and the connector direction is immediately reversed.

The previous example also added three other useful commands that are not shown in the ribbon:

*   **Center Drawing**: This moves all of the shapes on the page to the center of the Visio page

*   **Connect Shapes**: This connects one or more selected shapes together in the order they were selected

*   **Last Zoom**: This sets the Visio window back to the immediately previous view

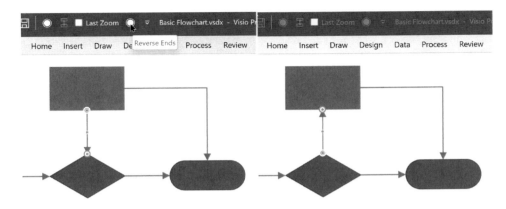

Figure 3.13 – Before and after using the Reverse Ends command

There is always a default routing style for connectors on a page, but this can be changed easily, as we will now learn.

Changing the routing style of connectors

We can change the routing appearance of all the connectors on a page using **Design | Connectors** in Visio online or **Design | Layout | Connectors** in Visio desktop. This allows us to change the appearance between **Right Angle**, **Straight Lines**, or **Curved Lines**, as shown in the following screenshot from the Visio desktop. To ensure that the changes are for the whole page, clear your shape selection by clicking the mouse in an empty area of the page, then clicking the **Connectors** button. The following screenshot shows the available options:

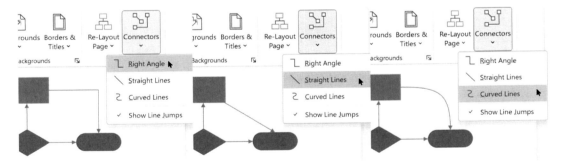

Figure 3.14 – The Right Angle, Straight Lines, and Curved Lines connectors

We can also change the routing style of one or more selected connectors by selecting them before clicking the **Connectors** button shown previously or by using the right-click context menu on a connector shape, as shown here:

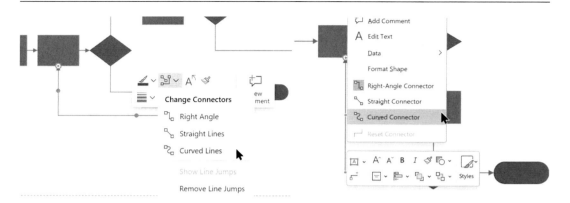

Figure 3.15 – Change connectors routing style in Visio web and desktop

We have been using the *dynamic connector* shape so far because that is the default one provided by Visio. However, we can change this for one of many other available connector shapes, as we will now learn.

Changing the type of connectors

Both the online and desktop editions of Visio can replace selected shapes with a selected alternative from a filtered drop-down gallery available from **Shape | Change Shape** online and **Home | Editing | Change Shape** on the desktop. In the following example, two connectors are selected before opening the **Change Shape** gallery:

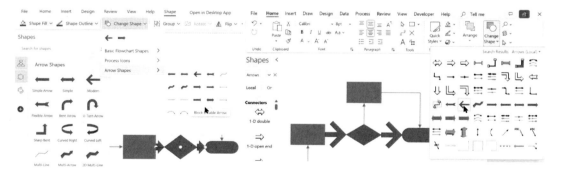

Figure 3.16 – Changing connector types in Visio web and desktop

If connector shapes are selected, then the list is filtered to display only *1D* shapes, so if a process flowchart shape is selected, then only **two-dimensional** (**2D**) shapes will be displayed.

The web edition only displays master shapes from the stencils that are included in the workspace. More stencils can be added using the + button at the bottom of the vertical stencil tabs below the **Search for shapes** input box, as described in the *Adding stencils to our workspace* section in *Chapter 2*.

There is always a default diagram layout style for a page, but this can also be changed to another style or direction of flow.

Automatically changing the diagram layout

We can automatically change the layout of a page, or a number of selected shapes, by choosing an alternate layout from the gallery drop-down available from **Design | Diagram Layout** in Visio online or **Design | Layout | Re-Layout Page**. There are more options available in Visio desktop, as shown here:

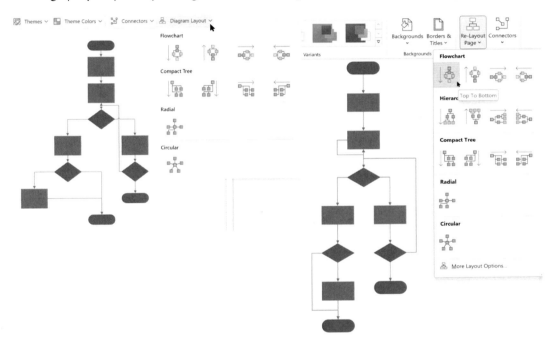

Figure 3.17 – Changing the diagram layout in Visio web and desktop

The connectors will automatically re-route, but it may be necessary to reposition some of the connector ends, as described in the *Gluing connectors to a specific position* section, but it should not be necessary to reverse the flow at all.

The next section details how to label the flowchart shapes and the decision outbound connectors.

Labeling shapes and relationships

All flowchart shapes should be labeled with a short description, and at least the connectors exiting a decision diamond should be labeled to differentiate the **yes** and **no** routes.

Every shape in Visio has a block of text, even if there are no characters in it, and this should always be used in preference to a separate block of text to the page because the text will stay with the shape whenever it is moved around. Editing the text of a shape is usually as simple as this:

1. Select a shape.
2. Type the text; this will enter *text edit* mode.
3. Hit the *Esc* key to exit *text edit* mode.
4. Hit the *Tab* key as required to advance to the next shape that needs text.
5. Repeat *steps 2* to *4*.

There is an extra step required in Visio desktop after using the *Tab* key because it does not automatically select the shape when we tab. It displays a gray rectangle around the shape tabbed to, indicating where the focus is, but then we need to hit the *Enter* key to actually select it before typing in any text:

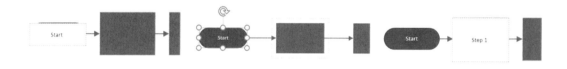

Figure 3.18 – Entering text on the first shape, tabbing, and entering text on the next shape

Note that hitting the *Enter* key after typing some text will automatically start a new line because Visio text can be split across multiple lines.

> **Important note**
>
> It is possible in desktop Visio to enable **Pressing the ENTER key commits shape text**. This setting is in **File | Options | Advanced | Editing options**, but then new lines within text blocks become difficult to type.

The default tab order of shapes in a Visio page is set by the order in which the shapes are added to the page. This may not be ideal if we do not drop the shapes strictly in the order of the flow, and indeed it is usually impossible to do this. However, desktop **Visio** has the **View | Show | Task Panes | Navigation** panel that allows the tab order to be edited.

The text of any shape can be re-edited by selecting a shape and then entering text edit mode. This could be double-clicking the shape, although this can be redirected to a different action in the desktop edition or selecting **Edit Text** from the right-click context menu. Additionally, this can be done with the *F2* key in the desktop edition.

The default text behavior for the flowchart shapes is to wrap within the enclosing rectangle, and if the text is too long to fit, then the shape will automatically increase in height, as in the following screenshot (the actual text is not important, just the amount):

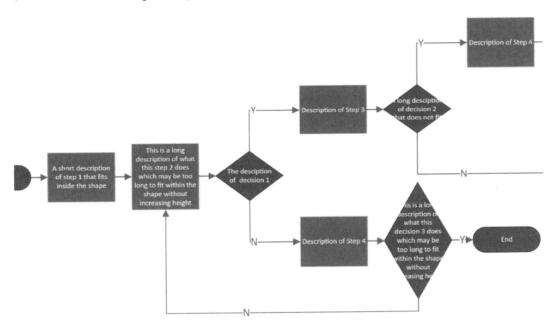

Figure 3.19 – Entering long text will increase the height of flowchart shapes

This does not make a professional-looking flowchart, so a label of two or three lines maximum should be considered the best solution. The flowchart shape could also be widened to allow the text to fit within the default height. The *Using ScreenTips to store a longer description* section in this chapter provides a way of adding more information for desktop Visio users.

We may decide to edit the text to be less verbose, so we need to know how to return the shapes to their default size.

Resetting flowchart shape sizes

If long descriptions are required, a right-click menu command, **Set to Default Size**, returns the width and height of the flowchart shape to its default, as shown in the following screenshot:

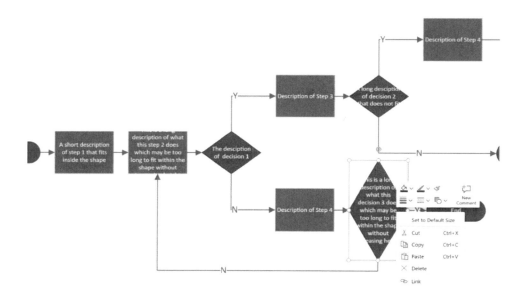

Figure 3.20 – The Right-click command to reset the flowchart shape size

Once the flowchart shape has been reset to its default size, another option to make a long text fit is to reduce the font size, as in the following screenshot, where the font size of the selected shape has been reduced from 8 pt to 7 pt:

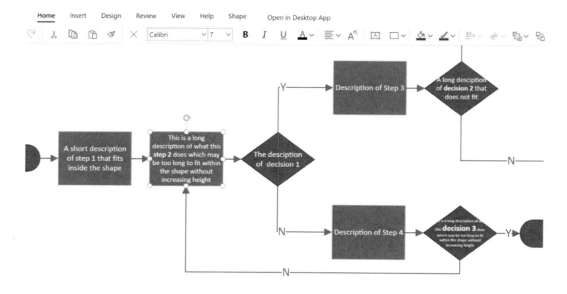

Figure 3.21 – Reformatting flowchart shape text

Notice that parts of the text within a text block in Visio can be formatted differently so that specific words can stand out by being a different style, size, or color.

The connector shapes also have text labels, which may need to be repositioned to make it clearer to read or understand which connector it relates to.

Moving the connector label

Unlike the flowchart shapes, the connector shape has a yellow control point that can be used to reposition the label. This is often necessary for the outbound connectors from a decision diamond to make it easier to see the flows, as in the following screenshot.

Take the following steps to perform this action:

1. Select the connector shape.

2. Move the mouse cursor over the yellow control point.

3. When the cursor changes from an arrow to a cross, drag it down with the left mouse button and move it to the desired position.

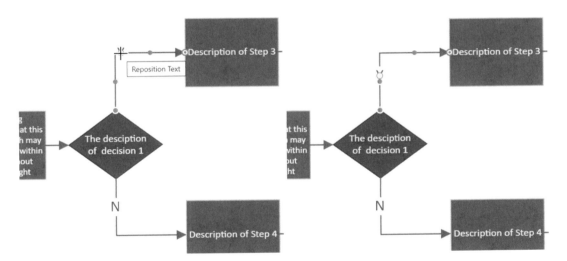

Figure 3.22 – Grabbing and moving the connector label control point

All of the actions described in this chapter so far have been possible in both the online and desktop editions, except where otherwise indicated.

The remaining sections are currently only available in the desktop editions. The last two *Creating subprocesses* sections and **Validating the structure of flowchart diagrams** are only available in Visio Plan 2 and Visio Professional.

Visio has some special container shapes that can be used to hold other shapes within them. As we will now learn, these special shapes are used in cross-functional flowcharts with swimlanes and separators.

Working with swimlanes and separators

The **Cross-Functional Flowchart** template, available in all editions of Visio except Visio in M365, provides a couple of swimlane shapes displayed horizontally by default. The orientation can be changed to vertical via the **Cross-Functional Flowchart** ribbon menu.

This template opens the **Cross-Functional Flowchart Shapes** stencil in addition to the **Basic Flowchart Shapes** stencil. This stencil contains horizontal and vertical versions of the **Swimlane** and **Separator** master shapes.

Swimlanes should be labeled with the actor responsible for process steps within it, and more swimlanes can be added.

Adding a swimlane to a cross-functional flowchart

There are two ways of adding another swimlane in Visio online. The first is as follows:

1. Select a swimlane, usually best done on the header, that you want to insert a new swimlane after. If you just want to add one at the end, then don't select anything.

2. Click the **Cross-Functional Flowchart \ Swimlane** button.

The second way is to do the following:

1. Click and drag the **Swimlane** master shape from the stencil over the outline of an existing swimlane where you want to insert a new one.

2. When an orange line appears, release the mouse button to drop the swimlane.

The following screenshot shows a **Swimlane** shape as it is dragged over the edge of an existing swimlane:

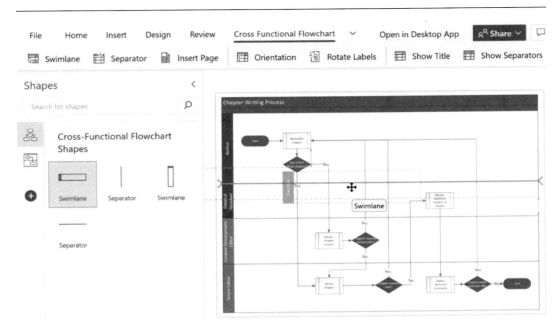

Figure 3.23 – Dragging and dropping a swimlane in Visio online

In desktop Visio, we can additionally choose **Insert 'Swimlane' Before** or **Insert 'Swimlane' After** from the right-click menu of a selected swimlane, as in the following screenshot:

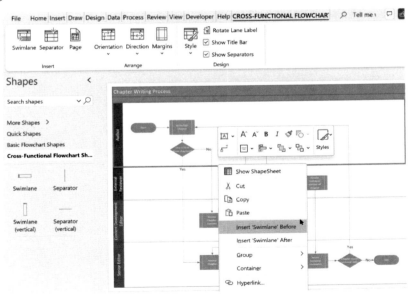

Figure 3.24 – Inserting a swimlane in Visio desktop

These swimlanes have a default height and width, but we may need to resize them or move them to suit our diagramming requirements.

Moving and resizing swimlanes

Swimlanes can be moved vertically if they are horizontal or horizontally if they are vertical simply by clicking on the header and dragging it. All of the shapes within them will stay inside of them as they are moved. They can also be resized by taking the following steps:

1. Move the cursor over the edge of a swimlane.

2. When the cursor changes to two vertical lines with arrows pointing away from them, click and drag the line with the left mouse button held down.

3. Release the mouse button when the edge line is at the required position.

Note that the edge line cannot be moved closer to its contained shapes than the predefined margin around them.

The **Separator** shapes can also be added across swimlanes to delineate distinct phases for a process.

Adding a separator to a cross-functional flowchart

The **Separator** shapes, labeled **Phase** by default, are always perpendicular to the swimlane shapes. They are used to break up the flow into phases and can be relabeled at the top right of each one.

They can be dragged and dropped similarly to swimlanes, as in the following screenshot, and although they can be resized, they cannot be moved:

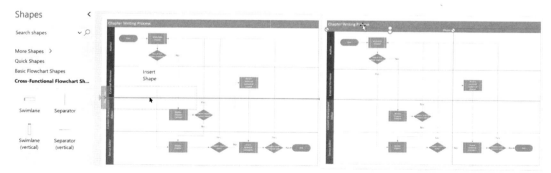

Figure 3.25 – Dragging a Separator shape into a cross-functional flowchart

Once they have been added, the **Show Separators** check box will be automatically ticked if it wasn't already. Unticking it will delete all of the separator shapes.

The second way to add a separator shape is to do the following:

1. Select an existing **Separator** shape.
2. Click the **Separator** button, and a new **Separator** shape will be added at the mid-point of the selected **Separator** shape.

The default flowchart shapes each have predefined **Shape Data** rows, and one of them, labeled **Function**, automatically displays the text of the swimlane that the flowchart shape is within. We will now learn about the other **Shape Data** rows in each flowchart shape. We can add more information to each flowchart step, or even the connector lines between them, using **Shape Data**. This information can then be read by viewers when they select a shape in either the web or desktop edition. This data can also be displayed in or around the shape as text, icons, or using **Data Graphics**, as we will learn in *Chapter 7*, or exported into a Word document along with images of the diagram, as shown in *Chapter 9*. It can also be synchronized with an Excel table, as we will learn about in *Chapter 5*.

Adding more detailed information to shapes

All shapes in Visio can store specific data with them. The name and type of data expected are often predefined in master shapes, such as flowchart shapes. Each of them has the following rows defined:

- **Cost**: Currency
- **Process Number**: Numeric
- **Owner**: Text
- **Function**: Text and displays the label of the swimlane if it is inside one
- **Start Date**: Date
- **End Date**: Date
- **Status**: A list that contains the **Not Started**, **In Progress**, **Completed**, **Deferred**, and **Waiting on Input** values, but we can add any other value too

We can enter values for each row, and they will be stored with the shape:

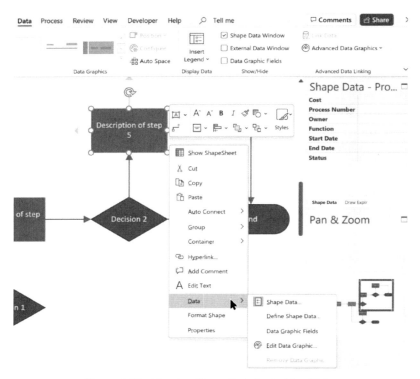

Figure 3.26 – Viewing Shape Data in desktop Visio

The **Define Shape Data…** command from the **Data** sub-menu of the right-click menu of one of the flowchart shapes opens a dialog that can be used to edit the existing definitions or to add more. However, the definitions are not normally edited for each individual shape. This feature will be discussed more in *Chapter 10*.

Although the **Shape Data** window cannot currently be seen in Visio for web in edit mode, it can be viewed in the **Shape Info** panel when in **Reader View** mode.

Ways of creating and updating data values from external data will be described in *Chapter 5*.

We normally have short but descriptive text within each flowchart shape, so it can be useful to display a longer description when the mouse cursor is paused over a shape. We can use the **ScreenTip** feature to provide this information.

Using ScreenTips to store a longer description

We have already entered a short description of each step or relationship as text, but we may want to store a longer description too. Fortunately, we can use the **Insert | Text | ScreenTip** button to open the **Shape ScreenTip** dialog, where we can add multiple lines of text. The first 252 characters will be displayed as a tooltip when the mouse is hovered over the shape, as shown in the following screenshot:

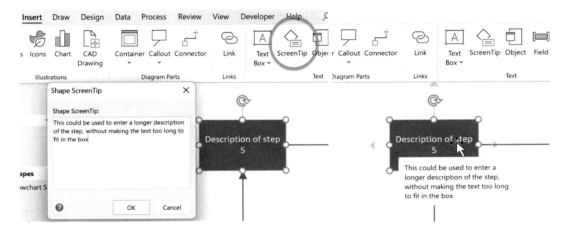

Figure 3.27 – Editing and viewing ScreenTip in desktop Visio

We do need to use the *Ctrl + Enter* keys in the **Shape ScreenTip** dialog to enter a new line character because just clicking *Enter* closes the dialog.

In fact, all editions of Visio shapes can hold up to 64,000 characters in each **Shape Data** value and in other areas of a shape.

We will now learn how Visio can help when we need to add more steps between existing ones or delete ones that are already connected.

Inserting shapes between existing ones

Another useful feature in desktop Visio is the ability to drag and drop a flowchart shape onto an existing connector shape, which then automatically splits the connector in two and then reconnects the connectors to the inserted shape. This is extremely useful when a forgotten process step needs to be inserted between existing ones, as shown in the following screenshot:

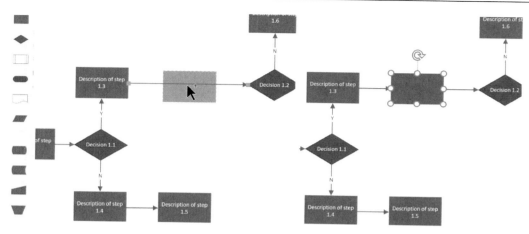

Figure 3.28 – Inserting a shape into a connector in desktop Visio

Also, if we delete a flowchart shape that is already connected to two others, then Visio will automatically delete the last connector in the direction of the flow and reconnect the first connector.

> **Important note**
>
> The ability to split a connector with a shape can be toggled on/off at **File | Options | Advanced | Enable Connector Splitting**.

We usually do not want each Visio page to be too overwhelming with the number of shapes on it, so we often need to break down complex processes into a number of subprocesses displayed on different pages. Subprocesses are dealt with in the next section.

Creating subprocesses

If we break down processes into smaller chunks, then each subprocess page should still have a logical beginning and one or more logical endings to the flow. These should be denoted with labeled **Start** and **End** shapes at each end of the flowchart and preferably with hyperlinks back to the parent process shape.

Desktop Visio, except for Visio Standard, has three specific ribbon buttons in the **Process | Subprocess** group to assist with these tasks, as shown in the following list:

- **Create New**: This can be selected when the subprocess has not been created yet.
- **Link to Existing**: Select this when a subprocess page has already been created.

- **Create from Selection**: Select this when you want to move a selection of shapes to a subprocess page and replace it with a single subprocess shape on the original page. This is often done after realizing that the original page is getting too complex and that some parts of the process can be moved to a separate page for clarity.

These actions are explained in the next sections.

Creating a new subprocesses page

The first button in the **Process | Subprocess** group will create a new blank page, named the same as the text in the selected shape. A hyperlink to this new page is added to the selected shape, as shown in the following screenshot:

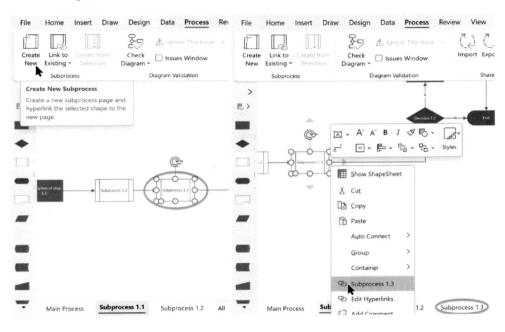

Figure 3.29 – Creating a new subprocess page from an existing shape

The subprocess should then be diagrammed on the new page, optionally with hyperlinks back to the original shape.

Linking to an existing subprocess page

The second button in the **Process | Subprocess** group simply creates a hyperlink to an existing page that exists in the active document or to an existing Visio document.

The following screenshot shows how this is done:

1. Select an existing *Process* shape.

2. Select an existing page from the **Link to Existing** drop-down list, as in the following screenshot:

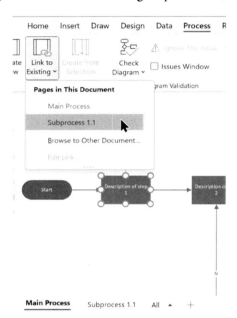

Figure 3.30 – Linking a shape to an existing page

3. If the existing shape is not a *Process* shape, then use **Home | Editing | Change Shape** to swap it for a **Subprocess** shape, as in the following screenshot:

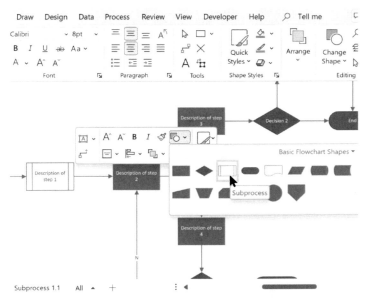

Figure 3.31 – Changing a Process shape for a Subprocess shape

4.   A link to the existing page is created, as shown here:

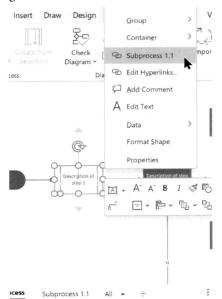

Figure 3.32 – Selecting a hyperlink to a page

5.   If necessary, rename the label of the *Subprocess* shape to match the target page name or vice versa.

Creating a new subprocess page from selected shapes

When the existing page looks too complex, we can use the third button in the **Home | Subprocess** group to move some of the flowchart to a new page as a subprocess. To do this, follow these steps:

1. Carefully select the flowchart shapes that could become a subprocess.

2. Click the **Create from Selection** command from **Process | Subprocess**, as shown here:

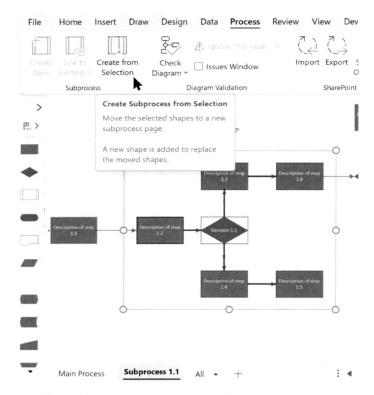

Figure 3.33 – Creating a subprocess from selected shapes

3. A new page will be created with the selected shapes moved to it.

4. The original selection is replaced by a **Subprocess** shape with a hyperlink to the new page, as shown in the following screenshot:

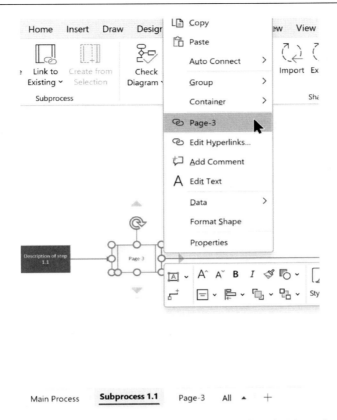

Figure 3.34 – A new page created with the existing shapes replaced with a subprocess shape

5. Rename the new page.

6. Rename the **Subprocess** shape to match the new page name, as seen here:

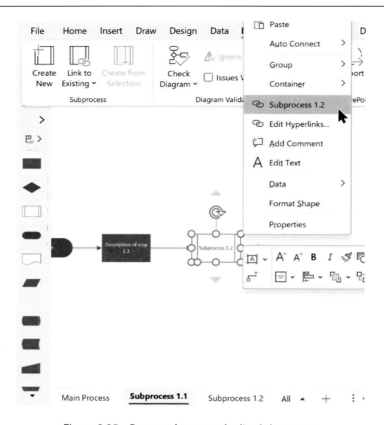

Figure 3.35 – Renamed page and edited shape text

For completeness, we should add a **Start** shape and an **End** shape at the beginning and end of the process shapes on the new page, which we will then add hyperlinks back to the new **Subprocess** shape. To do this, we need to get the name of the new **Subprocess** shape.

Once the **Subprocess** page is completed, we can return to the original page to read the name of the *Subprocess* shape using the **Shape Data** window. The name of the selected shape appears on the header of the **Shape Data** window. It can also be read from the **Shape Name** ribbon button found at **Developer | Shape Design**.

Then we go back to the subprocess page and add the same hyperlink to both the **Start** and **End** shapes. This is the procedure to add a hyperlink to a specific shape on a different page in desktop Visio:

1. Select a shape.

2. Open the **Hyperlinks** dialog with **Insert | Links | Link** (*Ctrl + K*).

3. Leave the **Address** field blank.

4. Click **Browse...** on the **Sub-address** row to open the **Hyperlink** dialog.

5. Select the page where the *Subprocess* shape is from the **Page** drop-down list.

6. Enter the name of the *Subprocess* shape in the **Shape** field.

7. Optionally enter a **Description** value for the hyperlink.

8. Click **OK** to close the **Hyperlink** dialog, then **OK** to close the **Hyperlinks** dialog.

The following screenshot shows this procedure:

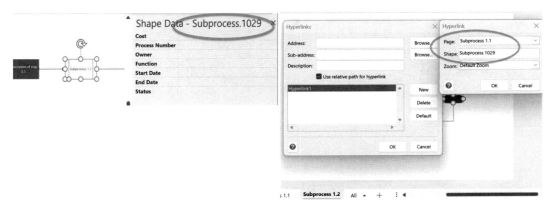

Figure 3.36 – Getting the subprocess shape name and then creating a hyperlink to it

> **Important note**
>
> It is possible to add a single hyperlink in online Visio to another page, as described in the *Using the Off-page (reference) shape* in *Chapter 1*.

The same hyperlink can be added to both the **Start** and **End** shapes of the subprocess page so that they return to the *Subprocess* shape on the previous page. The following screenshot shows the hyperlink being selected from the right-click menu:

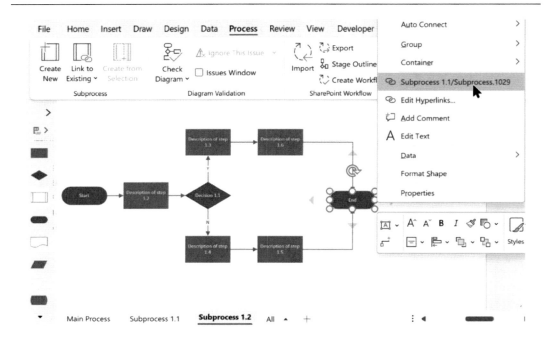

Figure 3.37 – Following a hyperlink to a page and shape

Simply hold down the *Ctrl* key and click a shape with a hyperlink to follow it. There is a right-click menu command to follow the link, but currently, we sometimes need to select the hyperlink command twice in Visio for it to actually work.

Validating the structure of flowchart diagrams

If we follow the advice in this chapter about connecting and labeling shapes, then we should have a well-structured flowchart diagram. However, if there are issues, such as missing labels and connections, then they can be easily revealed with the **Process | Check Diagram** button, as shown in the following screenshot:

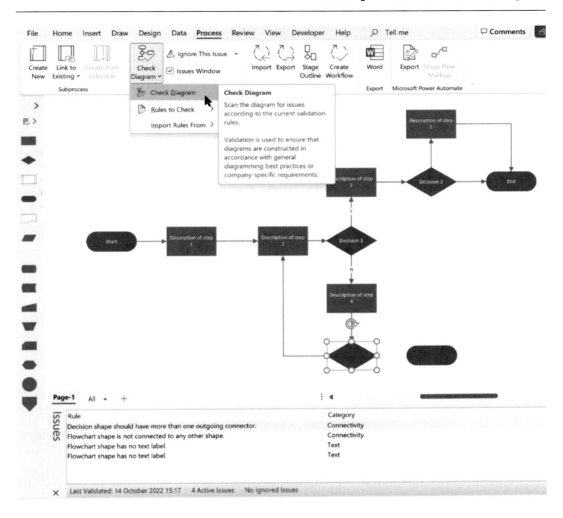

Figure 3.38 – Validating the diagram structure

Visio Plan 2 and Visio Professional include validation rules for *flowcharts*, and they can be modified or new rules created. This is the subject of the still valid book from Packt Publishing, *Microsoft Visio 2013 Business Process Diagramming and Validation* by David J Parker, and it can be referred to for more detail.

The **SharePoint Workflow** group in the **Process** ribbon tab will not be addressed in this book because it is superseded by the last ribbon group, **Microsoft Power Automate**, which will be covered in the next chapter. The other group, **Export**, will be covered in *Chapter 9*.

Summary

We learned about the techniques to manually create basic flowchart diagrams in this chapter. This included ways of breaking down complex flows into multiple pages with subprocesses and hyperlinks taking you backward and forward. We learned how to glue connectors to shapes so they stay glued to a particular point or move around it as the page layout is modified. We also learned how labels and more information can be stored with each shape.

In the next chapter, we will learn about one of the most popular standards for sharing process flowcharts, **Business Process Model and Notation** (**BPMN**).

4

Using Visio for Desktop with BPMN

We learned in *Chapter 3* how to create process flow diagrams in general, using the tools, features, and templates in **Visio**. This chapter now focuses on one specific diagram type and template – the **Business Process Model and Notation (BPMN)** template. Here, you will learn not only how to use the BPMN template and stencil but also the very specifics of how to use the more hidden features, allowing you to create full BPMN 2.0-compliant diagrams.

Specifically, we will cover the following main topics:

- The basic idea of the BPMN approach
- An introduction to BPMN
- The differences between BPMN and **cross-functional flowcharts** (**CFFs**)
- An overview of the components and shapes of a BPMN diagram
- A built-in scenario for the BPMN template – the **Power Automate** export

> **Note**
> Please note that this chapter does not cover the how and why of BPMN documentation – that could easily be a book by itself (and it actually fills a lot of content on the Object Management Group (OMG) website). This chapter focuses on using Visio as a tool to create BPM documentation in the BPMN notation /visualization style.

Technical requirements

The BPMN template and shapes are only available in **Visio Plan 2** or **Visio Professional**. So, if you want to create BPMN diagrams, you must have access to one of the following editions of Visio:

- **Visio Plan 2**: The desktop and web subscription app
- **Visio Professional 20xx**: A Windows one-time purchase only

> **Important note**
>
> You can also use Visio Online if your subscription is Visio Plan 2, and then your Plan 2 web portion will also contain the BPMN shapes. However, a regular subscription to Visio Plan 1 will not contain the BPMN template and stencils. At the time of writing, the BPMN shapes are only available in the web version for the **en-US** locale, but it is expected that they will become available for other locales within the first half of 2023.

The basic idea of the BPMN approach

Here, we will learn how and why the BPMN approach was introduced. Business process modeling and documentation with tools is nothing new – there have been tools available since the early 1990s. Whenever you need to describe a business process, the first question is, how do you depict the various components of a business process that needs to be described? In the past, there have been several approaches to achieve this.

One of the older approaches was introduced by the company **SAP AG** in the early 80s, which was one of the first approaches to document business processes in a standardized manner. It is known by its original German name, **Ereignisgesteuerte Prozesskette (EPK)**. The English term for this is an **Event-Driven Process Chain (EPC)**.

Also, the ISO consortium had another definition of how business processes should be documented in a visual standard – this standard is today one of the most commonly known and used, which we learned about in *Chapter 3* – with the standard symbols used there. The diagram type is known as **CFFs**.

There are several other visual standards, but they don't have a major market share. What is important is that as the process design, toolings, and IT tools matured, these old standards were not capable of completely describing a full system and environment.

Therefore, the **Object Management Group (OMG)** tried to define and establish a new standard on how processes and business processes could be described. This new approach also took into consideration that processes are not only things executed manually by people; there are also systems (IT systems especially) that take over a part of a task or operation. The standard they described was called **business process modeling and notation**. The full story and definition can be accessed on the OMG website at www.bpmn.org.

It is not the purpose of this book to introduce all the BPMN rules and regulations, but there is an extensive introduction, with all the visuals, what they mean, and what they should be used for, available at a special website that the OMG created: https://www.bpmnquickguide.com/.

Although you can download the guide, there is an easier way – the OMG provides a regularly updated online version at `https://www.bpmnquickguide.com/view-bpmn-quick-guide/`.

That way, you can always be sure to have the most up-to-date version of the quick guide.

> **Important note**
> The term *BPMN* can mean two things – *I approach* or *the visual standard.*

The terminology of BPMN

Nowadays, the term *BPMN* is used to refer to several things, the approach itself or the visual standard:

- **The idea of the whole approach**: The BPMN approach – how to model business processes and which notation to use (and also a file storage format suggestion).

- **The visual standard of how processes should be described**: The BPMN visual standard – how to visually describe processes using a specific *visual language*. Note that, in this chapter, we will focus on this interpretation of BPMN, since Visio is a tool that can use this visual standard.

Now that we have got a basic understanding of what BPMN is or can be, we will turn to how to start creating Visio diagrams that follow the BPMN visual standard.

Getting started with BPMN in Visio

For the purpose of this chapter, we will work in Visio Plan 2; however, Visio Professional will work equally well – there is no difference between these two editions regarding the descriptions in this chapter:

1. Start Microsoft Visio.
2. Select **Templates | Flowchart | BPMN Diagram** (i.e., the BPMN-related template).
3. Create a diagram.

> **Important note**
> We do not recommend (although it is possible) starting with the **Empty Diagram** template and then adding the BPMN stencils. Invoking the the **BPMN Diagram** template will make sure you have all the extra functions, toolings, and settings set so that you can create a correct BPMN diagram.

Now, we are ready to start creating the BPMN-based diagram type.

> **Please also note**
>
> This chapter is not intended to teach you the basics and principles of BPMN. There are whole courses and books that deliver training on this, and it would by far exceed the scope of this chapter to provide full training on BPMN. Instead, this chapter focuses on showing you how to create such documentation, adhering to the BPMN standards with the Microsoft Visio tool.

Finding the BPMN template

In this section, we will see how to get started with the BPMN template and how the Visio work environment will look once the template has been initiated correctly. The template can be found in several ways, but all are accessible through the start screen experience.

Figure 4.1 – Finding the BPMN template through the Flowcharts search category

To find the BPMN template and invoke it, there are multiple possible ways to get started, each of which will lead you to the BPMN template:

- Search for the template by entering the name in the search textbox

- In the initial **Office** view, select the **Flowcharts** search category

- Go to **Categories** | the **Templates** view (the second option in the top row of *Figure 4.1*) on the start screen and select the **Flowchart** category

In all cases, you will navigate to a screen and a templates overview, where you will find the BPMN Diagram template.

> **Important note**
>
> Like all other standards, BPMN is constantly extended and improved. The current version of BPMN is version *2.0*. The BPMN template for Visio is conformant with BPMN 2.0. This is the same version that is also delivered by Visio. The rule-checking engine in Visio is even able to check whether the diagram adheres to the BPMN 2.0 standard and rules.

The following screenshot shows how and where the BPMN template is visible in the Visio UI:

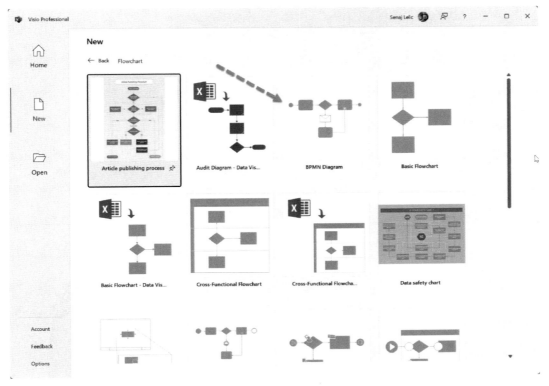

Figure 4.2 – The BPMN Diagram template

Click on the template to open it. Once you click on it, you will see the *starter* diagrams experience, as shown in *Figure 4.3*. This presents the option of using a pre-populated diagram or creating an empty one:

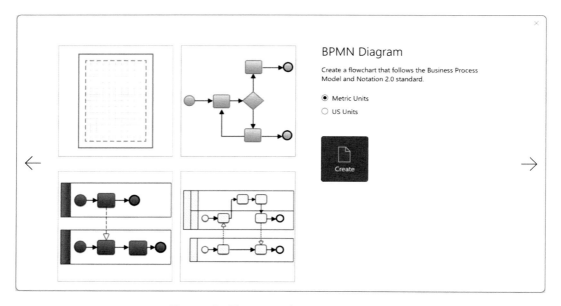

Figure 4.3 – The starter diagrams experience

It is up to you how you want to start. If one of the starter diagrams already looks similar to the diagram you need or you like the visual design and formatting, select the starter diagram; otherwise, start with an empty diagram.

> **Important note**
>
> Make sure you select the right units, since Visio has two types of measurement units, **Metric Units** and **US Units**. You will not break anything if you select the wrong one, but if you live in Europe, working with millimeters and centimeters would certainly be easier, while if you reside in the US, using inches might be easier. In both cases, the page size will be the one that is the standard in your region – **Letter** for the US and **DIN A4** for the rest of the world.

Working in the BPMN diagram environment

Here, we will be working with the BPMN diagram environment, which basically uses the different shapes that Visio provides. The basic UI does not differ from other Visio diagrams, so on the right-hand side, there is a drawing page in landscape (in the size you selected when you selected the template), and on the left-hand side, there is a stencil with the BPMN basic shapes.

The BPMN stencil delivers the following shapes:

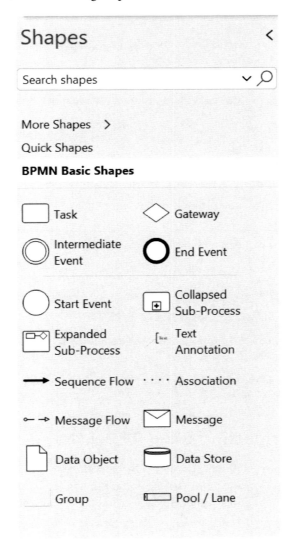

Figure 4.4 – The shapes in the BPMN Basic Shapes stencil

The shapes in the stencil are as follows:

- **Task**: Describes a task or process step
- **Gateway**: Describes a branch or decision
- **Intermediate Event**: An event between a **Start** and **End** event

- **End Event**: An indicator that the process is ending/has ended

- **Start Event**: An event that initiates the process

- **Collapsed Sub-Process**: A placeholder for a full process, described somewhere else (usually another file or page in the same drawing)

- **Expanded Sub-Process**: Creates a visual container that can be placed on the same page or another page to surround a process that is a sub-component of the current process

- **Text Annotation**: A shape that can be used to add comments, annotations, or remarks to the process elements

- **Sequence Flow**: A connector line that describes the flow of the process that progresses from element to element (e.g., from a task to a gateway or from a gateway to another task)

- **Association**: Not a flow but an indicator that two elements have a relation, which can have several variations

- **Message Flow**: The direction and flow of a message between elements

- **Message**: A message created or received

- **Data Object**: Some data created or received

- **Data Store**: A place of storage for data (e.g., a database)

- **Group**: A visual container for objects with a common topic (e.g., all elements that describe the storage of data)

- **Pool / Lane**: A method of indicating and containing elements for a specific participant (for example, department). Note that the BPMN standard defines both, a *pool* and a *lane*

Changes and formatting of all BPMN shapes

The BPMN standard defines every object not only by its initial configuration but also by several variations. For example, following the BPMN standards, **Start Event** can have several visual variations, and the container object can be either a pool or a lane. With normal diagramming tools, they would have to be different objects, but here, we use the Visio technology of **smart shapes**, which allows us to have one object with variations instead of various different objects. This section will show you how to manipulate the shapes and where to get the variation of the shape you need for your documentation.

Accessing the variations through metadata

All variations of a specific object can be set by setting the corresponding metadata. Metadata in Visio is called **shape data**. So, we start by opening **Shape Data Window** in Visio. Access to this window is placed on the **Data** ribbon tab:

Figure 4.5 – Access to Shape Data Window

To get there, execute the following steps:

1. Select the **Data** ribbon tab.
2. Check the **Shape Data Window** checkbox.

The **Shape Data** window will give you access to all the metadata of a selected shape, or the mutually existing metadata of multiple selected shapes. By selecting a specific value, the shape will change its appearance to the pre-coded variation of the shape.

So, for example, for the **Start Event** shape, the property called **EventType** will change the visual appearance of the shape.

Initially, the **Start Event** shape is an empty circle, and the shape data value is **Start**.

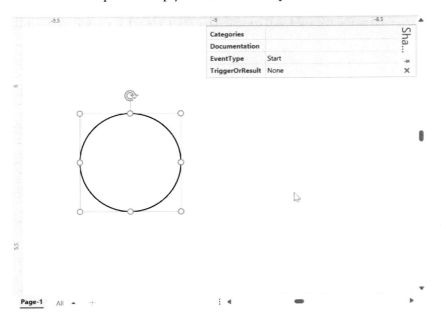

Figure 4.6 – The Start Event shape in its initial configuration

However, if we change the value of the **EventType** shape data element to the **Start (Non-Interrupting)** value, we see a change in the shape.

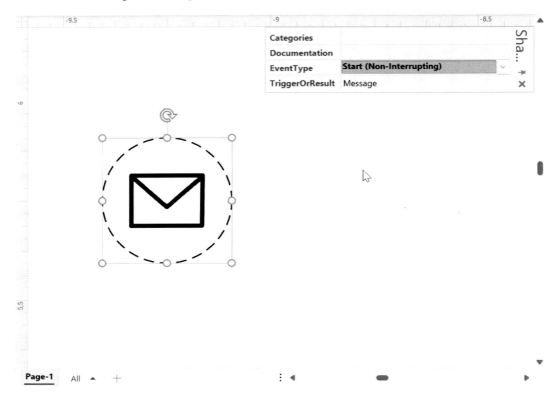

Figure 4.7 – The Start Event shape in the Start (Non-Interrupting) variant

The formatting has changed; the shape now has a dashed line as the line format. Also, in the inner part of the shape, a *letter* symbol is shown.

Setting the **EventType** value to **Intermediate** will again change the appearance of the shape – it will now show with a double line but no inner content.

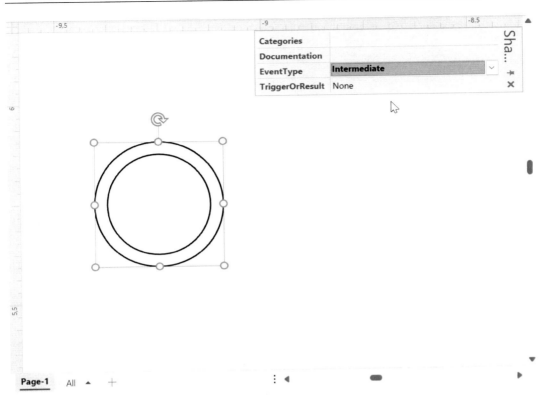

Figure 4.8 – The Start event shape in the Intermediate variant

So with this Visio-style approach, we can have many different visual objects being represented by only one single *master shape* in the stencil, but every shape can have numerous variations of the initial configuration.

> **Important note**
>
> Some value changes to metadata will only change the visual appearance, but there are values that will change even the structure of the metadata, so some properties/shape data elements might appear or disappear accordingly.

To show this, let's see the **Task** shape. In its initial configuration, it is an empty rectangle with rounded corners.

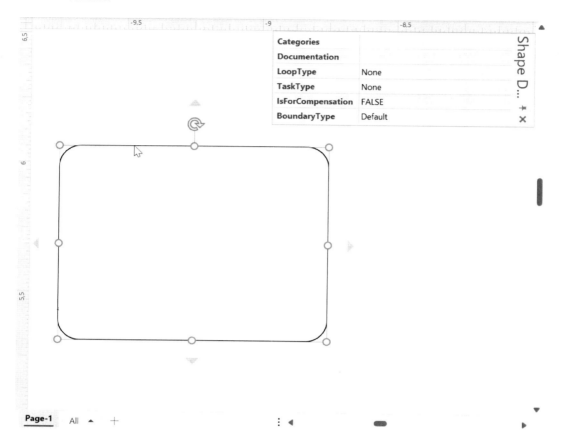

Figure 4.9 – The Task shape in its initial configuration

However, if we set the **TaskType** property to **Script**, two things happen:

- The shape gets a document paper symbol added to its inner area
- A new shape data element/property, **Script**, appears, which is only there for this specific task type

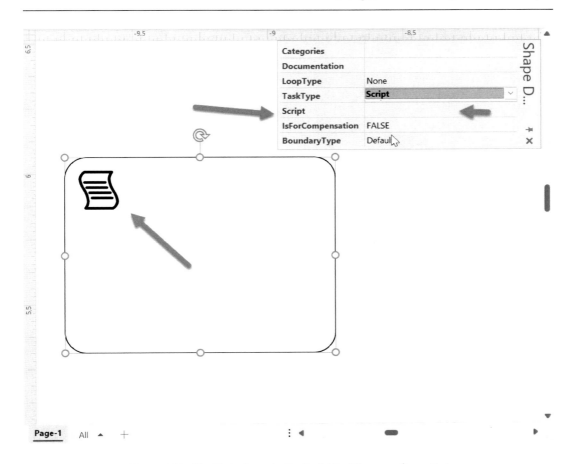

Figure 4.10 – The Task shape in the Script TaskType configuration

So, sometimes changing the type will not only change the appearance but also result in new metadata elements being added to the shape itself.

> **Important note**
> For many shapes, the visual configuration can also be done through the context menu. To achieve this, simply right-click on the shape and select the option from the context menu.

Getting started with placing the shapes and formatting the shapes

Here, we will create our first BPMN-type diagram and modify the shapes. Since a simple flow in BPMN always follows the same principle and contains at least the four basic elements, we will start with those. After that, we will see how to manipulate the appearance of the shapes (following the BPMN standard) by manipulating the shape data (i.e., the metadata of the shapes).

Adding the start event

The first step in a BPMN flow is an event initiating the flow – typically, a start event, so we place this shape on the page. Initially, it looks like a simple circle; however, the BPMN standard defines several variations to the start event (for a full description, please check out the aforementioned **BPMN quick guide**).

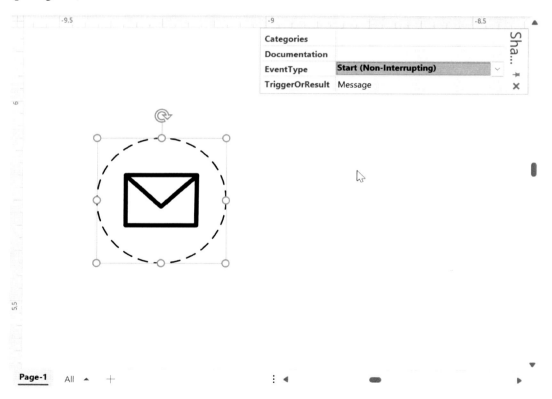

Figure 4.11 –The Start Event shape fully configured

Extending the diagram with a task

After this, the next step is to add the follow-up component, which would typically be a task. So, we add the **Task** shape to the diagram too.

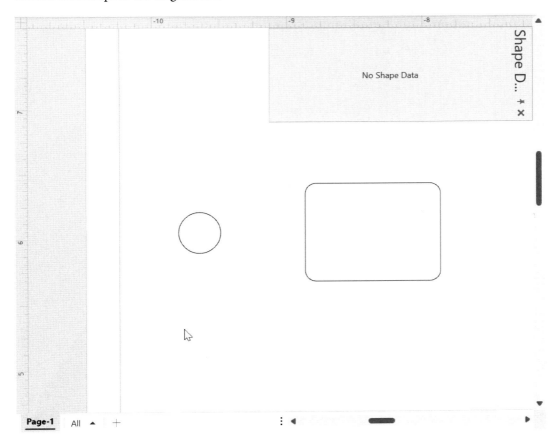

Figure 4.12 – A diagram with a start event and a Task shape

Connecting the shapes

Now that the shapes have been placed, the next step is to connect them. Since this indicates the flow of the process, the **Sequence Flow** shape is needed. It is basically a *connector* in Visio terms.

While dragging the shape on the drawing page, both of the process shapes will highlight their connection points to show where the shape can be connected and glued to. If the shapes are within a certain proximity, a drop would connect them immediately, but if not, a glue can be established afterward.

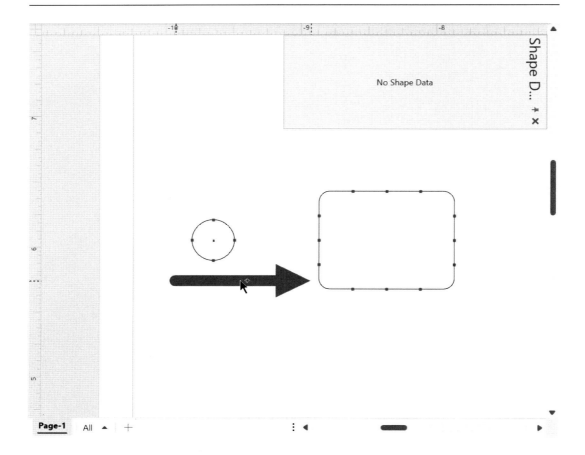

Figure 4.13 – Connection points during the dropping of the shape

There is nothing wrong with connecting the shape afterward, end to end, after dropping it. When connecting, make sure you use the **Sequence Flow** shape.

> **Important note**
> The shapes must be glued and connected so that they create a real flow. If a shape is not glued properly, an error will occur during the validation.

So, while dropping, we can already ensure that the begin and the end of the **Sequence Flow** shape are glued to the corresponding shape. However, as stated, it is not mandatory from the start.

Instead of picking one specific connection point, we can also drop the sequence flow above the two shapes – in this case, Visio will create what we call a dynamic glue. If you want to learn more about the different types of glue in Visio, please refer to *Chapter 3*.

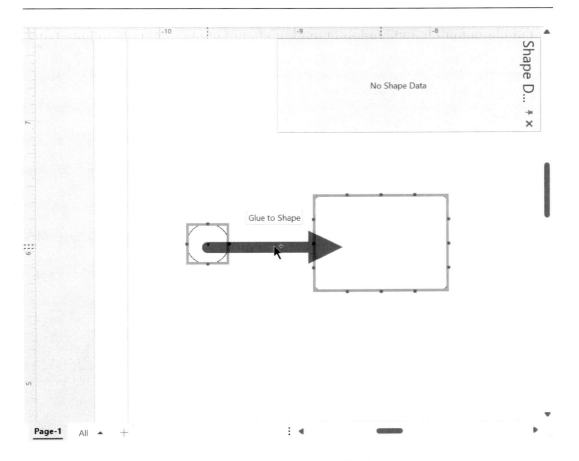

Figure 4.14 – Two shapes connected with a dynamic glue

Both shapes are now connected at the connection point that is the nearest to the other shape and minimizes the length of the connector (the **Sequence** shape).

Visio for the web and BPMN

At the time of writing this book, only Visio Plan 2 desktop is able to create, modify, and edit BPMN files.

However, the Visio team at Microsoft is actively working on extending Visio web with BPMN templates and also with capabilities to edit shape data in shapes, which would give you the ability to also create, edit, and modify any BPMN diagram file in Visio for the web – that is, the web portion of your Visio Plan 2 license.

> **Important note**
>
> Please ensure that you have the right Visio license. To edit BPMN diagram files, you will need a Visio Plan 2 license; a regular Plan 1 license will not contain the BPMN templates and not give you the ability to edit BPMN diagram files.

Validating the structure and syntax of BPMN diagrams

As shown in *Chapter 3*, Visio has a built-in engine to validate that a diagram adheres to certain standards. This validation will check for errors in the *graphical syntax*, such as the following:

- Are all shapes connected?

- Does a gateway shape have one or at least one incoming connection only (so does one arrowhead end at the gateway shape)?

- Does a gateway shape have at least two outgoing connections (so it is indeed a branch we documented)?

These and many more rules are already stored in the diagram template. So, all we need to do is to invoke the **Check Diagram** feature.rules checking.

Since Visio has a built-in rule-checking engine, we can use this and tell it to check this diagram according to the rules and standards of the BPMN notation rules. This will ensure that we will have a diagram that correctly follows the BPMN visual syntax:

Figure 4.15 – Access to the diagram validation feature

In this screenshot, you can see where you can access the rule-checking functionality.

To get there, follow these steps:

1. Select the **Process** ribbon tab.
2. Select **Diagram Validation** | the **Check Diagram** button.

However, to ensure the right ruleset is applied, check that the **BPMN 2.0** ruleset is loaded. To achieve this, select the small dropdown on the **Check Diagram** button and then **Rules to Check**.

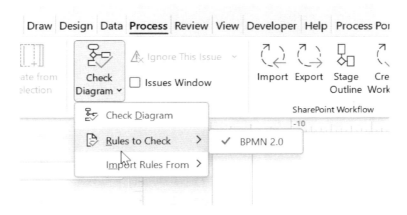

Figure 4.16 – Checking for the right set of rules

Now, if you selected the BPMN template at the beginning, this should always be correct, but if you started with the **Blank Drawing** template, then you might need to import the ruleset, which can be accomplished from the **Import Rules From** menu.

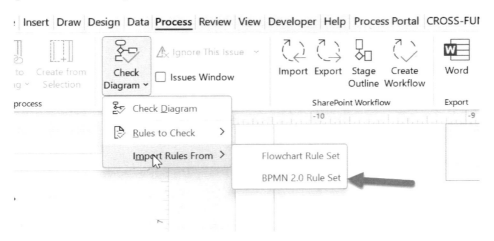

Figure 4.17 – Importing the BPMN 2.0 ruleset

Important note

Importing a set of rules will only be needed if you did not start with the BPMN diagram template.

If the diagram encounters errors, the error window will open and show a list of errors:

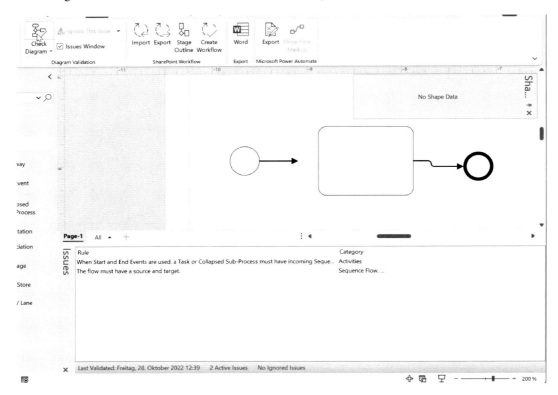

Figure 4.18– A BPMN diagram with validation errors

If no errors are found, Visio will report **Diagram validation is complete. No issues were found in the current document**.

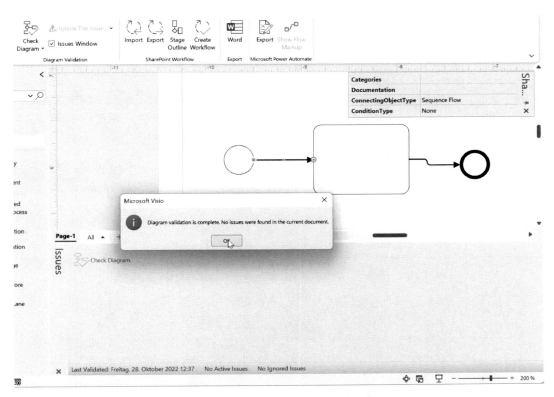

Figure 4.19 – A validation check completed without errors

> **Important note**
>
> The diagram check will check for errors in the optical syntax, meaning that it will report whether the diagram is technically correct. However, it will not check whether the process itself is logical or whether it is a correctly documented process. This is similar to spell checking, which will tell you if there are misspelled words but not whether your sentence makes sense.

Now that we have covered modeling in BPMN itself, let's briefly discuss a very interesting extension of the BPMN template – the ability to export the BPMN flow into Microsoft **Power Automate**.

A built-in scenario for the BPMN template – the Power Automate export

Now that we have covered BPMN in general, the question is whether there is more we can do than just document business processes. The answer is *yes*. The Visio team has added an extension to the Visio desktop client in Visio Plan 2, so a flow can be attached to Microsoft Power Automate and then exported. This allows us to model and design a Power Automate flow *"offline"* in Visio and then attach it to a specific **Microsoft 365** environment.

> **Important note**
>
> Microsoft made this feature exclusively for Visio Plan 2. That means it is not available in Visio web editions (even if you have Visio Plan 2 attached to your user account), nor is it available in Visio Professional.

To start, we simply open the BPMN template in Visio. There is also a specific BPMN Power Automate export template, **Microsoft Flow Diagram**, but basically, these two templates are the same. The only difference is that the latter already creates a very basic flow as a starter.

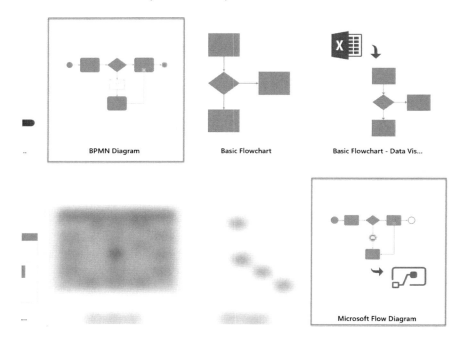

Figure 4.20 – The two templates for the Power Automate export

So, we pick either the **Microsoft Flow Diagram** or **BPMN Diagram** template. Here, we will start with the first one.

Once the template is instantiated, we are presented with the following starter diagram.

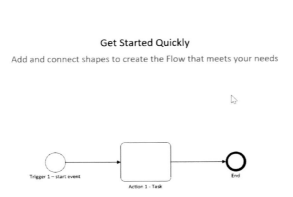

Figure 4.21 – The starting point for a flow

This diagram contains all a Power Automate flow needs – an initial *trigger*, an *action*, and the *end*.

Every Power Automate flow is initiated by an event. This could be a system event or a user doing something. The Power Automate flow then executes a series of actions or tasks (called an *action* in **Power Automate**, but a *task* in BPMN).

So, to successfully create a flow that works in Power Automate, we must first assign a *trigger* from the **Power Automate Flow** system to the *trigger/start* object. Then, we must assign an *activity* to the *task* object. That is all we need to do to enable the export.

Assigning the Power Automate elements to the shapes in the Visio diagram

The **Process | Microsoft Power Automate** tab has the buttons we need to assign Power Automate elements to shapes in the Visio diagram, as shown here.

Figure 4.22 – The Power Automate functions in the Process ribbon

To start, we simply click the **Export** button to open the panel with the buttons and settings for this solution, as shown in *Figure 4.23*.

> **Important note**
> To be able to use this function, you must be logged in to Visio with a **Microsoft 365** account, and your cloud-based account must have a **Power Automate** license assigned; otherwise, you will not be able to proceed.

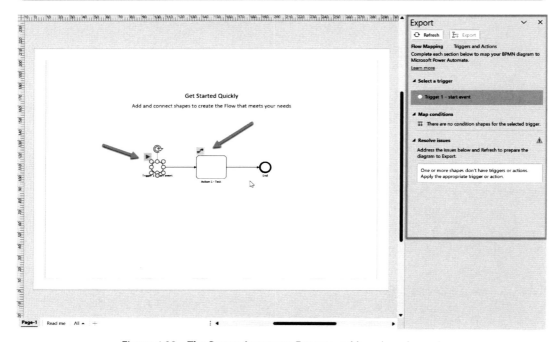

Figure 4.23 – The Power Automate Export workbench and panel

We can see, in the preceding screenshot, that each BPMN flowchart shape, except the **End** shape, displays a small graphical extension, which is the indicator that it is prepared for Power Automate.

On the right side, we can see the Power Automate **Export** panel. However, since the elements have not yet been assigned, we also see the **Resolve issues** section, which tells us what is preventing the flow from being exported right now.

To properly configure this, we must click on each of the graphical extensions:

- The green arrow for the *trigger*
- The gray flow symbol for the *task/action*

Let us first click on the green arrow next to the *trigger* or *start* event, as shown in the following screenshot.

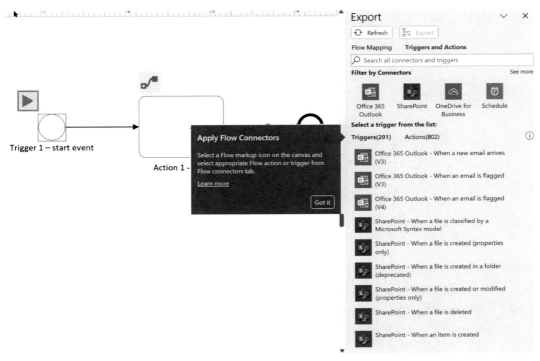

Figure 4.24 – The workbench with the preloaded trigger objects

Now, we can see a list of all trigger events available in the Power Automate flow system. Just pick one that fits your needs – in this case, **Office 365 Outlook - When a new email arrives (V3)** – by clicking on the entry on the right-hand side.

> **Important note**
>
> The loading of the list of connectors can take time. Sometimes, it takes several seconds until the elements are available and visible; the same applies to the process of assigning a trigger to an event object.

After the trigger event has been successfully assigned, the green arrow disappears and an icon of the component used as a trigger is shown – in our case, Office 365 Outlook.

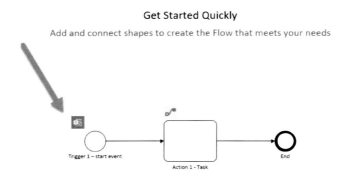

Figure 4.25 – The Outlook event successfully attached to the start event object

We can now proceed to configure the Power Automate elements for all other objects.

After that, we hit the **Refresh** button on the workbench, and then, if we did everything correctly, the **Resolve issues** section will report **There are no issues to resolve**.

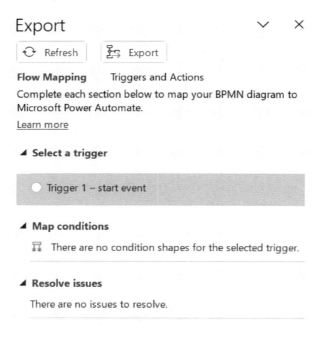

Figure 4.26 – A successfully configured flow

So, the flow is now fully configured, and we can initiate the export.

Exporting the flow to Microsoft Power Automate

Now, we can click on the **Export** button and start the export.

The export basically just requires us to log in with our Microsoft 365 credentials, give the flow a name, and then hit the **Export** button. This will open the necessary dialog.

Figure 4.27 – The login and export to the Microsoft 365 Power Automate backend

Please pay attention to the small red circle – you are required to log in with your Microsoft 365 credentials. The next figure shows you the details. This dialog can be accessed by clicking on the three dots next to the red sign (see red arrow in *Figure 4.27*).

Figure 4.28 – Picking the right connection for your Microsoft 365 backend

Once the connection has been validated, you can initiate the export to the Power Automate backend. Note that in the preceding screenshot, some connections have a red flag, which means they are not valid for the Power Automate export. When the connection is verified (the red flag turns to a green check), we are ready to create the flow.

Figure 4.29 – The validated connection and the flow ready to export

Once the connection is verified, the **Create flow** button becomes active, turns blue, and can be clicked to start the creation of the flow.

Once the flow has been created, Visio will report the success in a final dialog.

Figure 4.30 – Final confirmation of the creation of the flow

When Visio is finished, a final confirmation will be shown, meaning that the flow is now present in the Power Automate backend.

> **Note – completion of properties needed in the Power Automate backend**
>
> Once exported, we will need to complete the properties of each *action* and *trigger* in the Power Automate backend system because these are not available within Visio. These configuration settings depend on data that is only available in a specific selected tenant.

This section showed that we can use Visio Plan 2 desktop to easily plan and design Power Automate flows, which can then be easily exported to as many Microsoft 365 backends as desired.

Summary

In this chapter, we learned how to create a BPMN-type diagram in Visio Plan 2 or Visio Professional. We also learned how to configure the shapes to represent the various options the BPMN standard allows and defines. In the end, we also saw that rule checking in Visio can help us to validate and visually spell-check the diagram. So, with this chapter, we learned how to find the BPMN template, invoke it correctly, and also use the built-in mechanisms to create diagrams that are correct according to the BPMN visual standard. This approach ensures that we can quickly create diagrams with very few elements. Beyond that, Visio can check for us whether we have made some minor visual mistakes, ensuring we get a full BPMN-compliant diagram.

In the next chapter, we will learn how to use data sources in business process diagrams in Visio.

Utilizing Data Sources to Create and Enrich Business Process Diagrams

The previous chapters taught us how to manually create business process diagrams. However, there are ways of automating the creation or updating the diagram from external data and even updating the data from the diagram. So, in this chapter, we will review the no-code techniques available to us:

- Creating process diagrams automatically in Excel
- Creating process diagrams automatically from data in Visio for Desktop
- Creating Visio for Desktop and Excel process diagram templates for others
- Adding extra information to process steps

Technical requirements

The following are the Microsoft apps that are utilized in this chapter, and we should have access to at least one of the Visio subscriptions, but Visio Plan 2 subscribers will be able to use all of the features described:

- **Teams**: The desktop or web app
- **Visio Reading View**: The web-only app
- **Visio in Microsoft 365**: The web-only app
- **Visio Plan 1**: The web-only subscription app
- **Visio Plan 2**: The desktop and web subscription apps
- **Excel**: Microsoft 365 editions

The sample files of the chapter are placed here: `https://github.com/PacktPublishing/Visualize-complex-processes-with-Microsoft-Visio/tree/main/Chapter5`

Creating process diagrams automatically in Excel

A free add-in for Microsoft Excel, called **Microsoft Visio Data Visualizer**, is available from the **Office Store** via the **Insert | Add-Ins | Get Add-ins** button:

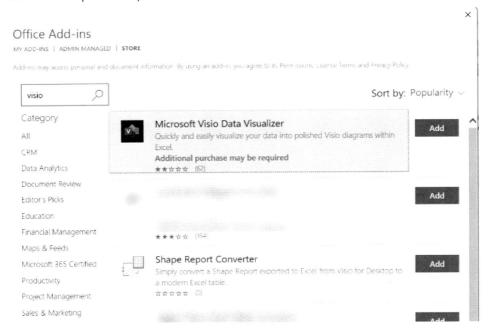

Figure 5.1 – Getting the Microsoft Visio Data Visualizer add-in for Excel

> **Important note**
> The **Shape Report Converter** add-in, listed third in the preceding screenshot list, is a handy free tool from **bVisual**, to quickly convert a *Visio Shape Report* that has been exported to Excel into a modern formatted table that can be used as a data source for *PowerQuery* and Visio.

The **Microsoft Visio Data Visualizer** add-in will be available with its own icon on the ribbon when it is installed. When the icon is clicked, a **Data Visualizer** object is inserted in the worksheet, as shown in the following screenshot, presenting a choice of different diagram types:

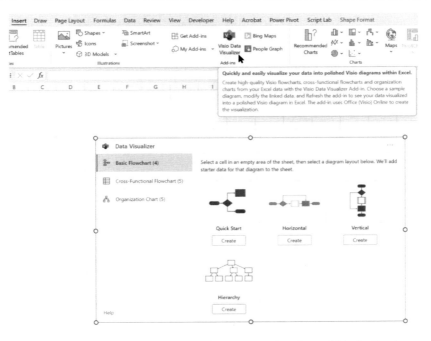

Figure 5.2 – Choices for the Microsoft Visio Data Visualizer add-in for Excel

This add-in requires an internet connection because it uses a web service to create the Visio diagram. When we click the **Create** button in the add-in object, it will insert a sample table and create one of three diagram types, **Basic Flow Chart**, **Cross-Functional Flowchart**, or **Organization Chart**, as a Visio diagram embedded in the worksheet:

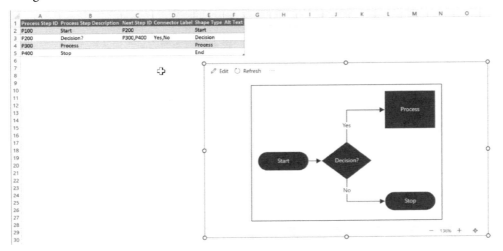

Figure 5.3 – Example data of the Visio Data Visualizer add-in

We can move the Visio diagram by clicking an edge and dragging it or resize it by clicking and dragging one of the corners or mid-point circles. We can now edit the table in Excel by inserting, editing, or deleting rows. Each of the rows should have a unique value in the **Process Step ID** column, and the **Data Checker** feature of the add-in will highlight in pink if a value is missing or duplicated, as in the following screenshot:

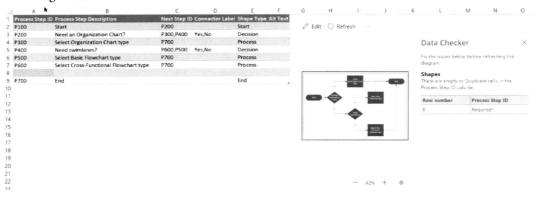

Figure 5.4 – The Visio Data Visualizer checks the data

The table contains the following columns:

1. **Process Step ID**: This is a unique value for each row.

2. **Process Step Description**: This is the text that will be inserted into the flowchart shapes.

3. **Next Step ID**: This should contain only values that exist in the **Process Step ID** column. Multiple target IDs should be separated by a comma. **Data Checker** will highlight any invalid values and list them in a panel in the **Data Visualizer** frame.

4. **Connector Label**: This can optionally contain the text that should be applied to the connectors between the flowchart shapes, and they should be separated by commas in the same order as the **Next Step ID** values.

5. **Shape Type**: This value should be one of the following from the names of the flowchart shapes on the **Basic Flowchart** stencil:

   • **Process**

   • **Decision**

   • **Subprocess**

   • **Start**

   • **End**

   • **Document**

   • **Data**

- **Database**
- **External Data**
- **On-page reference**
- **Off-page reference**
- **Custom 1**
- **Custom 2**
- **Custom 3**
- **Custom 4**

6. **Alt Text**: This is an extra description that can be read by screen readers for accessibility.

Once the rows have been edited, simply click the **Refresh** button in the header bar of the **Visio Data Visualizer** diagram frame to see the diagram updated, as in the following screenshot:

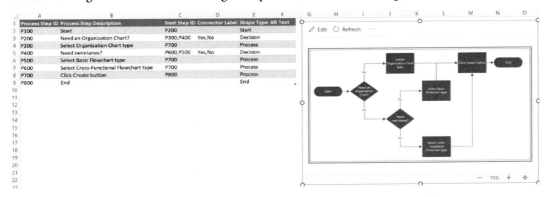

Figure 5.5 – Updated data redrawn by the Visio Data Visualizer add-in

We should save the Excel workbook before using the **Edit** button in the **Data Visualizer** frame because the add-in needs to create a Visio document in the cloud first. The **Edit** button will only work for Visio Plan 1 or Visio Plan 2 subscribers; Visio for M365 does not have this capability.

Editing in Visio online

If we click the **Edit** button to open the diagram online with Visio for the Web, we should immediately rename it as something more useful than the **Drawing xx** name automatically assigned by **Visio Data Visualizer**. In the following screenshots, we have clicked on the default **Drawing 20** name in the header bar and given it a more meaningful name. Then we edited the page in Visio for the Web by a title using **Home** | **Insert** | **Text Box**, above the **Data Visualizer** rectangular container and applied a different theme:

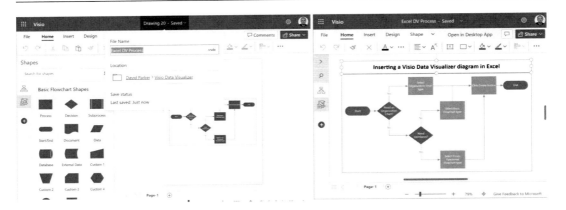

Figure 5.6 – Immediately rename in Visio online and edit as required

We can also change the layout by using the **Design | Diagram Layout** options, as described in the *Automatically changing the diagram layout* section in *Chapter 3*. These edits will be simultaneously applied to the diagram in the **Data Visualizer** frame in Excel.

Editing in desktop Visio

There is even an **Open the diagram in the Desktop App** option if you have Visio Plan 2, when the diagram is opened in Visio online (Visio for the Web). The diagram has been opened in Visio Plan 2 in the following screenshot, a different layout has been applied, and rounded corners have been added to the shapes. Also, notice that the **Shape Data** window displays the values that are synchronized with the Excel table rows. The right-hand image is the updated diagram in Excel after it was saved by the Visio desktop app:

Figure 5.7 – Edited in Visio desktop and refreshed in Excel

> **Important note**
> It may be necessary to close and reopen the Excel workbook to see the name of the Visio diagram updated in the **Data Visualizer** frame and to click the **Refresh** button.

There are limits to the edits you can make to the layout because it will be updated by the **Data Visualizer** add-in. Therefore, we must use one of the preset layouts only because any manual rearrangements will be lost when the add-in refreshes the layout.

Using the example Cross-Functional Flowchart of the Data Visualizer process

So far, we have used the **Basic Flowchart** template with the **Data Visualizer** wizard, but there is the **Cross-Functional Flowchart** type too. This allows us to use two extra columns, **Function** and **Phase**, as in the following table that describes the **Data Visualizer** wizard process, which is the next section's subject:

Figure 5.8 – Top of the example Cross-Functional Flowchart table

In fact, this is just the first 14 of 39 steps in the table that can be found in the supplied example `Data Visualizer Process.xlsx` file.

The values in the **Function** column will become the text of the **Swimlane** headers.

The values in the **Phase** column will become the text in the **Separator** headers.

The sample data produces the following horizontal **Cross-Functional Flowchart** diagram:

Figure 5.9 – The top of the example Cross-Functional Flowchart table

The flowchart shapes are sequentially arranged within their respective horizontal swimlanes and vertical phases (separators).

The swimlane container has a header labeled **Title**, which can only be edited with a Visio subscription license:

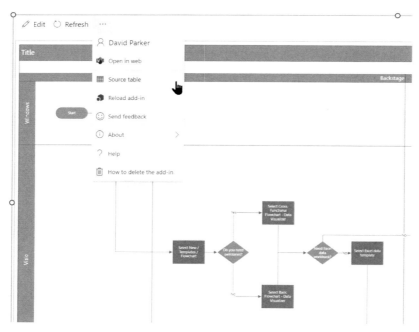

Figure 5.10 – The top of the example Cross-Functional Flowchart table

The main options on the drop-down menu of the **Data Visualizer** frame are as follows:

- **Open In web**: You will need to create a Visio document first before opening it in the browser

- **Source table**: This changes the active selection in Excel to the source table

- **Reload add-in**: This will reload the add-in in case there is an issue or update

- **Help**: This will open the following Microsoft support page about the **Visio Data Visualizer** add-in for Excel: `https://support.microsoft.com/office/create-a-diagram-in-excel-with-the-visio-data-visualizer-add-in-bee3b5aa-aaaf-4401-acc6-276b711c763c`

This particular example describes the process for creating a linked Visio flowchart and Excel table, which will be expanded on in the next section.

Creating process diagrams automatically from data in Visio for Desktop

We have now learned about the **Visio Data Visualizer** add-in for Excel, but it is only one small part of the **Data Visualizer** tool. It can also be used to create separate Visio and Excel documents that can be synchronized with each other.

In fact, if we have Visio Plan 2 installed, we can start **Data Visualizer** from either Visio, shown on the left, or Excel, shown on the right in the following screenshots:

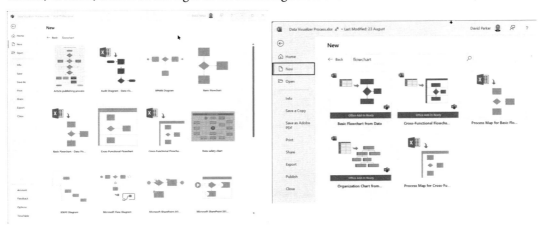

Figure 5.11 – The Data Visualizer templates with the Excel icon in the top left

If we click one of the Visio templates, such as **Cross-Functional Flowchart – Data Visualizer**, then we will be offered a button to start a new Excel workbook from one of the templates that would be opened from Excel.

Understanding and editing the Data Visualizer Excel workbook

The Excel template workbook displays four tabs, but there is also a hidden one that is used for a lookup:

- **Visio Data Visualizer**: This is a quick-start guide
- **Understand the Process Map**: This is a description of the required and optional columns
- **Process Map**: This is the `ProcessMapData` table
- **Visio Trial**: This is a link to a web page to get a Visio subscription trial at `https://aka.ms/VisioPlans_DVExcelAdd-in`
- **Shape Notation Mapping**: This is a hidden list of the master names used by the **Shape Type** column in the process map table

In the following screenshot, we have opened the **Cross-Functional Flowchart** template:

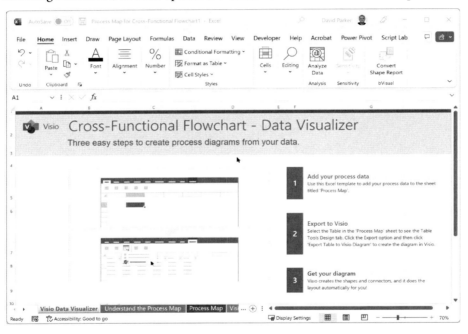

Figure 5.12 – The Data Visualizer Excel template

The Excel template has a table that is very similar to the one inserted by the **Visio Data Visualizer** add-in for Excel, but with some subtle differences.

The following screenshot is of the **Process Map** worksheet after the suggested optional columns labeled **Owner**, **Cost**, **Start Date**, **End Date**, and **Status** were deleted, and rows from the earlier *Data Visualizer Process* worksheet were pasted in:

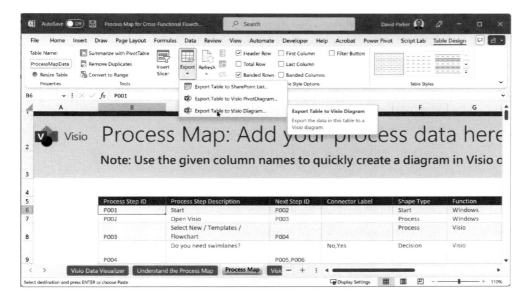

Figure 5.13 – Process Map with non-required columns removed

Note that the **Alt Description** column is the same as the **Alt Text** column used by the Excel add-in earlier.

The **Shape Type** values must be selected from the provided drop-down list created from the hidden **Shape Notation Mapping** worksheet. The next screenshot shows the lookup list of the values in the hidden worksheet:

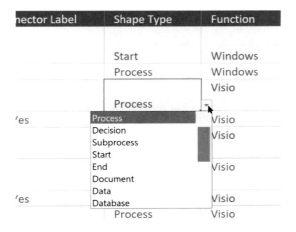

Figure 5.14 – The drop-down list in the Shape Type column

We should have at least one row of data in our Excel table for **Data Visualizer** to make a successful link between Excel and Visio, and we should save the workbook before starting **Data Visualizer**.

Running the Data Visualizer wizard in Visio

There are three ways that the **Data Visualizer** wizard can be started:

1. In Excel, select any cell within the table to be made into a diagram:

    A. Click the **Table Design | External Table Data | Export | Export Table to Visio Diagram** command, as shown in *Figure 5.13*.

    B. Visio will open with a new document created from a flowchart template.

    C. The **Data Visualizer** wizard labeled **Create Diagram from Data** will open with the Excel workbook path and the table name already filled in.

2. In Visio, select **File | New | Templates | Flowchart | Cross-Functional Flowchart – Data Visualizer** or **Basic Flowchart – Data Visualizer**:

    There is also an **Audit Diagram – Data Visualizer** template that uses a different list of shape types from the **Audit** stencil.

3. In Visio, on any page, click the **Data | Create from Data | Create** button.

To perform **Step 1**, shown on the left in *Figure 5.15,* do the following:

1. Select the type of diagram from the first drop-down list:

    A. **Basic Flowchart**

    B. **Cross Functional Flowchart (horizontal)**

    C. **Cross Functional Flowchart (vertical)**

2. Select or enter the Excel workbook path.

3. Select or enter the name of the table or custom range in the workbook.

4. Click **Next**.

Step 2, shown on the right in *Figure 5.15,* is only shown if a **Cross Functional Flowchart** type is selected because the **Basic Flowcharts** option does not include swimlanes:

1. Drag a column from **Available Columns** into the **Function or Swimlane** box.

2. Optionally drag a column from **Available Columns** into the **Phase or Timeline** box.

3. Optionally check to retain the order of column values for the following options:

    A. **Function or Swimlane**

    B. **Phase or Timeline**

4. Click **Next**.

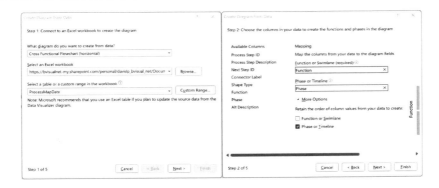

Figure 5.15 – Selecting the source table, swimlane, and phase columns

Step 3, shown in *Figure 5.16,* is the same as **Step 2** for **Basic Flowcharts**:

1. Drag a column from **Available Columns** into the **Process Step ID/Activity ID** box.

2. Optionally drag a column from **Available Columns** into the **Process Step/Activity Description** box.

3. Optionally drag a column from **Available Columns** into the **Shape Type for Process Steps / Activities** box.

4. Optionally drag a column from **Available Columns** into the **Shape Alt Description** box.

5. Click **Next**.

Step 4, shown in *Figure 5.16,* is the same as **Step 3** for **Basic Flowcharts**:

1. Drag a shape from the list of the **Basic Flowchart Shapes** stencil on the right side into the relevant **Shapes** box that matches the **Shape Type** to represent.

   Note the **More Shapes** button does allow you to open other installed stencils.

2. Click **Next**.

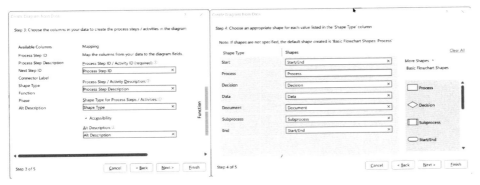

Figure 5.16 – Mapping the process data columns and type shapes

Step 5, shown in *Figure 5.17,* is the same as **Step 4** for **Basic Flowcharts**:

1. Choose how to connect the process steps from the following:

    A. **Connect using column**

    B. **Connect sequentially**

    C. **Don't connect**

2. If connecting using a column, then drag a column from **Available Columns** into the **Specify column name** box.

3. If connecting using a column, ensure that the correct **Next Step ID** or **Previous Step ID** option is selected.

4. If connecting using a column, select the correct delimiter in the text that separates multiple step IDs and their labels from the following:

    A. **(none)**

    B. **, (comma)**

    C. **; (semicolon)**

    D. **: (colon)**

    E.   **space**

5. Optionally drag a column from **Available Columns** into the **Connector Label** box.

6. Click **Finish**.

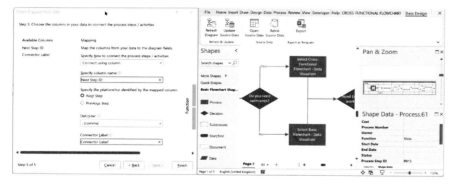

Figure 5.17 – Mapping the connection columns and creating the diagram

The diagram will now be drawn using the default layout arrangement within a special **Data Visualizer** container labeled **Heading**, as shown in the following screenshot. Also, notice that there is a **Cross Functional Flowchart** container labeled **Title**. Both of these can now be edited to be more relevant.

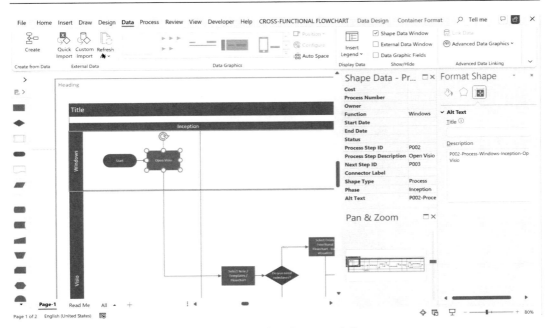

Figure 5.18 – Reviewing the created diagram

Despite our best efforts, we rarely get it all correct when entering data in a table, so it is very fortunate that **Data Visualizer** can also update the source table after editing the graphics.

Updating the source table from Visio

In this example, there are a couple of rows that should have been a **Decision** shape in the table, but they were incorrectly entered as a **Process** shape, so they appeared as a **Process** shape in the diagram, as shown here:

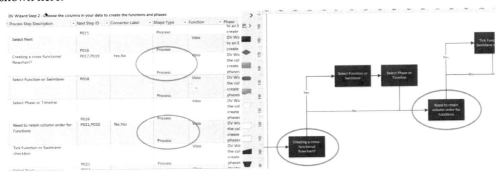

Figure 5.19 – Noticing errors

In Visio, we can use the **Home | Editing | Change Shape** drop-down gallery to swap the **Process** shapes for the **Decision** shapes:

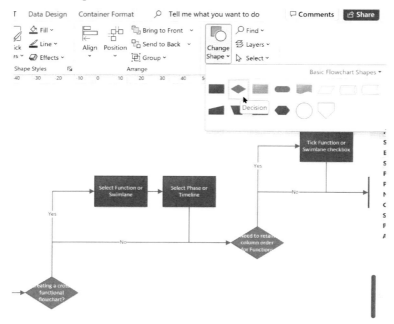

Figure 5.20 – Changing shapes

Connectors can also be moved to the vertices of the **Decision** shape to make the routing clearer.

> **Important note**
>
> The **Data Design** and **Container Format** ribbon tabs are contextual tabs, and these tabs will only appear when we select the special **Data Visualizer** container shape or one of the flowchart shapes within it.

After we have made the edits in Visio, we should ensure that the Excel workbook is closed before clicking the **Data Design | Refresh & Update | Update Source Table** button, as shown in the top left of the following screenshot. We will get an error message if we do not close the workbook first. We can see that the updates are done when we reopen the Excel workbook, as shown in the image on the right in the following screenshot:

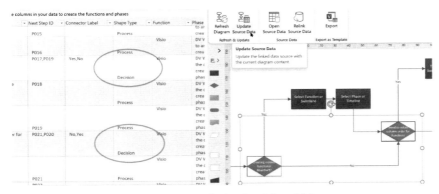

Figure 5.21 – Updating Excel from Visio

We only made a simple shape change in this example, but we could have deleted shapes, added more flowchart shapes, connected them, and labeled them too. The source table will be updated with all of the changes.

Although we created a straightforward **Cross-Functional Flowchart** diagram in this example, we could have added more columns in the Excel table, and the data fields with values would be added to the shape data. In addition, we could have edited the hidden Excel worksheet, **Shape Notation Mapping**, to use shape names from a different stencil.

Creating Visio for Desktop and Excel process diagram templates for others

We have been using the instance of master shapes from the **Basic Flowchart Shapes** stencil in this chapter. We have seen, for a given shape, that in addition to pre-defined shape data fields, additional shape data fields with values as specified in our source data table are appended to **Shape Data** when the diagram has been created using *Data Visualizer*. The pre-defined **Shape Data** fields on each of these shapes will have no data placed in them apart from the **Function** row. These pre-defined fields are explained here:

The default **Shape Data** rows (or fields) are as follows:

- **Cost**: This must be numeric and is displayed as currency
- **Process Number**: This must be numeric
- **Function**: This is inherited from the text of the swimlane that it is contained in
- **Start Date**: This must be a date
- **End Date**: This must be a date
- **Status**: This can be selected from a default drop-down list or any other text value

Data Visualizer will update the values in these **Shape Data** rows if the Excel table column names are *exactly* the same as the label. They must be the same case too!

> **Important note**
>
> If we relabeled the **Step ID** column as **Process Number** in Excel, then **Data Visualizer** would change the **Process Number** data type to text for all flowchart shapes that are within the special container. In this case, we would have one less **Shape Data** field. We may also choose to relabel **Next Step ID** as **Next Process Number**.

The **Status** option of the **Shape Data** row has a variable list to select a value from, so we could add a similar list to provide the Excel user with a list to select from. In the following screenshots, we have added a new worksheet with a table that contains the same rows as the list in Visio, and then used **Data | Data Tools | Data Validation** on the **Status** column of our table:

Figure 5.22 – Adding a Status lookup column

We can add all of the default **Shape Data** rows as column headings and add even more if we want to. The following screenshot is of an **Excel** workbook that was originally created from the provided Excel **Data Visualizer** template, but the explanatory worksheets have been deleted, along with the extra rows above the `ProcessMapData` table and the extra columns on the left. This meant that the hidden **Shape Notation Mapping** worksheet was left intact, and the new **Status** worksheet was also hidden:

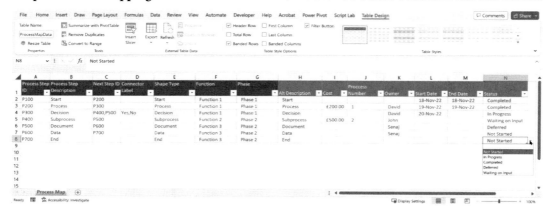

Figure 5.23 – The Excel template with extra columns

We can include some rows of data in the table because it is helpful to others to see how the Excel data is transformed into a diagram in Visio. Of course, the table and the diagram can be edited by the users, and each one used to update the other.

Then we can use the **Table Design | External Table Data | Export | Export Table to Visio Diagram** command to create a new Visio document, as shown here:

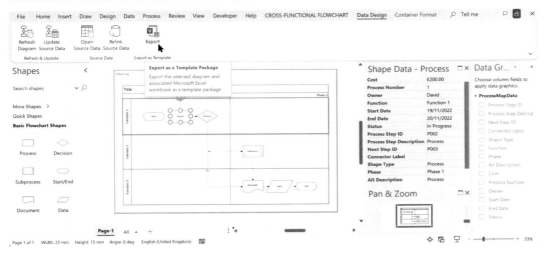

Figure 5.24 – Exporting a package from Visio

We can then click the **Data Design | Export as Template | Export** button to save a template package, as in the following screenshot. This package can then be given to others, and they can simply open it to install the Visio and Excel templates, as indicated by the dialog shown as follows:

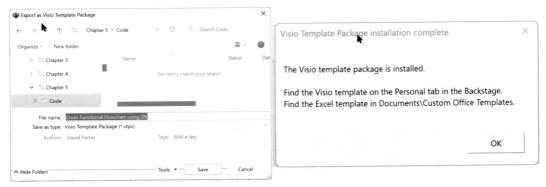

Figure 5.25 – Exporting a package from Visio

We started with an Excel `*.xlsx` workbook and a Visio `*.vsdx` document, but they will be installed as an Excel `*.xltx` template and a Visio `*.vstx` template.

> **Important note**
>
> None of the Excel or Visio documents included in the package are allowed to contain any macros. **Data Visualizer** will not create a package if they do. Also, the Excel workbook must be closed when the **Export** button is clicked in Visio.

If we have mapped any shape types from open custom stencils in the **Visio** workplace when exporting the template, then they will also become part of the package file and will be installed in the `Documents\My Shapes` folder on the workstation when the package is installed.

Once installed, the templates will be available from the **Personal** category in each application, shown as follows:

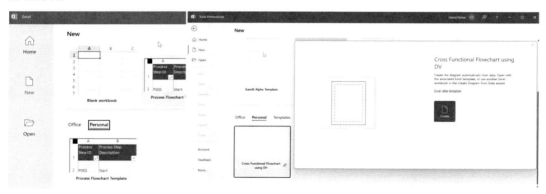

Figure 5.26 – Creating new documents from the custom templates

Now that we have learned about **Data Visualizer** in Visio Plan 2, we will now look at some capabilities that are also available in Visio Professional.

Adding extra information to process steps

One of the best features of Visio Plan 2 is the ability to link data to shapes. So, even if we do not use **Data Visualizer** to create process flowcharts automatically, we can add data to shapes from a variety of data sources. This capability is covered in the book *Mastering Data Visualization with Microsoft Visio Professional 2016* by Packt, and this is still current for Visio Professional and Visio Plan 2. This technique can also be used to enhance diagrams created by **Data Visualizer**.

For example, if we create another Excel table with a column name that matches a unique identifier of the process flowchart shapes in the diagram, then we can link more data, including hyperlinks, to specific shapes. In this example, we have used the **Process Number** column and added a **Url** column that contains more information:

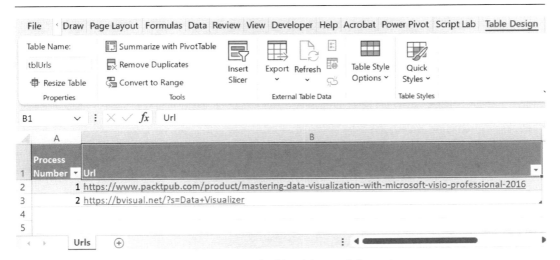

Figure 5.27 – An Excel table with extra information

The **Data | External Data | Custom Import** button in desktop Visio Plan 2 (and Visio Professional) can be used to import data from a number of different sources, and then each row can be linked to one or more shapes in the Visio document. The data will be shown in the **External Data** window, as in the following screenshot, and a row can be dragged and dropped onto an existing shape to add the extra information:

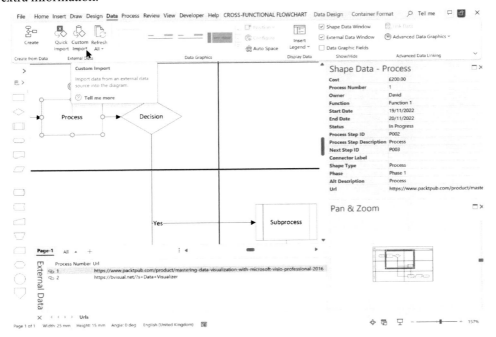

Figure 5.28 – Extra Shape Data, including hyperlinks, added to shapes

If the value is a hyperlink, as in this example, then one or more hyperlinks will be created on the shape. These hyperlinks can be used in online Visio, as in the following screenshot, to access further information about a process step or even to send an email:

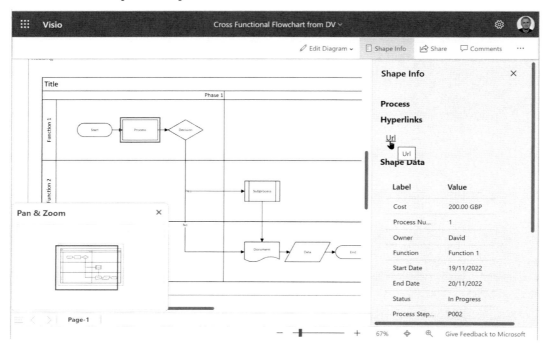

Figure 5.29 – Following a hyperlink online in Visio Reading View

These Visio process flowcharts could become a visual navigation system within Teams or **SharePoint** for company standard operating procedures with links to all of the related information for each step.

These process flowcharts could also be overlayed with data in a custom Teams or SharePoint app or within a **Power BI** dashboard.

We will also learn in *Chapter 7*, about using **Data Graphics** in desktop Visio itself to highlight important information.

Summary

In this chapter, we learned how we can automatically create a business process flowchart diagram from an Excel table. We have also learned how to update the Excel table from the Visio diagram and add more information to each process flowchart shape. Additionally, we also learned how to package combined Visio and Excel templates for others to use.

In practice, many organizations already have tables of steps for different processes. The **Data Visualizer** feature of Visio provides an opportunity to visualize these steps and often results in better understanding and analysis.

In the next chapter, we will learn some useful techniques for augmenting our process diagrams and some more efficient working practices.

6

Learn How to Diagram Efficiently

We learned how to automatically and manually create business process diagrams in the previous chapters; however, we often need to make some manual enhancements to improve the arrangement or add visual impact. We want to perform these tasks quickly and efficiently, so in this chapter, we will go through some skills to make our lives easier. We will learn how to make some useful hidden commands visible and some shortcut keys and keys combined with mouse actions that can speed up diagramming. We will also learn how to select a group of shapes and align or distribute them. Finally, we will go through the options for adding annotations to shapes and including borders and title blocks.

In this chapter, we will cover the following topics:

- Editing the built-in ribbon to provide more options
- Learning useful shortcut keys
- Banding shapes together
- Controlling the layout
- Adding callouts for annotations
- Adding borders and titles
- Printing process diagrams

Technical requirements

These are the Microsoft apps that are utilized in this chapter, and we should have access to at least one of the Visio subscriptions, but Visio Plan 2 subscribers will be able to use all of the features described:

- **Teams**: The desktop or web app
- **Visio Reading View**: The web-only app

- **Visio in Microsoft 365**: The web-only app
- **Visio Plan 1**: The web-only subscription app
- **Visio Plan 2**: The desktop and web subscription apps

The sample files of the chapter are placed here: `https://github.com/PacktPublishing/Visualize-complex-processes-with-Microsoft-Visio/tree/main/Chapter6`.

Editing the built-in ribbon to provide more options

The ability to customize the ribbon is only available in desktop Visio; however, this is where it is most useful since there are many more commands available to us in the desktop version than there are in the web versions. When Microsoft decided to rewrite the user interface in the Office applications many years ago, the ribbon interface with multiple tabs was introduced along the top of the application window. They based this concept on a hand-held clipboard with its ability to grip useful items along the top.

Previously, the user interface had numerous command bars with buttons that could be dragged independently around the screen, so locating them often wasted time. So, having a consistent location along the top saves time, but Microsoft had to limit the immediately available buttons to the most used ones because of space constraints and to provide simplicity. This means that many available buttons are missing unless you decide to add them back in.

> **Important note**
> The ribbon display can be changed between **Show tabs only** and **Always show Ribbon** from the **Ribbon Display Options** button at the bottom- right corner of the ribbon. It also provides the option to toggle the visibility of **Quick Access Toolbar** and to enter **Full screen Mode**.

We have already learned how to add some useful commands to **Quick Access Toolbar** in the *Reversing the direction of flow* section of *Chapter 3*, but now we will look at adding more command buttons to the ribbon.

Creating a new ribbon tab, group, and buttons

Fortunately, desktop Visio makes this easy with the **Customize Ribbon** section on the **Visio Options** dialog that can be opened from **File | Options | Customize Ribbon** or by selecting the **Customize the Ribbon…** option from the menu that appears when you right-click on any unused area of the existing ribbon.

In the following screenshots, we have added a new tab called **My Extras**, and a new group, called **Connections**, which will include the **Reverse Ends** and **Connect Shapes** commands:

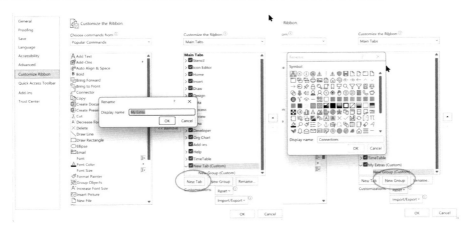

Figure 6.1 – Adding a new ribbon tab and group

We can change the name of the tabs, groups, and commands, and even change the icon to display from a gallery of 180 possible icons. Solution developers can use different icons, either from those provided by the Visio library or custom-installed images, but it is not possible to do this without writing some code.

The following screenshot shows that the **Reverse Ends** command is chosen from the **Commands Not in the Ribbon** option and then selecting **Symbol** from the **Rename** dialog.

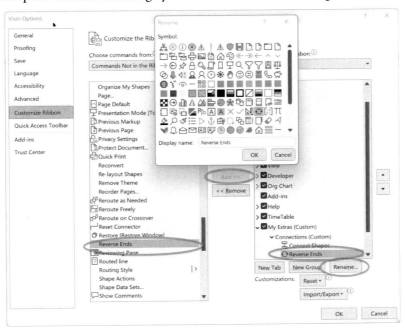

Figure 6.2 – Adding a command to a custom ribbon group

The following screenshot of a custom ribbon contains mostly commands that are not already in the ribbon and are useful for working with process flow diagrams:

Figure 6.3 – A custom ribbon tab

Next, we will explore these commands to understand when they can be useful.

The Connections group

These are some useful commands for use with connectors, especially the **Reverse Ends** one:

- **Connect Shapes**: This creates connections between the sequentially selected shapes
- **Reverse Ends**: This swaps the direction of the selected connectors
- **Connector**: This draws connections between shapes that already exist

The Arrange group

These are useful commands for a selection of process flowchart shapes:

- **Distribute Middle**: This evenly spaces the selected shapes vertically
- **Distribute Center**: This evenly spaces the selected shapes horizontally
- **Re-layout Shapes**: This relays the selected shapes or the whole page if none are selected
- **Center Drawing**: This moves all shapes (unless locked) to be in the center of the page
- **Align**: This opens the **Align Shapes** dialog to act on the selected shapes
- **Multiple Select**: This is a toggle button that allows multiple selections without holding down the *Ctrl* or Shift key

The View group

These are extra commands for changing the view, especially **Last Zoom**, because it cannot be done with any keys or mouse actions:

- **Zoom In**: This zooms in one level
- **Zoom Out**: This zooms out one level
- **100%**: This zooms to the actual size
- **Last Zoom**: This returns to the previous zoom position

We can save our customized ribbon and **Quick Access Toolbar** to a file using the **Import/Export** drop-down button on the **Customize the Ribbon** tab (see *Figure 6.2*) and then import again later or on another computer. However, be aware that importing will remove any existing customizations, so they should be exported first if required again.

The preceding ribbon commands are useful, but there are also a large number of shortcut keys that can really speed up the drawing process.

Learning useful shortcut keys in Visio

There are many shortcut keys available in Visio; however, the following shortcut keys can be utilized to efficiently create or edit process diagrams.

Firstly, some shortcut keys are common to both the desktop and web editions of Visio:

Shortcut keys common in Visio and most M365 and Office applications

Some commands available from key combinations are common to Visio and most Microsoft Office applications:

- *Ctrl + A*: This selects all shapes (unless they are not selectable)
- *Ctrl + S*: This saves the document, however, saving is usually continuous on the web
- *Ctrl + K*: This opens the **Hyperlinks** dialog
- *Ctrl + C*: This copies selected shapes to the clipboard
- *Ctrl + X*: This cuts the selected shapes to the clipboard
- *Ctrl + V*: This pastes the clipboard
- *Delete*: This deletes the selected shapes
- *Esc*: This exits the current edit status
- *Ctrl + B*: This toggles the bold format to the selected text
- *Ctrl + I*: This toggles the italics format to the selected text
- *Ctrl + U*: This toggles the underline format to the selected text
- *Ctrl + F*: This opens the **Find** dialog, or similar

Visio-specific common shortcut keys

Then there are keys that are only applicable to Visio:

- *Ctrl + D*: This duplicates the selected shapes to an offset position

- *Ctrl* + drag: This duplicates selected shapes to the position when the left mouse button is released
- *Shift* + drag: This moves the selected shapes orthogonally until the left mouse button is released
- *Ctrl* + *G*: This groups the selected shapes
- *Ctrl* + shift + *U*: This ungroups the selected shapes
- Arrow keys: These nudge the selection in the direction of the arrow, or pans the page if no shapes are selected
- *Shift* + arrow keys: This moves the selection pixel by pixel in the direction of the arrow
- *Ctrl* + arrow keys: This scrolls the window in the direction of the arrow
- *Enter* or spacebar: This enters the text edit mode of the first selected shape unless it is locked

> **Important note**
>
> It is not recommended to group flowchart shapes together because they will become sub-shapes of the group shape. This will change the routing of connectors and hide their **Shape Data**. Also, ungrouping shapes will remove any **Shape Data** and smart behavior that was added to the group shape.

Many more key combinations are only available in desktop applications.

Using short keys in desktop Visio

Desktop Visio has additional keys that can be used to access commands. For example, there are keys that can be used to navigate around the ribbon. Simply press the *Alt* key to reveal the keys that can be used to access other tabs, groups, and buttons, as shown in the following screenshot:

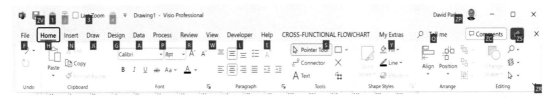

Figure 6.4 – The Alt ribbon keys in desktop Visio

Then there are also a number of useful actions accessed with the *function* keys:

- *F1*: This opens the **Help** pane
- *F2*: This enters the text edit mode of the first selected shape unless it is locked
- *F3*: This opens the **Format Shape** pane
- *F4*: This repeats the last edit action, if possible

- *F5*: This launches the **Full Screen** mode for presentation
- *F6*: This cycles your focus around the **Visio** panes
- *F7*: This checks the spelling of the selected shapes
- *F8*: This opens the **Align Shapes** dialog
- *F9*: This enters **Insert Field** mode
- *F10*: This toggles the display of the ribbon shortcut keys, the same as *Alt*
- *F11*: This opens the **Format Text** dialog
- *F12*: This opens the **File Save As** window

Then there are some more useful commands accessed by holding down the *Ctrl* and *function* keys together:

- *CTRL + F1*: This toggles the ribbon visibility
- *CTRL + F2*: This opens the **File | Print** window
- *CTRL + F4*: This closes the active window, which could be the document

There are even some commands accessed by holding down the *Ctrl*, *Shift*, and *function* keys together, but this one is useful when showing the view to others:

- *Ctrl + Shift + F1*: This toggles the ribbon and menu visibility of the Visio UI, for instance, **Full Screen Mode**

> **Important note**
> Some keyboards may have different key mappings and could be re-assigned. This chapter describes the normal mapping of most keyboards.

Getting quick access to the tools

There are a number of useful actions available with a combination of the *Ctrl* key and another key. The following list can all be seen in the **Home | Tools** ribbon group:

- *Ctrl + 1*: This selects the **Pointer** tool
- *Ctrl + 2*: This selects the **Connector** tool
- *Ctrl + 3*: This selects the **Text** tool
- *Ctrl + 4*: This selects the **Pencil** tool
- *Ctrl + 5*: This selects the **Freeform** tool
- *Ctrl + 6*: This selects the **Line** tool

- *Ctrl + 7*: This selects the **Arc** tool
- *Ctrl + 8*: This selects the **Rectangle** tool
- *Ctrl+ 9*: This selects the **Ellipse** tool
- *Ctrl + 7*: This selects the **Arc** tool

There are a couple more tools in the ribbon group that can be useful and we will review them next.

Moving around the page in desktop Visio

When we are working on or presenting a process flowchart, we often need to pan and zoom around a page:

- *Ctrl + Shift + W*: This allows you to zoom to the whole page, but do not use this key combination on the web! It closes the browser immediately!
- *Ctrl* + arrow keys: This pans the page to the corner of the page indicated by the arrow

In fact, holding down the *Ctrl + Shift* keys changes the cursor to a zoom icon, and then there are a number of actions that can be made with the mouse with those keys held down:

- Left mouse button click: This zooms in one level
- Right mouse button click: This zooms out one level
- Left mouse button held down: This drags a rectangle to zoom into that area

Another useful combination can be used when the mouse is moved over the edge or corner of a page with the *Ctrl* key held down. The cursor changes to a double-headed arrow and then clicking the left mouse button and dragging will resize the page.

So, now that we are more familiar with shortcut keys, we can look at some of the actions often used in process flowcharts.

Banding shapes together

It is quite simple to select multiple shapes and move them without physically grouping them with the **Group** command, and there are different ways of selecting multiple shapes and keeping them banded together.

As mentioned earlier, ungrouping instances of master shapes dragged from a stencil can have a detrimental effect because it can accidentally break them apart and remove their smartness, including any data associated with them.

Selecting multiple shapes

We can multi-select by holding down the *Ctrl* or *Shift* key while clicking the left mouse button and clicking on shapes, or by holding down the left mouse button on the page and dragging a rectangle over shapes. In desktop Visio, there is also a **Lasso Select** command available from the **Home | Editing | Select** drop-down menu.

Using the built-in containers

Desktop Visio users have the ability to add other containers to band shapes together besides the **Swimlanes** masters from the **Cross-Functional Flowchart Shapes** stencil and the **Pool/Lane** or **Group** masters from the **BPMN Basic Shapes** stencil. These can be found on the **Insert | Diagram Parts | Container** gallery, as shown here:

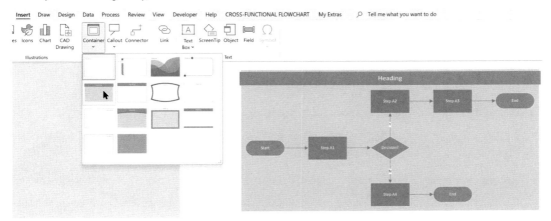

Figure 6.5 – Adding a container around selected shapes

An extra tab, **Container Format**, appears whenever we select one of these container shapes. This tab has a number of actions that can be used to control the size and style or to lock and select shapes within them.

Regardless of which container shape we choose, we do have the ability to swap it for one of the other styles and to re-position the header or hide it completely, using the **Container Format | Heading Style** drop-down gallery, as shown here:

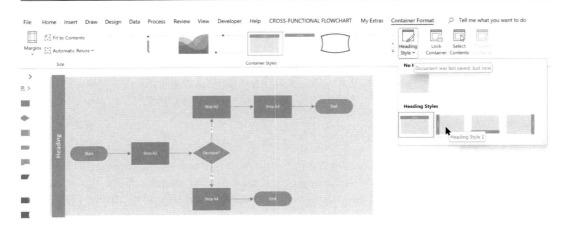

Figure 6.6 – Changing a container header style

The **Margins** drop-down list has a few preset sizes that can be applied as the distance between the edge of the container and its contained shapes. This is also applied if the **Lock Container** toggle button is down and we move any of the contained shapes beyond the extent of the container.

The **Automatic Resize** drop-down menu has the following three options:

- **No Automatic Resize**: The container will not automatically resize to fit the member shapes when they are moved
- **Expand as Needed**: The container will extend to fit the member shapes when they are moved
- **Always Fit to Contents**: The container will resize to fit the member shapes when they are moved

The **Container Format** ribbon has a useful **Select Contents** button so the member shapes can then have other actions, such as the layout, distribution, and alignment options.

Controlling the layout

We learned how we can set up the defaults for layout and routing in the *Aligning shapes with Smart Guides and Dynamic Grid* section in *Chapter 3*, but we also need to know how to apply different arrangement options to selected shapes.

Aligning shapes

We can select multiple shapes and align them relative to the first shape selected. In the following screenshots, the **Align Middle** option is chosen from the context menu:

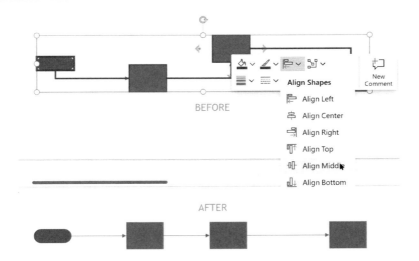

Figure 6.7 – Aligning selected shapes

Desktop Visio has an additional **Auto Align** option that will align either horizontally or vertically, depending upon the selection. We earlier added the **Align** button to the **My Extras** ribbon group, and this, or the shortcut key *F8*, can be used to open the following dialog for the selected shapes:

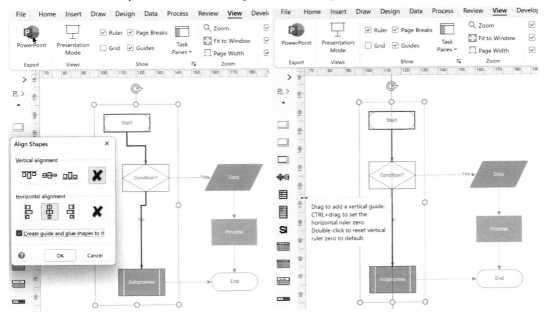

Figure 6.8 – The Align Shapes dialog

This dialog has the extra option of adding a guideline and gluing the selected shapes to it. We can also create a guideline by holding down the *Shift* key while clicking the left mouse button on the edge of the ruler and dragging it onto the page. Shapes can be glued to these guidelines and will remain where they are if layout styles are applied. There are both vertical and horizontal guidelines, and they never print. They provide another way of ensuring shapes are aligned perfectly, and we can left-click the mouse button on a guideline and move it by dragging it. Guide points can also be created by clicking and dragging the cross at the top- left junction of the vertical and horizontal rulers.

> **Important note**
> **View | Show | Guides** must be checked for the **Create guide and glue shapes to it** option to be available. **View | Show | Ruler** must be checked to be able to create guides by clicking and dragging.

Distributing shapes evenly

We can also distribute the shapes evenly, either horizontally or vertically by using the **Home | Arrange | Position** drop-down menu in desktop Visio or the **Home | Position Shapes** drop-down button in online Visio, as shown here:

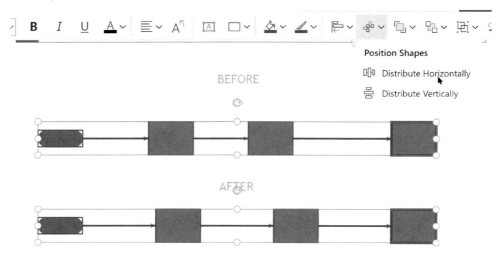

Figure 6.9 – Distributing selected shapes evenly

Desktop Visio has an additional **More Distribution Options…** command that opens the following **Distribute Shapes** dialog:

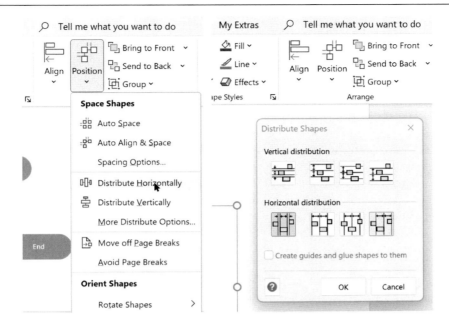

Figure 6.10 – Desktop Visio distribution options

There is also a **Home | Arrange | Position | Spacing Options** dialog available for desktop Visio that allows us to change the spacing between the selected shapes, as in the following screenshots:

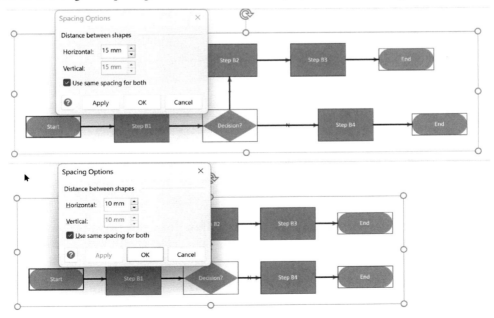

Figure 6.11 – Spacing shapes in desktop Visio

Now that we have learned more ways of enhancing the layout, we can display more information about the shapes.

Adding callouts for annotations

We sometimes need to add extra annotations to our diagrams, which could be done by just adding text blocks onto a page, but often these notes are related to specific process shapes. In this case, we can add callout shapes to our process diagram that are associated with these process flowcharts and BPMN shapes. The two shapes should remain glued to each other when they are moved. Interestingly, Visio's desktop and web versions provide quite different **Callouts** stencils. In either case, it is generally good practice to glue callouts to their target shapes because they keep the relationship between them, and code could be written to export all of the steps and their associated callout information later if required.

Getting Callout shapes in Visio for the web

The callout shapes in the web version merely have a leader that can be repositioned near a target shape. However, searching for `callout` displays a horizontal and vertical of a **Simple** callout that can be glued to other shapes and remains glued when either shape is moved.

The following screenshots show the **Callout** shapes available in online Visio:

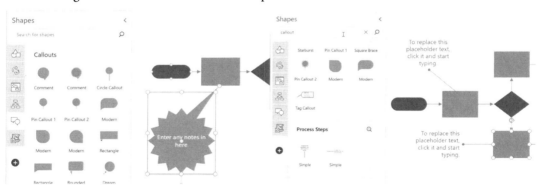

Figure 6.12 – The Callouts shapes in online Visio

Getting the Callout shapes in desktop Visio

Desktop Visio has the **Insert | Diagram Parts | Callout** drop-down gallery to provide a variety of special callout shapes that can be added to the selected shape unless that shape is a connector or another **Callout** shape. We can associate multiple **Callout** shapes with each shape, and these special **Callout** shapes automatically resize to fit any text typed in. Most of these **Callout** shapes can also be re-sized manually.

A callout shape is added to the selected **Process** shape in the following screenshots, which show a callout shape being added:

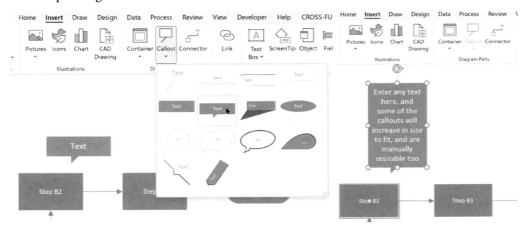

Figure 6.13 – Insert Callout shapes in desktop Visio

The yellow control point is glued to the selected shape, but it can be clicked and dragged to glue to a different shape if necessary. Desktop Visio also has a **More Shapes | Visio Extras | Callouts** stencil with many different types of callout shapes that can be added to a page and then glued to other shapes. These behave a little differently from the special callouts described previously because we need to click and drag the endpoint at the end of the leader line to move it, as shown here:

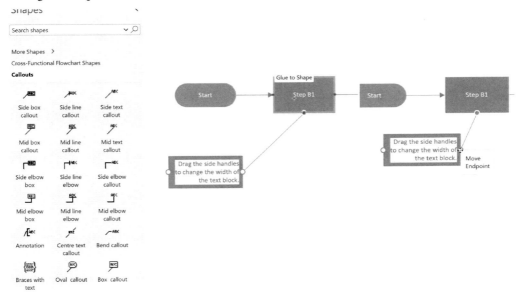

Figure 6.14 – Adding Callout stencil shapes in desktop Visio

There are three very special shapes at the bottom of the **Callouts** stencil, called **Custom callout 1**, **Custom callout 2,** and **Custom callout 3**, as shown here:

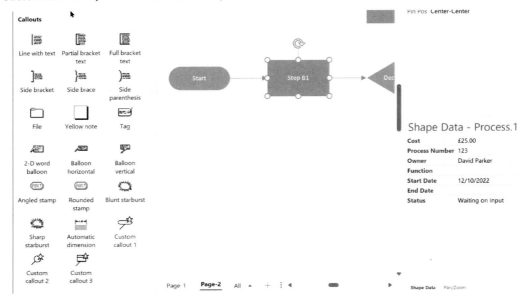

Figure 6.15 – Insert Callout shapes in desktop Visio

These three callout shapes have the ability to display selected **Shape Data** values of the shape that they are glued to. A **Configure Callout** dialog is automatically opened when the callout is glued to a shape. This dialog can also be opened from the menu that appears when you right-click the callout shape, shown as follows:

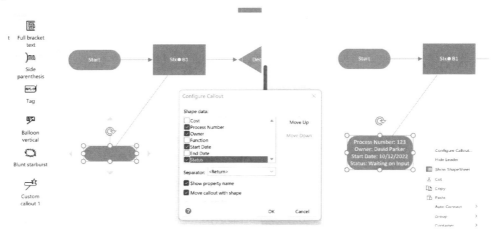

Figure 6.16 – Custom Callout shapes in desktop Visio

If we add these Visio callout shapes in desktop Visio, then they still have the same smartness if edited in online Visio afterward. They will stay associated, move, and resize in the same way as they did in desktop Visio. However, the **Configure Callout** dialog is not available in the web version of Visio because it is a desktop Visio-only feature.

Adding borders and titles

We often need to add a title to each page and possibly a border too. This is less necessary for **Cross-Functional Flowcharts** because of the container that has an optional title bar.

There is a **Banners** stencil in online Visio that contains a number of pre-formatted title and sub-title blocks that can be added to the page, as shown in the following screenshot:

Figure 6.17 – Titles in online Visio

However, desktop Visio has a **Design | Backgrounds | Borders and Titles** drop-down gallery that can be used to add a pre-formatted border and title to the page. In fact, it does not add it directly to the page but creates a background page that can be viewed through the foreground page. For example, notice the **VBackground-1** tab in the following screenshot:

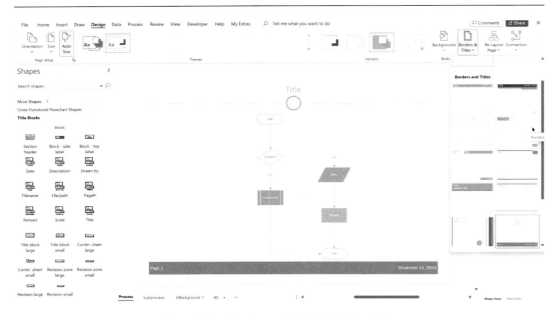

Figure 6.18 – Borders and Titles in desktop Visio

In desktop Visio, we can use **Insert** | **Text** | **Field** to add automatically updating values, such as the page name or number, as shown in the following screenshot, to any shape:

Figure 6.19 – Inserting fields in desktop Visio

We can also display document information and dates in the same way, and custom formulas can be inserted too, such as the `="Page "&PAGENUMBER()&" of "&PAGECOUNT()` formula in the previous screenshot.

Desktop Visio can also create background pages with the **Design | Backgrounds** drop-down gallery or by changing the **Type** value of an existing page in the **Page Setup | Page Properties** dialog. This dialog can also be used to assign a background page to an existing page, as in the following screenshot:

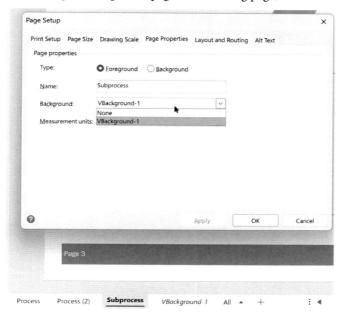

Figure 6.20 – Assigning a background page in desktop Visio

If we choose to **Insert** or **Duplicate** from a page that already has a background page, then both online and desktop Visio will create the new page with the assigned background, as in the following screenshots:

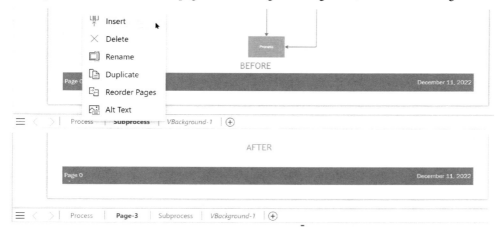

Figure 6.21 – Inserting a page in online Visio

We can edit the background page and edit or enhance the shapes on it, and these edits will be seen on all foreground pages that have the background page assigned.

It is even possible to assign a background page to another background page, and you can add watermark shapes that are not visible in normal Visio use but are visible if the file is printed.

> **Important Note**
>
> In the preceding screenshots, there is a page number label in the bottom -left corner. This is actually using an inserted formula, PAGENUMBER(), that should show the foreground page number, even when the formula is in a shape on the background page. There is currently an issue in online Visio that prevents the number, or a similar function PAGENAME(), from showing the foreground page values. Therefore, these formulas should be removed from the background page shapes if they are intended to be viewed online.

Alternatively, there is also a **More Shapes** | **Visio Extras** | **Title Blocks** stencil that contains a number of title block shapes that can be added to the page.

Editing headers and footers

There is one other feature of desktop Visio that we need to be aware of if we need to physically print a page that covers multiple sheets of paper or to PDF. In the following screenshot, we have a Visio page that will print to seven sheets of paper, which we could then overlap to reconstruct the whole page:

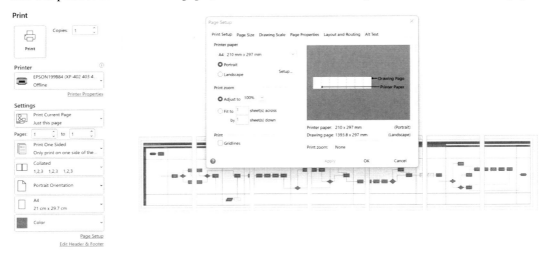

Figure 6.22 – Page Setup in desktop Visio

This could also have been multiple sheets vertically, and it would be quite easy to get confused about which printed paper sheets are joined to each other. Fortunately, there is a **Header and Footer** dialog that can be opened from the button at the bottom of the **Print** window. This dialog allows for up to 128 characters of text to be inserted in each of **Left**, **Center,** or **Right** of **Header** and **Footer**. This text can include special placeholders for page, date, time, or file properties, as shown in the following screenshot:

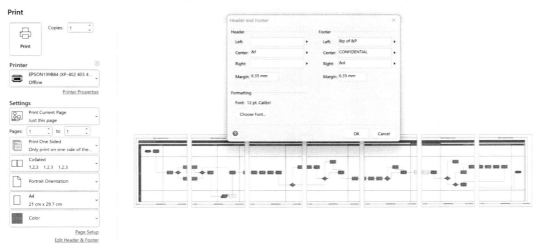

Figure 6.23 – Header and Footer in desktop Visio

These codes can be selected from the arrow buttons to the right of each textbox in the preceding dialog, or they can be entered as follows:

- &p: The page number
- &n: The page name
- &P: The total printed pages
- &t: The current time
- &d: The current date (short)
- &D: The current date (long)
- &f: The file name
- &e: The file extension
- &f&e: The file name and extension

These header and footer settings are applied to all pages when printed from desktop Visio, as can be seen in the first two printed pages in the following screenshot, which can then be cut or overlapped to provide a perfect join:

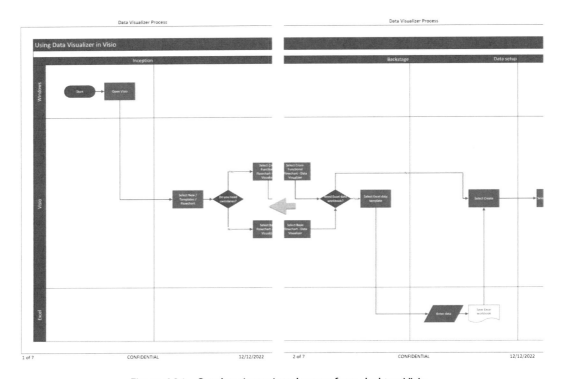

Figure 6.24 – Overlapping printed pages from desktop Visio

Some users like to create process flowcharts that span multiple pages, as here, but others prefer to break them down into multiple smaller pages. In either case, the purpose of the flowchart must be clear and visible, whether viewed onscreen, online, or printed.

Summary

In this chapter, we learned how to customize the ribbon and about some useful shortcut keys. We also learned some techniques for aligning and distributing shapes to improve the arrangements. Finally, we added annotations to specific shapes and title our pages.

In the next chapter, we will learn more about preparing diagrams for presentation and collaboration.

Preparing Diagrams for Presentation and Collaboration

Now that we know how to create process diagrams automatically and manually, we will now focus on making them more inviting to our intended audience. We are more likely to induce others to collaborate with our diagrams if they are visually appealing and accurate. This can be done by using themes and variants to quickly apply colors, effects, and connector styles, or by using automatically applied visual elements, *data graphics*, to highlight specific data values. In this chapter, we will learn about the options available to us.

In this chapter, we will cover the following key topics:

- Using themes to enhance the appearance of pages
- Applying different styles to shapes
- Adding **data graphics** to highlight information
- Using layers to control visibility and color
- Considering accessibility
- Options for multi-language versions

Technical requirements

These are the Microsoft apps that are utilized in this chapter, and we should have access to at least one of the Visio editions, but Visio Plan 2 subscribers will be able to use all of the features described:

- **Teams**: Desktop or web app
- **Visio Reading View**: Web-only app
- **Visio in Microsoft 365**: Web-only app
- **Visio Plan 1**: Web-only subscription app
- **Visio Plan 2**: Desktop and web subscription apps

The sample files of the chapter are placed here: `https://github.com/PacktPublishing/Visualize-complex-processes-with-Microsoft-Visio/tree/main/Chapter7`

Using themes to enhance the appearance of pages

We looked at some parts of the **Design** ribbon tab in the previous chapter, but now we will look in more detail at the **Themes** gallery. A diagram without a theme, as in the following screenshot of desktop Visio, can look unfinished and uninviting to some audiences, so we often enhance the look by using a theme:

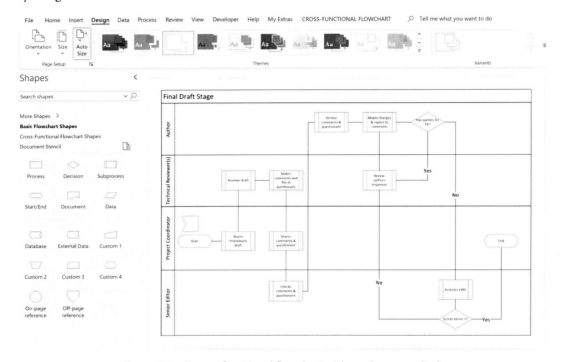

Figure 7.1 – A cross-functional flowchart with no theme applied

Themes are applied on a page-by-page basis, so it is possible to have different themes on different pages in the same document, but there can only be one theme per page.

There are a number of built-in themes available in the gallery, and we may decide to use a different theme on the same diagram at different stages of the development of a process flowchart. For example, we may use one of the **Hand Drawn** themes initially to convey the intention that the diagram is still being analyzed and change to one of the themes in the **Professional** category, as in the following screenshot, once stakeholders have reviewed it and agreed that the flow is correct:

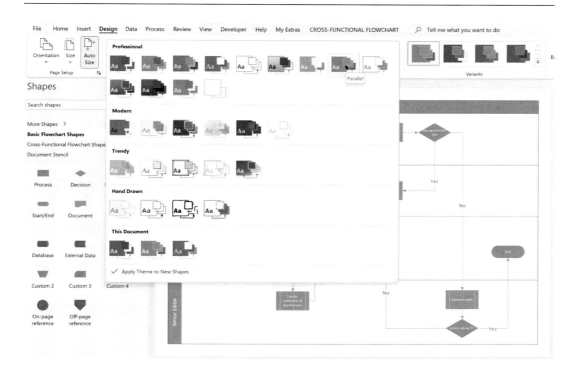

Figure 7.2 – A cross-functional flowchart with a theme applied

A preview of the theme is applied to the active page shapes when the cursor is moved over one of the themes in the gallery, and the theme is applied to the shapes in the visible stencil when a theme selection is actually made.

The choice of themes is currently smaller in Visio for the web and each theme has a different color palette available in the drop-down gallery under **Theme Colors**, as shown on the right side of the following screenshot:

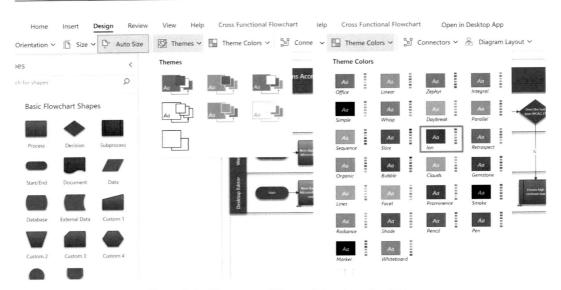

Figure 7.3 – Themes and Theme Colors in online Visio

The **Theme Colors** in online Visio are similar to **Variants** available in desktop Visio.

Using variants in desktop Visio

Each theme has four **Variants** that can be selected to quickly apply a different look and effects within the same theme. In addition, **Colors**, **Effects**, and **Connectors** can be varied using the drop-down galleries, as in the following screenshots:

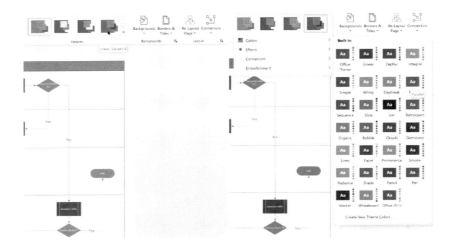

Figure 7.4 – Theme variants and colors in desktop Visio

Desktop Visio has further options to apply **Embellishment** to the formatting and effects. These options are **Low**, **Medium**, **High,** and **Automatic** to influence certain parts of the geometry to display, from understated to elaborate. Each built-in theme sets this value automatically.

In desktop Visio, you can also create custom theme colors, based on the currently selected theme, by clicking **Create New Theme Colors…** from the bottom of the **Colors | Built-In** gallery. This provides the ability to create a branded set of colors, as in the following screenshot:

Figure 7.5 – New Theme Colors in desktop Visio

The **New Theme Colors** dialog shown in the preceding screenshot clearly demonstrates how the designers of the built-in process flowchart shapes applied different theme colors to each of them. For example, the **Process** shape uses the **Accent 1** color by default, and the **Decision** shape uses the **Accent 3** color. As we will learn later in this chapter, these are the default colors, which can be overwritten on the page by other operations, such as applying an alternative style or color because of a specific **Shape Data** value.

Once created, this custom palette will be available from the top of the **Colors** galley in the **Design | Variants** tab group.

The **Effects** and **Connectors** galleries on the **Variants** group of the **Design** tab, as shown in the following screenshots, can also change the look of each shape and connector:

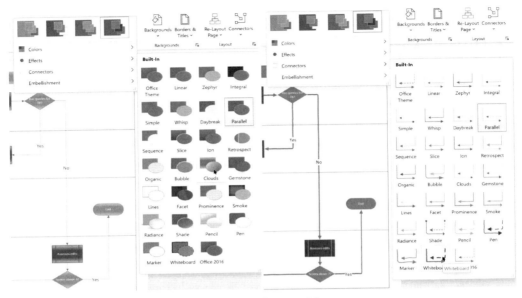

Figure 7.6 – Theme Effects and Connectors

> **Important note**
> The ability to create custom **Effects** and **Connectors** styles was removed in Visio 2013.

This section has been about applying a theme and variant to a whole page, but the next section will look at changing the style of selected shapes.

Applying different styles to shapes

The **Shape Styles** group on the **Home** tab of desktop Visio contains the **Fill**, **Line**, and **Effects** drop-down menus to change these properties of the selected shapes, but it also contains the **Quick Styles** gallery to make pre-defined changes for all of these in one selection, as shown in the following screenshot:

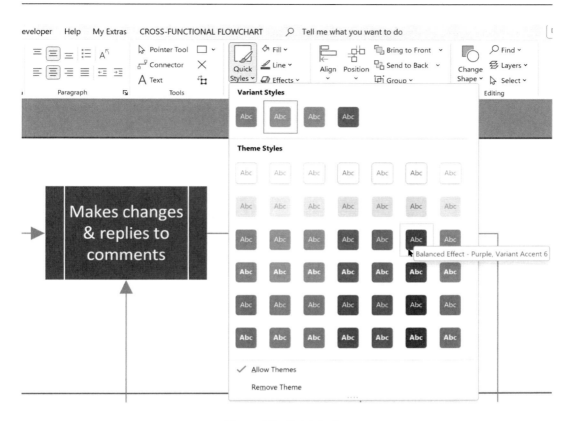

Figure 7.7 – Quick Styles

Important note

Quick Styles is displayed as a button to open a gallery in the preceding screenshot, but one row of the styles may be displayed within the ribbon on larger displays, with the remaining rows of the gallery available with a drop-down button. This depends upon the resolution of the display.

There are many more options in desktop Visio than online Visio to format shapes. For example, there is currently no option to use **Effects** in Visio for the web, as shown in the following screenshots:

Figure 7.8 – Online Visio Shape Fill and Shape Outline options

Desktop Visio also has the **Format Shape** side panel, which can be opened with the **Fill Options…** and **Line Options…** commands at the bottom of the **Fill** and **Line** drop-down galleries, as shown here:

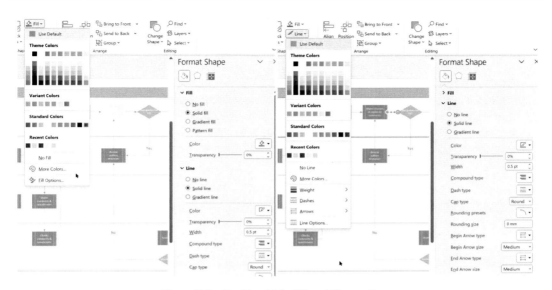

Figure 7.9 – Desktop Visio Fill and Line options

Desktop Visio also has multiple **Effects** that can be applied to the selected shapes and an **…Options…** command below each gallery to open the second tab, **Effects**, of the **Format Shape** side panel:

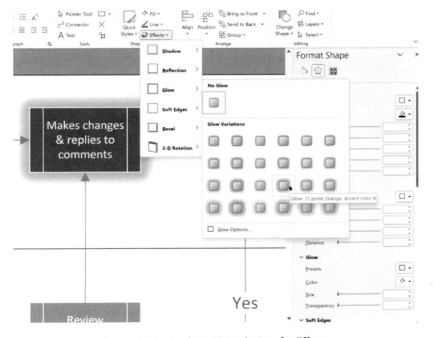

Figure 7.10 – Desktop Visio choices for Effects

The **Format Shape** panel can also be opened from the right-click menu of a selected shape and from the dialog box launcher button in the bottom-right corner of the **Shape Styles** ribbon group.

> **Important note**
>
> Online Visio does not currently support editing the gradients and effects that can be applied with desktop Visio. Search the web for the Microsoft pages titled *Limitations to file editing in Visio for the web* and *Use design features in your drawing that are compatible with Visio for the web* to read more about this.

We have now learned how to apply themes and styles to our shapes, but sometimes we need to visually display data to make it easily understandable. The next section is about another desktop Visio feature that can do this automatically.

Adding data graphics to highlight information

This section is an introduction to a subject that is covered in more depth at `https://www.packtpub.com/product/mastering-data-visualization-with-microsoft-visio-professional-2016`.

Data graphics is a feature available in Visio Plan 2 and Visio Professional that allows us to automatically display the values of **Shape Data** visually. These can be simply a different color for a specific value or a range of values, such as a text callout, a set of icons, or data bars. Each data graphic can be a collection of multiple text callouts; icon sets, or data bars, which can be positioned in a number of locations in and around each shape. It can also contain multiple color by value rows, but only the first row will be applied.

Data graphics can be created, edited, and applied manually to selected shapes using the **Data | Advanced Data Linking | Advanced Data Graphics** drop-down menu, as shown in the following screenshot:

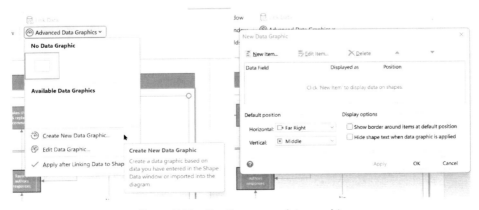

Figure 7.11 – Creating a new data graphic

Once a data graphic has been created, it will then be displayed in the drop-down gallery, where it has a right-click context menu with several options, including **Edit…** opens the **Edit Data Graphic** dialog, as seen in the following screenshot:

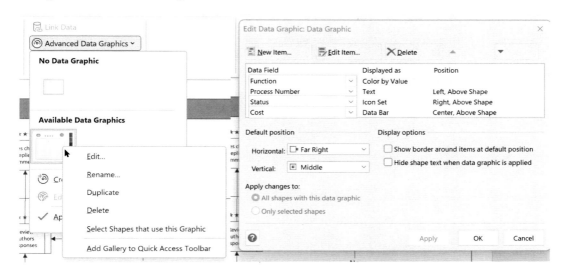

Figure 7.12 – Editing a data graphic

Data graphics can also be created via the **Data Graphic Fields** panel – the **Data Graphic Fields** panel contains each of the external data record sets created by *Data Visualizer* (**Data | Create from Data | Create**) – or by using **Data | External Data | Quick Import** and **Data | External Data | Custom Import**.

The **Data Graphic Fields** panel will open automatically when Data Visualizer is used, but it can always be opened with the **Data | Show/Hide | Data Graphics Fields** option. The panel will be enabled if there are one or more shapes linked to external data on the page and no shape is selected. It will also be enabled if a selected shape has one or more links to external data. Selecting a field in the panel will enable the **Data | Data Graphics** gallery, which can then be dropped down to show some selected options, as in the following screenshot:

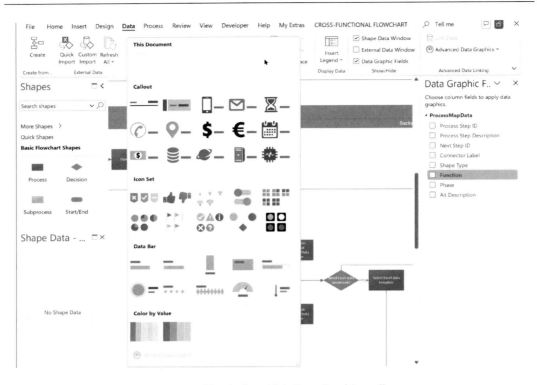

Figure 7.13 – The desktop Visio Data Graphics gallery

In fact, the gallery does not show the complete list of variants for each category, but these can be accessed via the **Data | Data Graphics | Configure** button. The following screenshots are of the **Text** (called **Callout** in the previous gallery screenshot), **Data Bar**, and **Icon Set** styles:

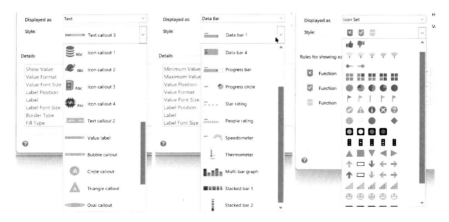

Figure 7.14 – Choosing a graphic item style

These graphic items are inserted into the related shapes as sub-shapes so that they will move with the shape that they are part of. The position of each of them can be configured using **Data** | **Data Graphics** | **Position** or **Configure**.

> **Important note**
> Shapes that are controlled by Data Visualizer should only have their data graphics set with the **Data Graphic Fields** panel.

Text / Callout

There are 24 built-in **Text / Callout** graphic items to choose from, and each one has a list of options in the **Details** panel, as shown in the following screenshot:

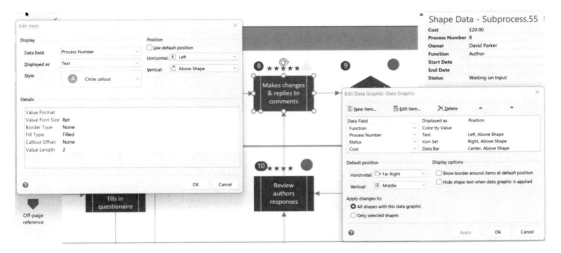

Figure 7.15 – Configuring a Text / Callout graphic item

Data Bar

There are 13 built-in **Data Bar** graphic items to choose from, and each one has a list of options in the **Details** panel, as shown in the following screenshot:

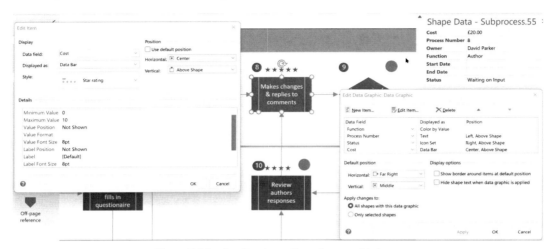

Figure 7.16 – Configuring a Data Bar graphic item

Icon Set

There are 17 built-in **Icon Set** graphic items to choose from, and there are a maximum of 5 icons in each **Icon Set**. The match criteria can be set for each icon, as shown in the following screenshot:

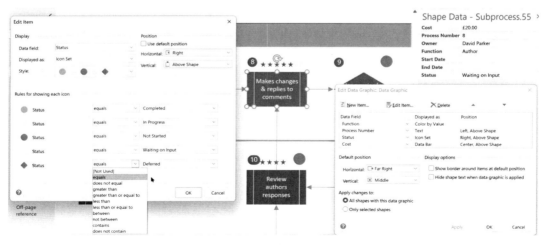

Figure 7.17 – Configuring an Icon Set graphic item

Using Color by Value

There are two options for **Color by Value** if the data type is numeric. The following screenshot shows the option for **Each color represents a unique value** on the left, and **Each color represents a range of values** on the right. The latter option only appears if **Data Field** contains numeric values, which also includes dates:

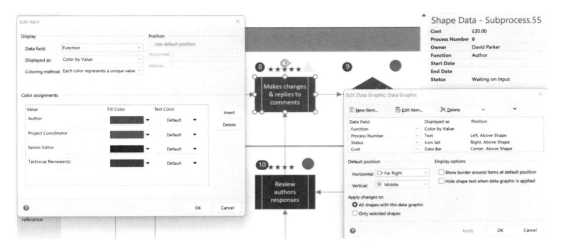

Figure 7.18 – Configuring Color by Value

Notice that we can edit **Fill Color** and **Text Color** and use the **Insert** or **Delete** options to insert or delete rows.

The default colors are extremely bright, so we invariably need to choose more muted values.

Inserting a legend

We can add a legend to the page after we have applied our data graphics using the **Data | Insert Legend** drop-down option:

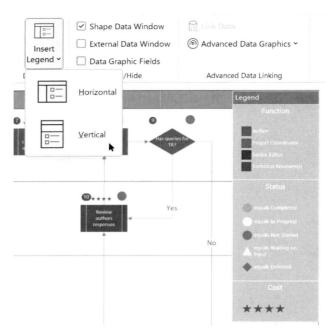

Figure 7.19 – Inserting a legend

The legend shape is always dropped in the top-right corner, but it can be edited and formatted and moved, even onto a different page if necessary.

> **Important note**
>
> Data graphics are not editable in Visio for the web and Visio diagrams embedded in **Power BI** do not display any data graphics.

Now that we know how to create data graphics, we can learn how their assigned layer can be controlled.

Using layers to control visibility and color

Layers in Visio are like different sheets of acetate, one on top of another, like we used to do with overhead projectors at school many years ago. We could add or remove these acetate sheets to show or hide their contents. However, Visio is more complex because all shapes in Visio can be optionally assigned to one or more layers, and all of the flowchart shapes have been pre-assigned to a layer called **Flowchart**. The **Dynamic connector** shape has been pre-assigned to a layer called **Connector**.

Each layer has seven properties, in addition to its name, that can control the appearance and behavior of every shape assigned to it. The seven properties are as follows:

- **Visible**: This toggles the visibility of shapes.

- **Print**: This toggles the printability of shapes.

- **Active**: If checked, then any new shapes that do not already have layer assignments will be assigned to this layer.

- **Lock**: This prevents the shapes from being selectable.

- **Snap**: This toggles the ability to snap to the shapes.

- **Glue**: This toggles the ability of other shapes to glue to the shapes on the layer.

- **Color**: This changes the display color of the shapes and their transparency. It does not change the actual color of the shape, just the display.

Desktop Visio has a dialog that is opened using **Home | Editing | Layers | Layer Properties** that allows for shapes on a layer to be temporarily assigned a color, made invisible or unprintable, and other options, as shown in the following screenshot:

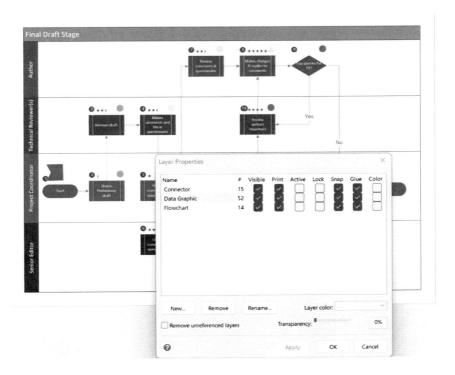

Figure 7.20 – The Layer Properties dialog

The column with the # label is the count of shapes on each layer, but that may be misleading because it also counts sub-shapes within group shapes.

Layers can temporarily hide shapes, as in the next screenshot, where the **Data Graphic** layer is made invisible:

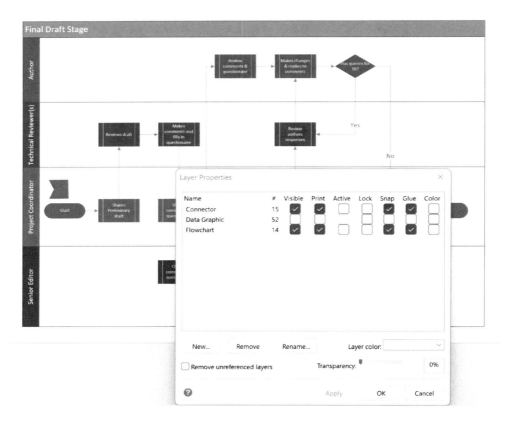

Figure 7.21 – Using layers to hide shapes

We can even set a layer to be invisible but remain printable, which can be used to create a watermark or copyright mark if printed or saved to PDF.

If we really want the data graphics to stand out, we can set **Color** of the **Flowchart** layer and, optionally, the **Connector** layer. This will have the effect of suppressing the normal color of these shapes, as in the following screenshot:

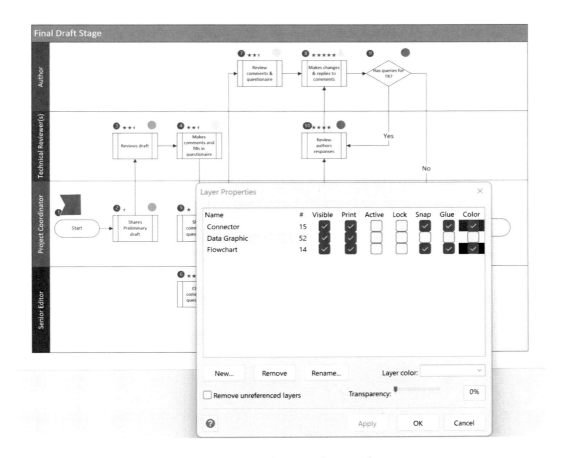

Figure 7.22 – Using layers to change colors

> **Important note**
> Visio for the web does not currently support editing documents with **Lock**, **Color**, or **Transparency** of any layer set.

We have now learned how to enhance diagrams to create more interest, but we should be mindful that not everyone has the same quality of eyesight or understanding. So now we will look at how we can make our diagrams more accessible.

Considering accessibility

It is possible that some users or viewers of the process diagrams are visually or cognitively impaired, or it may be a legal requirement that the diagrams are accessible. Both online and desktop Visio include a **Check Accessibility** button on the **Review** ribbon tab. The Visio for the web version is shown in the following screenshot:

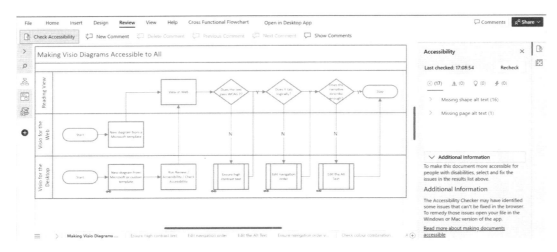

Figure 7.23 – Running the online Visio accessibility checker

Note that some accessibility fixes cannot be done within online Visio, so the diagram may need to be opened in desktop Visio. The **Check Accessibility** feature in desktop Visio is shown as follows:

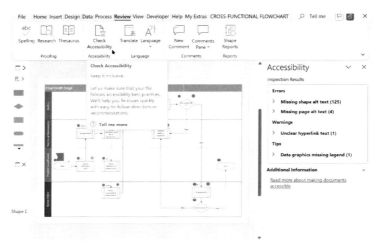

Figure 7.24 – Running the desktop Visio accessibility checker

There is a free guide to best practices for Visio accessibility available at `https://bvisual.net/resources/vision-up-your-visio-diagrams/`, but in summary, we need to be aware of the following:

- The contrast between any text and its background
- The titles and descriptions spoken by screen readers
- The tab order around each page

Use high contrast to ensure text is legible

Choose a good contrast between any text and its background, and if in doubt, there is a free contrast checker available at `https://webaim.org/resources/contrastchecker/`.

Most of the built-in themes do provide a suitable contrast, but not all.

Alt text titles and descriptions

The **Accessibility** results panel opened by the **Check Accessibility** tool will list all shapes that do not contain any **Alt Text** titles, but the description is optional. Screen readers will speak the title first and will only speak the description if the user pauses for it. The following screenshot shows **Alt Text** on the third tab of the **Format Shape** panel:

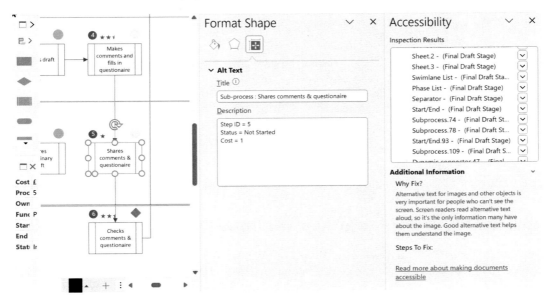

Figure 7.25 – Editing Alt Text of a shape

The shape is automatically removed from the **Inspection Results** list when some text is entered into the **Alt Text | Title** box.

Diagram navigation

The order in which the tab key jumps from shape to shape defaults to the order in which shapes are dropped onto a page. This may not necessarily be the best order for a vision-impaired user, so the **Diagram Navigation** panel , which can be opened with **View | Show | Task Panes | Navigation,** is used to drag and reorder the shape names vertically into a more logical order:

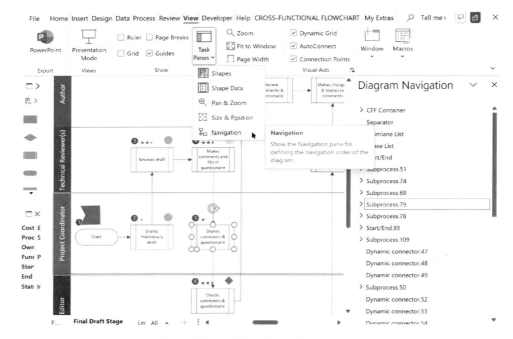

Figure 7.26 – Editing the navigation order

There is also an **Alt Text** tab on the **Page Setup** dialog for setting **Title** and **Description** for each page.

Options for multi-language versions

There are different language versions of Visio available, but the usual need is to present the same process diagrams in multiple languages without maintaining multiple copies.

One solution is to have translations in Excel for each process and then regenerate each diagram in the required language version of Visio using Data Visualizer, but that will lose any manual customizations done to the diagrams.

Another solution is to host the diagrams in a **SharePoint** portal where the end user can select the language to view, as available at `https://www.oneassist.de/`.

Also, there is a desktop Visio add-in available at `https://bvisual.net/products/multi-language-text-for-visio/` that provides the option to store multiple alternate language text for shapes, pages, and hyperlinks.

Summary

In this chapter, we learned how we can enhance our process flowchart diagrams with themes, variants, and shape styles. We also saw how we can visualize data by using color by value or adding text callouts, icon sets, and data bars. We then learned how we can control the visibility and color of many shapes simultaneously using layers.

With all these abilities to mix many colors of shapes and text, we also became aware of the need to make our diagrams accessible by providing sufficient contrast and alternative text, and sorting the tab navigation order. We will learn more about this in *Chapter 11*.

Finally, we considered the options for producing flowcharts in multiple languages.

In the next chapter, we will understand how we can control access to our documents while providing the ability to review, comment, and collaborate with the necessary individuals or teams.

8

Securing and Providing Access to Diagrams

In this chapter, we will see how we can make **Visio** diagrams available to others through Microsoft **SharePoint**, Microsoft **OneDrive**, and Microsoft **Teams**, while ensuring that the file and content are kept safe. For example, business process diagrams can contain information that is only intended for specific audiences; therefore, their security and targeted permission to edit, comment on, or even view needs to be controlled.

We will cover the following topics:

- Primary questions for sharing
- Options to store **Visio** files for broader sharing
- Publishing **Visio** files in a (shared) **Teams** channel
- Ways of collaboration – co-authoring in **Teams** and **SharePoint**

Technical requirements

In this chapter, we will publish the **Visio** document using several Microsoft technologies. Therefore, we should have at least some basic knowledge of **SharePoint**, **Teams**, and **OneDrive**, and also have access to these file-sharing or collaboration technologies, and of course, they should be properly configured.

Depending on our choice, access to the following is needed:

- Microsoft **OneDrive** or **OneDrive for Business**
- Microsoft **SharePoint** (in this chapter, we will utilize **SharePoint Online**)
- Microsoft **Teams**
- **Visio in Microsoft 365** – a web-only app (not in personal editions of Microsoft 365)
- **Visio Plan 1** – a web-only subscription app

- **Visio Plan 2** – desktop and web subscription apps
- **Visio Professional** – a Windows desktop one-time, purchase-only app
- **Visio Standard** – a Windows desktop one-time, purchase-only app

> **Important note**
> If we want to use shared Teams channels for external participants, our organization must have configured our tenant for external sharing – please refer to the Microsoft documentation to achieve this, as this is not activated by default.

Primary questions for sharing

When we plan to make a **Visio** file available to share with others, the first and most important question is whether the file should be just viewed by them or whether they also should be allowed to contribute to the file and edit it. This first question has some implications that will influence the way the file is distributed:

- *Co-authoring/editing*: We share the original file with specific rights for editing. We want to avoid having several copies of the file, so all users work with the very same file and add their input to the file.
- *View only*: Others are only allowed to open the file in **Reader View** (even if the data in it is updated). However, they are not able to modify or edit the file. Here, we can choose whether we give them access to the original file in a view-only manner or whether we create a copy of the file to view only in a separate location.

Now that we have made our first decision, let us understand where the files could be stored.

Options for storing Visio files for broader distribution

When making **Visio** files available, they usually will already reside in some online repository (not in our local filesystem). However, if the file is on our desktop computer, then we would have to upload it first to an online repository. The following options support **Visio** file viewing, commenting, and co-authoring:

- A **SharePoint Online** document library, where robust permission management is required, for sharing within an organization, group, or team
- A Microsoft **Teams** file storage section within a channel (which technically means that the file is stored in Microsoft **SharePoint** in an area controlled by Microsoft **Teams**), which is intended for project-oriented work
- A **OneDrive for Business** folder, which syncs with the desktop and is intended for work in progress and sharing with specific individuals, rather than a team or group

Which option we choose is determined by how we want to make the file available to other users. If we just want to share the actual file, then **OneDrive** is a good option. This pretty much feels as if we have a file on our own hard drive:

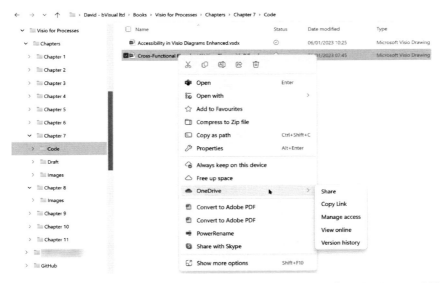

Figure 8.1 – A Visio file located in OneDrive for Business – with an online viewing capability

If we want to embed the file in a modern UI, then maybe Microsoft **SharePoint** is a better option.

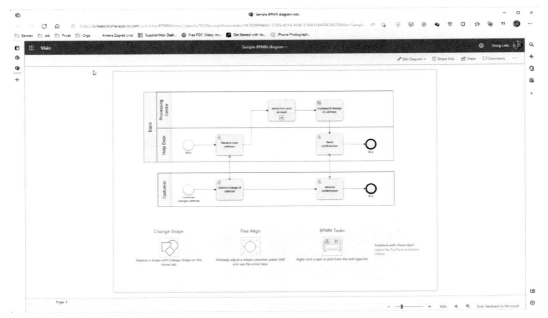

Figure 8.2 – Sharing a Visio file in a SharePoint page environment

If the primary purpose is to share a file with internal users for direct viewing and potentially collaboration, sharing within Microsoft **Teams** is a very good option.

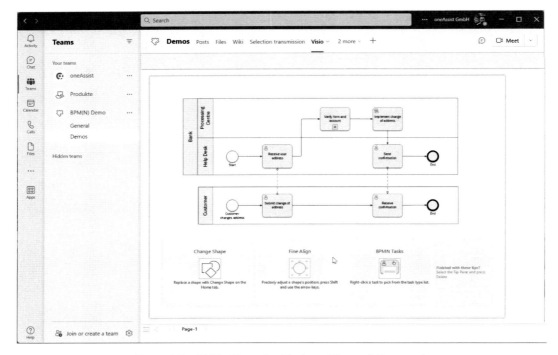

Figure 8.3 – A Visio file embedded as a Microsoft Teams tab

So, after covering the storage and display of the file in **Teams**, we will now focus on the next technology for file storage in the Microsoft universe – Microsoft **OneDrive** and **OneDrive for Business**.

Storage in OneDrive and OneDrive for Business

Microsoft provides a personal **OneDrive** online storage capability that can be used to store **Visio** files, but they are outside of the control of any organization. It does not have any auditing, reporting, and industry compliance that is available with Microsoft **OneDrive for Business**. Microsoft 365 accounts default to using **OneDrive for Business**, but **Visio Plan 2** desktop can connect to both editions of **OneDrive**, and **SharePoint** folders, as shown in the following screenshot:

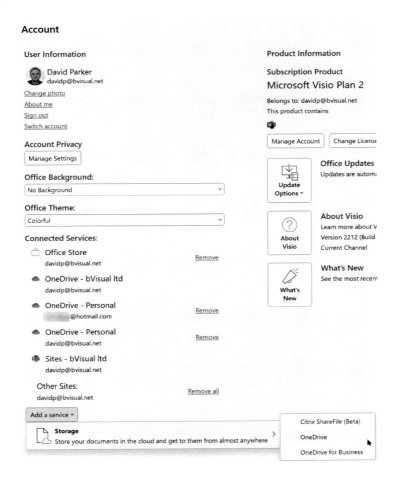

Figure 8.4 – Visio Plan 2 desktop options for connected services

The preceding screenshot shows the *Office Store* as a **connected service**. **Visio** documents cannot be saved there, but some **Visio** content is retrieved from here.

Storage in SharePoint Online

If you work with Microsoft 365, then the default way to store files on a corporate level is **SharePoint Online**, which provides a central and secure file repository for all your files. To store, access, and utilize a **Visio** file in **SharePoint**, we simply need to save it the *SharePoint way* – that is, in a **SharePoint** document library. This can happen in two ways.

Creating a file from the drop-down menu in a SharePoint document library

The following screenshot shows the **New** drop-down menu in a **SharePoint** document library, which will display **Visio drawing** if we have Visio license.

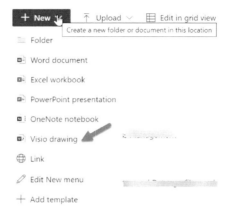

Figure 8.5 – Creating a Visio file within a SharePoint document library

By selecting this entry, a new **Visio** file will be created in the document library we are in. Note that with this approach, there is no selection of a specific template; instead, we just get an empty **Visio** diagram with a blank page. This means that we have to manually open the stencils we want to work with.

We can add an existing **Visio** document, either a template or a drawing, with the **Add template** command. Then, we will be able to create a new copy of this **Visio** document easily.

> **Important note**
>
> Another way to add a Visio template to the menu is to upload it to **SharePoint** and assign it to a content type. Then, we get an entry for this specific **Visio** template in the dropdown. This method is beyond the scope of this book.

However, from a working point of view, we can now open the stencils needed and create our diagram.

Creating a file in the Office.com website and storing it afterward in a SharePoint document library

The second option gives us full access to all the specific templates our **Visio** license is capable of.

Navigate to `http://portal.office.com` to see the following:

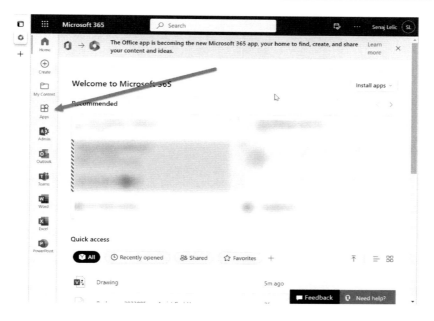

Figure 8.6 – The Microsoft 365 (Office) portal website

There, select the **Apps** tile, after which we will get access to all other apps in our account.

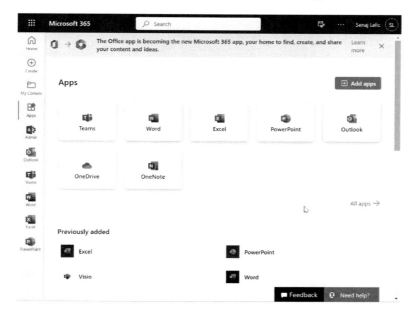

Figure 8.7 – Selecting the Visio app

Now, if we have used **Visio** before, we will see **Visio** in the **Previously added** section; otherwise, click on the **All apps** link to find the **Visio** link.

Scroll down to **Visio** and select it:

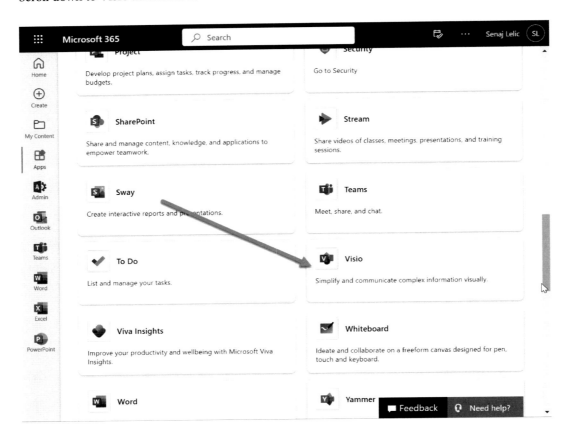

Figure 8.8 – Selecting Visio on the All apps page

We will navigate to the **Visio** app start experience, where we can select the desired template:

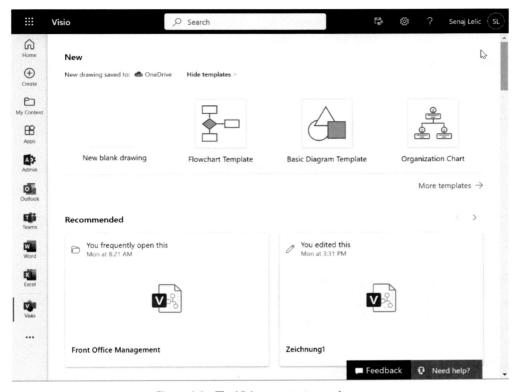

Figure 8.9 – The Visio app start experience

Once we have created the file, select **File | Save As | Save As**, and we will be presented with a simple save dialog:

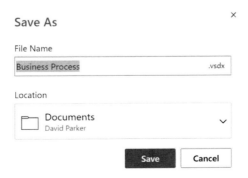

Figure 8.10 – The Save As dialog

From there, we can select the location, which will contain **OneDrive for Business** and **SharePoint** locations:

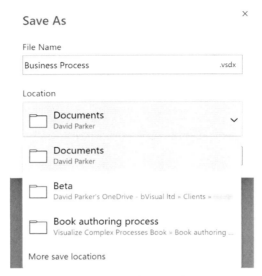

Figure 8.11 – A list of storage locations

Note that this list displays both **SharePoint** and **OneDrive** locations, so make sure you know which location you want to store your file in.

Once the file is saved, it will reside in your **SharePoint** Document library.

> **Another way to get a Visio file in SharePoint**
>
> We can also create the **Visio** file with a desktop version of **Visio** and then upload it to a **SharePoint** Document library. However, this may result in a **Visio** file that we cannot edit in the browser-based **Visio** version, since we might use a template not supported for editing in the browser, so be cautious with this option.

Adding Visio documents to Teams channels for reviewers (including shared channels)

The alternative to storing the **Visio** file in **OneDrive** or **SharePoint** is to store it in Microsoft **Teams**. The benefit of this approach is that we can not only store but also publish the file prominently as a *tab* in Microsoft **Teams**. The first step is to add the **Visio** file to our Microsoft **Teams** environment.

Adding a Visio file to Microsoft Teams

Apart from uploading a **Visio** file to the **Folder** tab in Microsoft **Teams**, we can also create it directly in Microsoft **Teams**. To achieve this, select the **Files** tab, and then select **Visio drawing** in the dropdown. The approach is similar to the approach for Microsoft **SharePoint**.

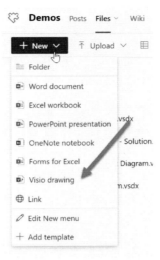

Figure 8.12 – Creating a Visio file directly in Microsoft Teams

Once the file has been created and stored, we can add it as a *tab* in Microsoft **Teams**.

Publishing a Visio file in Microsoft Teams on a tab

To create a tab, hit the + button in the Teams menu.

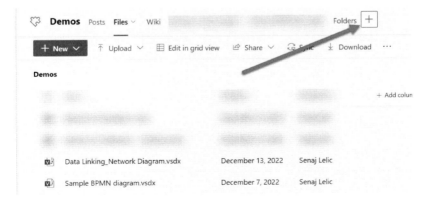

Figure 8.13 – The plus button

After that, in the app selection dialog, select the **Visio** app from the list of apps.

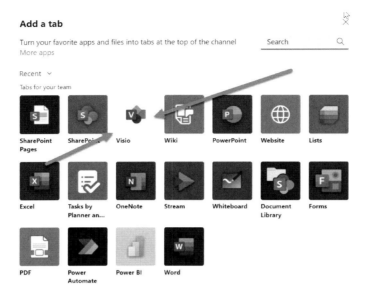

Figure 8.14 – Selecting the Visio app

The next step is to select the location of our **Visio** file. Note that with the **Visio** app, we can even pull the file from **SharePoint** locations.

Figure 8.15 – Storage locations for Visio files in the Visio App for Microsoft Teams

Note that with the **Visio** app, we can pick *either* a file within Microsoft **Teams**, a file from **SharePoint**, or a file from **OneDrive for Business**.

The selector allows us to pick a file from both:

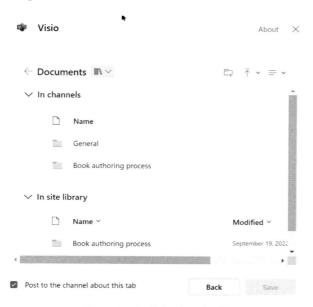

Figure 8.16 – Selecting the file

After selecting the file, it will be visible as a new tab in Microsoft **Teams**.

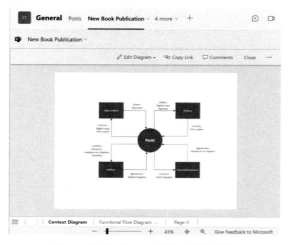

Figure 8.17 – The published Visio file

> **Publishing in shared channels**
>
> The same approach can also be used for **Teams** *shared channels*; just keep in mind that the file should reside in a location that is isolated so that you don't point to a different **SharePoint** document library. Storing it in the **Files** section of that channel would be the best option.

We now need to learn ways to collaborate using commenting and co-authoring in **Teams** and **SharePoint**.

Using conversations and comments with Visio documents

Visio documents that are stored in **OneDrive**, **Teams**, or **SharePoint** can be referenced in *conversations* in **Teams**, and with *comments* in the **Visio** file itself.

First of all, we need to understand the difference between the two ways of referencing all or part of a Visio diagram:

- **Conversations**: This is a **Teams**-only feature that allows us to include a reference to an accessible **Visio** file within a threaded **Teams** channel chat. We can use @mentions in the conversation to invite participation on a referenced file.

- **Comments**: This is a **Visio** feature that allows us to add threaded comments to a specific page or shape within a page. We can also use @mentions to invite other users to collaborate on a specific page or shape.

If we use @mentions to invite specific individuals to collaborate, then the way that they get notified is different by default. When used in a Teams channel conversation, then the individual will receive an activity indication within Teams.

In the following screenshots, the first user (**David Parker**) has added both a **Teams** chat message and a Visio comment in the left image, each with @mentions to **Fab Rikam** and **Claus Romanowsky**. The middle part of the screenshot shows that they get notified in **Teams**, and the right image shows the message in the **Teams Feed**.

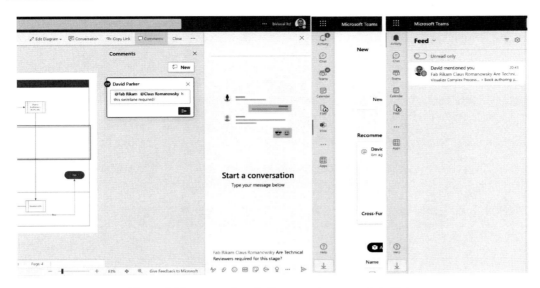

Figure 8.18 – @mentions in Teams and comments in Visio

If either of these users clicks on the message in **Teams**, it will open the **Visio** document within Teams, as shown in the following screenshot, where Claus can see not only the message in the **Teams** chat panel but also the Visio shape-specific comment indicator. There is also a **Comments** pane that can be displayed within the **Visio** interface.

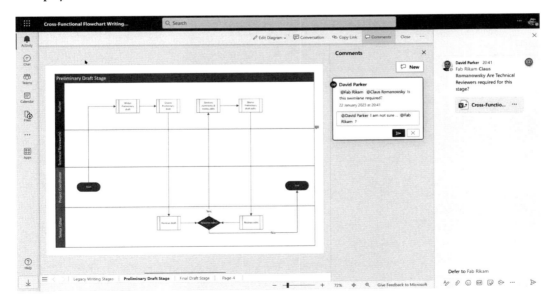

Figure 8.19 – Following a Teams channel chat link to a Visio document

Note that there is a small chat icon at the top right of the second swimlane shape in the preceding screenshot. These are the unprintable *tips* that are displayed when the **Comments** toggle button is pressed in the header bar.

The **Teams** user does not have to have any specific **Visio** license to view or add comments to the **Visio** file, provided they have been given suitable access permission.

However, if the **Teams** user does have an applicable **Visio** license, then they can use the **Edit Diagram** drop-down menu, which shows the **Edit in Teams**, **Open in Desktop App**, and **Open in Browser** options.

The following screenshot shows the file opened on **Visio Plan 2** desktop, where **Comments Pane** has been opened using the drop-down button in the **Review | Comments** ribbon group:

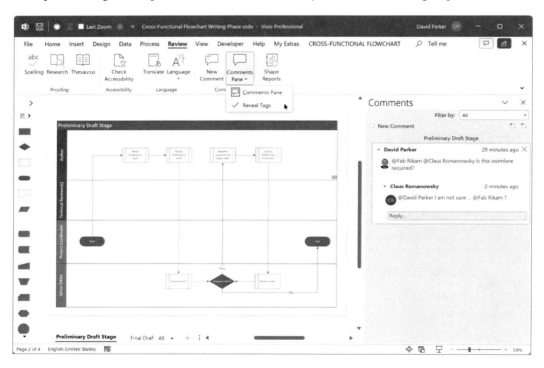

Figure 8.20 – Viewing Visio comments on Visio desktop

Comments can be filtered using the **Filter by** drop-down list, as shown in the following screenshot:

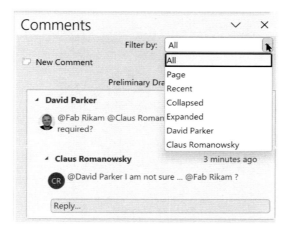

Figure 8.21 – The filter options for Comments on Visio desktop

The @mentions in the **Visio** comments will be notified by email with an image and a link, as shown in the following screenshot of **Outlook**:

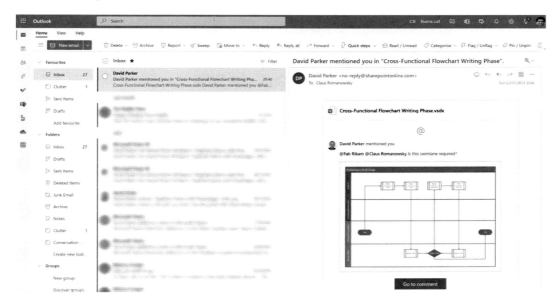

Figure 8.22 – The filter options for comments on Visio desktop

Clicking on this link will not open the **Visio** document in **Teams**, but it will open it in the browser instead, as shown here:

Figure 8.23 – Following a link from an email to Visio in the browser

If we are mentioned by someone using **Visio** comments, the **Microsoft 365** start screen and the **Visio** desktop start screen should display these files in the **Recommended** section along with an indication of who mentioned us and when. The following screenshot shows how this is displayed in the **Microsoft 365** app and **Visio Plan 2** desktop:

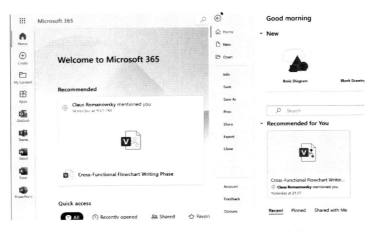

Figure 8.24 – Comments in Visio become recommended at startup

Comments in **Visio** diagrams are sometimes used to inform other collaborators of changes that have been made, or should be made, and it may not be suitable for these messages to persist forever, especially if a document passes through to production for more general consumption. Fortunately, there is a way that these comments can be removed.

Removing comments from a Visio document

Desktop editions of **Visio** can open a **Remove Hidden Information** dialog from the **File | Info | Check for Issues | Remove Personal Information** drop-down button, as shown here:

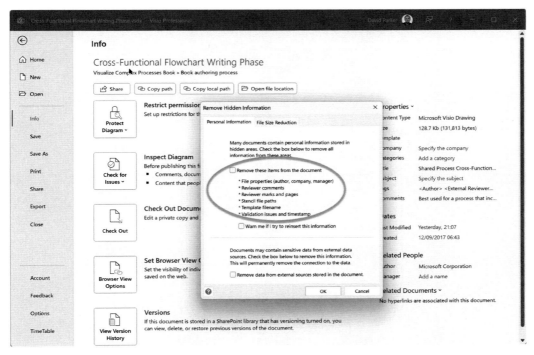

Figure 8.25 – Removing comments in Visio desktop

The top option will remove a number of items, including *reviewer comments, marks, and pages* when ticked, and then click **OK**.

This will delete all of the **Visio** comments in the document, and there is also an option to be warned if a user tries to add any future comments or other personal information.

Co-authoring in Teams and SharePoint

Co-authoring is also possible for **Visio** documents that are stored in **OneDrive for Business**, **Teams**, or **SharePoint**. Each of the co-authors requires permission to edit a document and a suitable **Visio** license for the features in the document. For example, a **Visio for M365** license is not sufficient to edit a cross-functional flowchart diagram because it needs a **Visio Plan 1** or **Visio Plan 2** license.

The following screenshot shows that **Claus**, on the left, has added a connector to the diagram in **Visio** within **Teams**, and Fab has the same page open for editing in the browser in **Visio for the Web**. She that sees a co-author, indicated in a circle with the initials **CR**, has the connector labeled **Recruits?** selected, and both users can see that **DP** also has the ellipse labeled **Technical reviewer** selected.

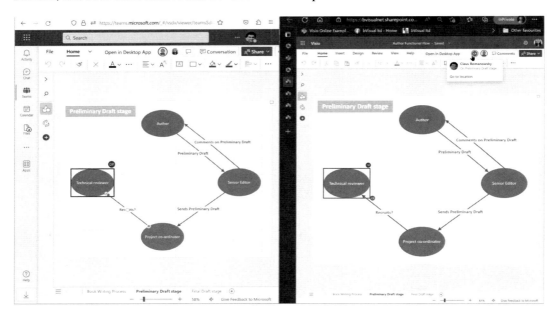

Figure 8.26 – Co-authoring in Visio, in Teams, and the browser

Note that the **DP** user has the document open for edit in the browser elsewhere.

> **Important note**
>
> Co-authoring is also possible if multiple users edit a **Visio** document using **Visio Plan 2** desktop simultaneously; however, it is not currently possible to co-author simultaneously with users within the web and the desktop editions.

Visio does not have a feature like **Review | Track Changes** in Microsoft **Word** or **Review | Show Changes** in **Excel**, but **OneDrive**, **Teams**, and **SharePoint** do have version control. Version history can be viewed under **File | Info | View Version History** on **Visio** desktop, and earlier versions can be restored.

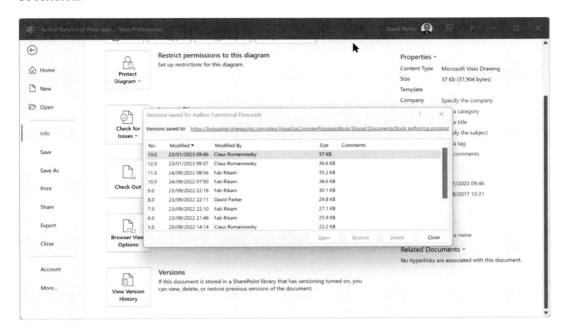

Figure 8.27 – Viewing version history in Visio

Sharing a Visio file

We are not limited to sharing a **Visio** document with others within a **SharePoint** Document library, **Teams** channel, **OneDrive** folder, or by using @mentions within **Teams** conversations or **Visio** comments. We can also share a **Visio** document using **File | Share** on **Visio** desktop, as shown here:

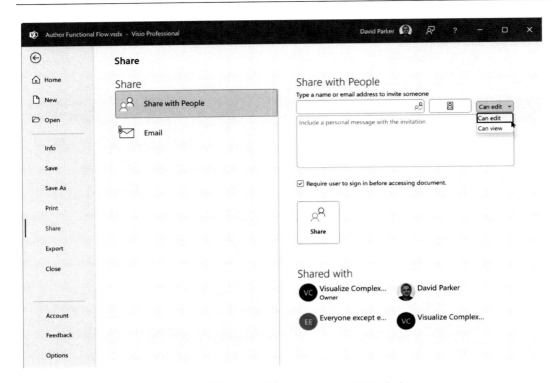

Figure 8.28 – Sharing a Visio document on Visio desktop

We can select people or groups and choose whether they have edit- or view-only permission, and then send them an accompanying message.

The **Email** button in the preceding screenshot has four options:

- **Send as Attachment**: This is discouraged, as the end user may not have a Visio license, and this also bloats email system storage

- **Send a Link**: This is the best option for files stored in OneDrive, Teams, or SharePoint because access can be controlled

- **Send as PDF**: This saves the file as a PDF, so this is the best option for end users who do not have any Visio license or cannot use controlled links to our storage system

- **Send as XPS**: This saves the file in the XPS format, and some end users might prefer this format to PDF; however, it is being used less and less

We can share a **Visio** document within **Teams** or the browser, and select a suitable setting for the link, as shown in the following screenshots:

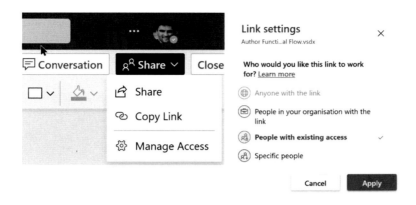

Figure 8.29 – Sharing a Visio document in Visio online

A link can also be shared from **Visio** in **Reading View** mode, and this link can be assigned with the **Edit** or **View only** permission.

Protecting a Visio document from viewing

Visio desktop, like the other Microsoft 365 apps, has the ability to use **Information Rights Management** (**IRM**) to restrict access to documents stored in **Teams**, **SharePoint**, or **OneDrive**, using **File | Info | Protect Document**, as shown here:

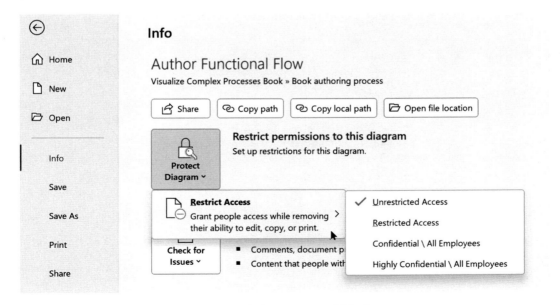

Figure 8.30 – Restricting access to a Visio document

The most onerous control is the **Restricted Access** option, which enables us to specify who can read or change the document, whether they can copy or print the contents, and even whether they can set an expiry date for the file, as shown in the following screenshots of the dialogs opened from **Restricted Access | More Options**:

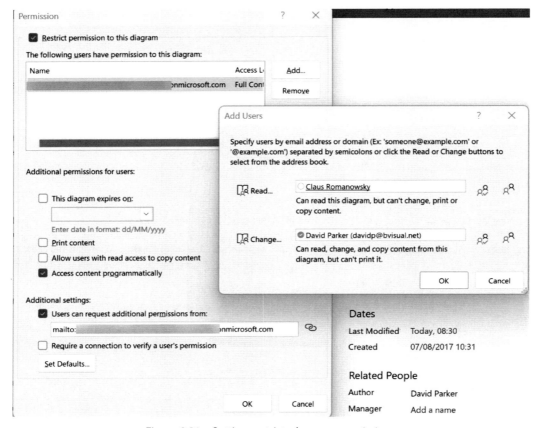

Figure 8.31 – Setting restricted access permissions

The IRM settings will prevent any opening of the **Visio** document in the browser.

Protecting a Visio document or parts from edits

We can discourage some elements of a **Visio** document from being edited, even if it is shared with others, by protecting them as follows:

1. On the **Developer** tab, in the **Show/Hide** group, select **Drawing Explorer**.

2. In the **Drawing Explorer** window, right-click the name of the drawing that you want to protect from changes, and then click **Protect Document**.

3. Select the items that you want to prevent people from changing, and then click OK.

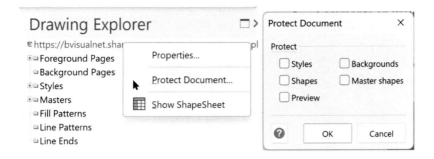

Figure 8.32 – Protecting document elements from edits

The **Shapes** option appears to have no effect, but the other options in the **Protect Document** box will disable the editing menus and commands. These types of edits cannot be done within the browser anyway.

We can also discourage editing some of the properties of shapes within a page too, as follows:

1. Select the shapes on the drawing page.

2. On the **Developer** tab, in the **Shape Design** group, click **Protection**.

3. Select the checkbox next to **From selection**, and any other options you want.

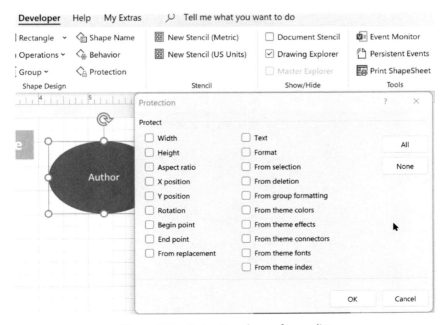

Figure 8.33 – Protecting shapes from edits

Ticking any of these options will prevent the whole document from being editable within the browser, and we will only be able to edit it within **Visio** desktop.

Both of these methods are only a discouragement because they can be changed by another user with permission to edit the file.

Summary

In this chapter, we have learned how we can securely store our **Visio** documents and provide access to them to an organization, groups of users, teams, channels, or specific individuals. We have also seen how we can add comments in **Visio** diagrams or include them within a Teams chat, and how to invite others to collaborate, using @mentions or by sharing a controlled link with them.

In the next chapter, we will learn how **Visio** can be integrated with other Microsoft apps – **Word**, **PowerPoint**, **Excel**, and **Power BI**.

Integrating Visio with Other Microsoft Apps

Microsoft Visio is great for creating process diagrams that can contain data and hyperlinks within each shape. These diagrams are more than just pictures; they can be exported to or embedded within other Microsoft apps for documentation, presentation, integration, and interaction. An image of each step of the process and a table of all the information within it can be automatically exported to **Microsoft Word** to create a comprehensive record. Named rectangular areas of Visio diagrams can be exported to **Microsoft PowerPoint** to create a presentation with titled slides, complete with transitions, to create storyboards of processes for group discussions. Data from process shapes can be exported to **Microsoft Excel** for analysis or integration with other systems. Process diagrams can be embedded within **Microsoft Power BI**, and steps can be linked to data from many other sources to provide an interactive dashboard with text or color overlays. We will go through all of these features to learn how we can use them effectively. The following are the specific topics that will be covered in this chapter:

- Exporting processes to Microsoft Word for documentation
- Exporting diagrams to Microsoft PowerPoint for presentation
- Exporting data to Microsoft Excel for integration
- Embedding diagrams in Microsoft Power BI for interpretation and interaction

Technical requirements

These are the Microsoft apps that are utilized in this chapter, and you should have access to at least one of the Visio subscriptions, but Visio Plan 2 subscribers will be able to use all of the features described:

- **Visio Plan 2**: Desktop subscription app
- **Word**: Desktop subscription app
- **Excel**: Desktop subscription app

- **PowerPoint**: Desktop subscription app

- **Power BI**: Desktop subscription app

We will be using the `Functional Flow Diagram from DV.vsdx` document throughout this chapter as an example because it contains a reasonably sized flowchart with **Shape Data**. This file and others can be found in the GitHub repository at `https://github.com/PacktPublishing/Visualize-complex-processes-with-Microsoft-Visio/tree/main/Chapter9`.

Exporting processes to Microsoft Word for documentation

We looked at some parts of the **Process** ribbon tab in previous chapters, but now we will concentrate on the **Export | Word** button that is available in the desktop Visio Plan 2 edition:

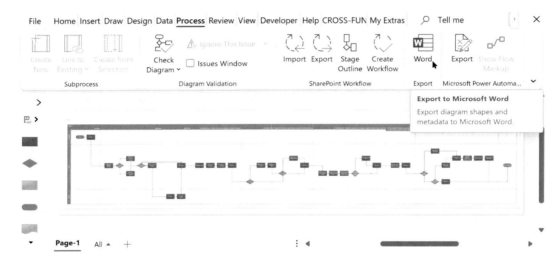

Figure 9.1 - The Process | Export | Word option

This command opens an **Export To Word** panel with two tabs: **Preview** and **Settings**, as shown in the following screenshot:

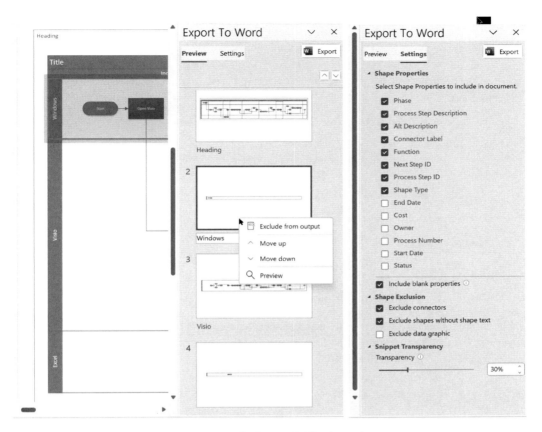

Figure 9.2 - The Export To Word panel

The **Preview** tab displays a preview image of each of the container shapes, titled with their header text, and other shapes that respect the options on the **Settings** tab. By default, all 2D (*non-connector*) shapes with a label are included.

The subject shape of each preview item is selected on the page whenever the preview image is selected. The preview image has a right-click context menu that displays the following commands:

- **Exclude from output**: This prevents the item from being included in the export to Word. The item is grayed out if selected, and the label changes to **Include in output**.

- **Move up**: This moves the item up in the display order. You can also use the up arrow at the top right of the panel.

- **Move down**: This moves the item down in the display order. You can also use the down arrow at the top right of the panel.

- **Preview**: This zooms into the area.

The **Settings** tab has the following options:

- **Shape Properties**:

  - A checkable list of all discovered **Shape Data** rows. Those with values will be automatically checked.

  - **Include blank properties**: This will include all **Shape Data** rows, even if they do not have a value.

- **Shape Exclusion**:

  - **Exclude connectors**: This is checked by default.

  - **Exclude shapes without shape text**: This is checked by default.

  - **Exclude data graphic**: This is not checked by default.

- **Snippet transparency**:

  - Transparency slider and up/down box.

The following screenshot shows the **Decision.133** shape in context, with its **Shape Data**. Notice that the preview, item *17*, has captured this shape with all of the other shapes that it is connected to. The preview item has been automatically titled with the label text:

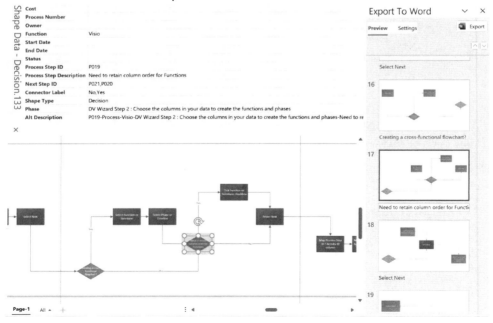

Figure 9.3 - The Export To Word panel selects the subject shape

If the shape does not have any label text, it will be initially set to the shape name, but it can be edited manually by simply clicking the image title.

We can also change the order of the images with the up and down buttons or just by clicking and dragging an image vertically.

Once we have edited the image titles, set the options in the settings, marked any images we want to exclude, and re-ordered them to suit, then we are ready to try an export to Word.

Enhancing the Word document

When we click the **Export** button on the **Export to Word** panel, then all of the included preview images and the data of each shape will be exported to Word, shown as follows:

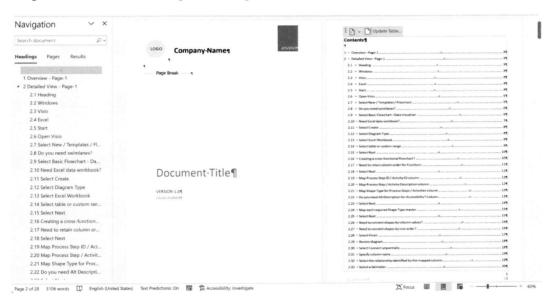

Figure 9.4 - The export Word document title page and table of contents

We can then enhance the Word document to create a more polished record of the process steps.

The author's name is copied from the Visio document in **File | Info | Related People | Author**. However, it can also be manually edited.

> **Important note**
> To update the **Table of Contents** table, place the insertion point under **Contents** in the Word document, and then select **Update Table**.

The following screenshot shows a section of the Word document with the same **Decision.133** shape from Visio, and the table of included data.

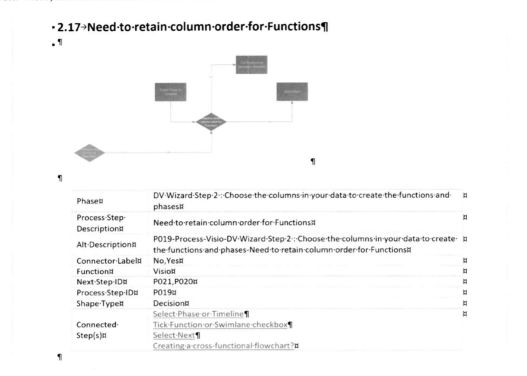

· 2.17→Need·to·retain·column·order·for·Functions¶
· ¶

Phase¤	DV·Wizard·Step·2·:·Choose·the·columns·in·your·data·to·create·the·functions·and· phases¤	¤
Process·Step· Description¤	Need·to·retain·column·order·for·Functions¤	¤
Alt·Description¤	P019-Process-Visio-DV·Wizard·Step·2·:·Choose·the·columns·in·your·data·to·create· the·functions·and·phases-Need·to·retain·column·order·for·Functions¤	¤
Connector·Label¤	No,Yes¤	¤
Function¤	Visio¤	¤
Next·Step·ID¤	P021,P020¤	¤
Process·Step·ID¤	P019¤	¤
Shape·Type¤	Decision¤	¤
Connected· Step(s)¤	Select·Phase·or·Timeline¶ Tick·Function·or·Swimlane·checkbox¶ Select·Next¶ Creating·a·cross-functional·flowchart?¤	¤

Figure 9.5 - Example shape image and data in Word

Now we know how we can create a comprehensive breakdown of our process for records or collaboration, we will learn how we can make a PowerPoint presentation to clearly explain the flow of processes next.

Exporting diagrams to Microsoft PowerPoint for presentation

We looked at some parts of the **View** ribbon tab in the previous chapter, but now we will concentrate on the **Export | PowerPoint** button. This button in desktop Visio Plan 2 will open the **Slide Snippets** panel on the right, shown as follows:

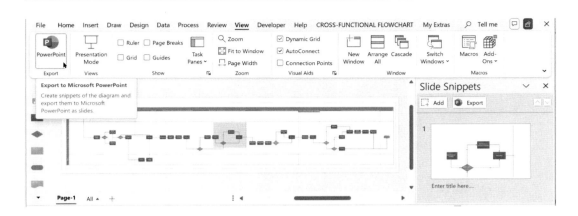

Figure 9.6 - The Slide Snippets panel

We can click the **Add** button at the top of the **Slide Snippets** panel, and a **Slide Snippet** rectangular shape is dropped in the center of the view. A preview image is added to the list in the **Slide Snippets** panel. The title of this snippet can be edited in the panel, and the rectangular shape can be resized, moved, and deleted. It is just a special Visio shape locked to a particular layer, and it will not be deleted if the **Slide Snippets** panel is closed; it will simply become invisible because the **Slide Snippets** layer will be made invisible. This is useful because these shapes are saved with the Visio document and can also be added to other pages. This means that we can make storyboards that flow over multiple pages, unlike the **Export to Word** feature, which only exports a single page at a time.

If we overlap these **Slide Snippet** shapes in Visio, as in the following screenshot, then we will get a better transition in PowerPoint between slides. This is because the export will automatically apply the **Morph** transition in PowerPoint, which creates a smooth animated transition between one slide and the next:

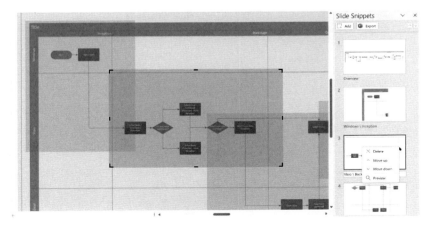

Figure 9.7 - Overlayed Slide Snippets

Clicking on a preview item in the **Slide Snippets** list will select the shape on the Visio page and change the page if necessary. The right-click menu of the preview image has the following options:

- **Delete**: This deletes the list item and **Slide Snippet** shape.

- **Move up**: This moves the selected item up in the list. You can also use the up arrow button at the top right of the panel.

- **Move down**: This moves the selected item down in the list. You can also use the down arrow at the top right of the panel.

- **Preview**: This zooms into the **Slide Snippet** shape.

The following screenshot of the slides created in PowerPoint using the **View | Presentation Views | Slide Sorter** view shows how each slide is titled, and the image of the area covered by the **Slide Snippet** shape is inserted on the right side of the slide:

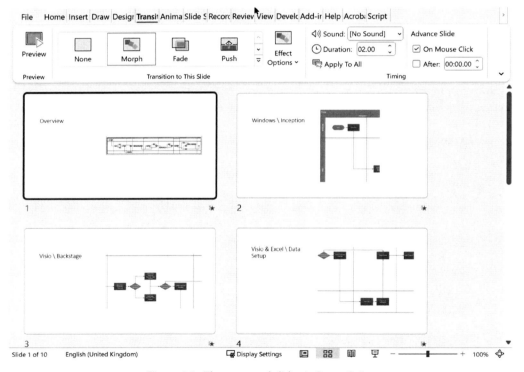

Figure 9.8 - The exported slides in PowerPoint

The presentation can then be enhanced and used to describe the flow of a process to an audience that might be intimidated by trying to navigate a large complex flow on one screen.

Although this export is very useful, there is a commercial Visio add-in, written by one of the authors of this book, that adds even more features.

Optional Visio add-in to provide extra features

There is a desktop Visio Plan 2 add-in, **SS Plus**, available at `https://bvisual.net/products/slide-snippets-plus/`. This adds the ability to add formatted notes and hyperlinks to each **Slide Snippet** shape and to choose the PowerPoint **Smart Layout** to apply. This means that it may not be necessary to manually enhance the slides after exporting to PowerPoint, as shown in the following screenshot of **Slide Sorter View** in PowerPoint:

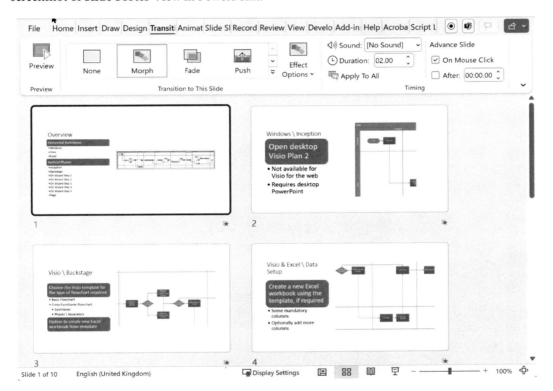

Figure 9.9 - Enhanced export to PowerPoint

We have learned how to document and present flows using Word and PowerPoint, so we will now see how we can export data from Visio diagrams for analysis or integration with other systems.

Exporting data to Microsoft Excel for integration

Our process flowcharts are a precious source of knowledge about our business, and we have learned how we can create diagrams automatically using the *Data Visualizer* feature, as described in *Chapter 5*, and how we can update a linked Excel table from the Visio flowchart. However, we may not have created our flowchart from an Excel table, or we may have used a query in Excel as a source, in which case, we are unable to update with Data Visualizer. We may want to check or analyze the data in our flowchart diagrams or integrate the data with another app or system, such as Power BI, as discussed in the next section.

Creating a report definition

We have previously looked at some parts of the **Review** ribbon tab in previous chapters, but now we will concentrate on the **Shape Reports** button. This button will open the **Reports** dialog, as shown here:

Figure 9.10 - The Review | Shape Reports dialog

This dialog will only display reports that are possibly relevant to the types of shapes on the active page. These reports can be defined in an external file with a `.vrd` extension for *Visio Report Definition* or within the document itself. The reports are stored in an XML format. This feature was written many years ago and is intended for producing lists of shapes, along with their data, and can also aggregate some values, if required.

The **New…** button on the **Reports** dialog will open **Report Definition Wizard**, as shown in the following screenshot, which we can use to create or edit our reports:

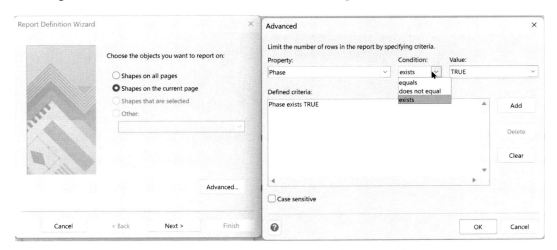

Figure 9.11 - The Report Definition Wizard | Advanced dialog

Our first option is to choose whether to include shapes on all pages, the current page, or just the selected shapes. The last option was permanently disabled by Microsoft after they acquired Visio back in 2000.

We can then further refine the shapes to be included by clicking the **Advanced…** button to open the **Advanced** dialog, shown on the right of the screenshot.

The **Advanced** dialog allows us to add multiple rows to the **Defined criteria** list:

- **Property**: Select from a list of shape properties, a list of discovered **Shape Data** rows, and **User-defined Cell** values. We will learn more about the latter in the next chapter.

- **Condition**: This normally includes **equals**, **does not equal**, or **exists**, but there are more options for numeric data.

- **Value**: Enter or select the required value.

We can check **Case sensitive** if we want to ensure that there is a perfect match for the values.

After saving any criteria with the **OK** button, we can proceed to the next screen with the **Next >** button. This screen will default to the shape properties and the discovered **Shape Data** rows, but we could extend this list to include *User-defined Cells* with the **Show all properties** option:

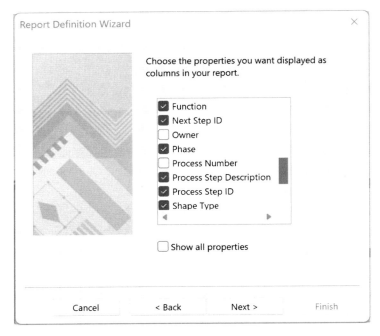

Figure 9.12 - The properties selector dialog

Once we are happy with our list of properties to report on, we can click **Next >** to go to the next screen.

This screen, as shown in the following screenshot, is where we can enter a title for the report, and open up other dialogs to define any grouping with subtotals, the order to sort by, and the format of numeric data. We can define an optional property to group by using the **Subtotals** dialog, shown here:

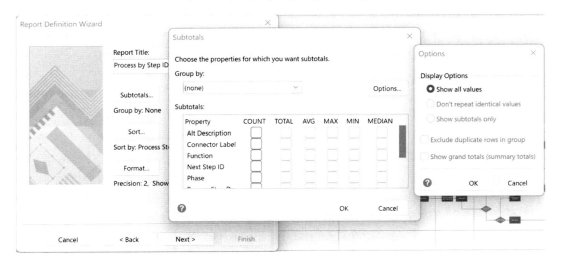

Figure 9.13 - The Subtotals dialog

We can choose to include **COUNT** of the same values or to add columns for **TOTAL, AVG, MAX, MIN,** and **MEDIAN** for numeric values if we have selected a property to group by using the **Group by** option.

We can also change **Display Options** for the data using the **Options…** button to vary some row display choices.

The **Sort…** button opens a dialog where we can define the order of the columns in the output and, optionally, **Sort by** of up to three properties in the specified **Row order**, shown as follows:

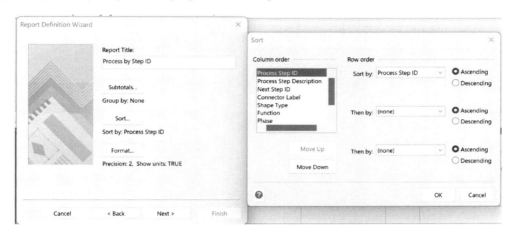

Figure 9.14 - The Sort dialog

The last button, **Format…**, allows us to specify the number of decimal places for numeric values and an option to display the units:

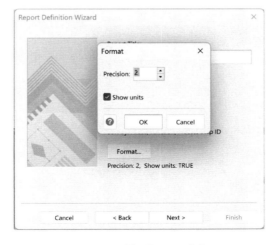

Figure 9.15 - The Format dialog

Once we are happy with these settings, then we can proceed using the **Next >** button to give the report a **Name** value and a **Description** value. We can also choose **Save in a file** to save externally or **Save in this drawing** to save within the document:

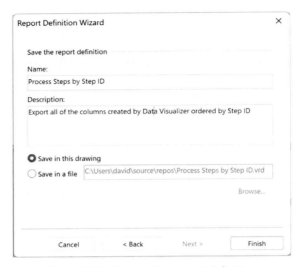

Figure 9.16 - Naming the report definition

Running a report definition

The **Review | Reports | Shape Reports** button also contains the **Run…** button to run the report and will then offer us four choices for the output, as shown in the following screenshot:

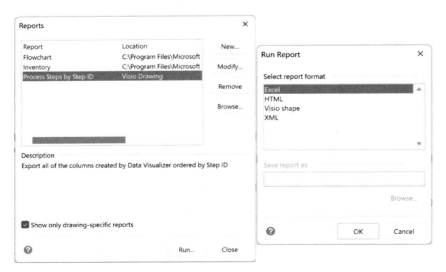

Figure 9.17 - The Run Report dialog

Report definitions can be modified or removed, and externally stored report definition files can be selected using the **Browse...** button.

In addition to the **Excel** option, the report can be exported to an **HTML** file or an **XML** file. The **Visio shape** option creates an embedded Excel worksheet on the current page. The following screenshot shows the report formatted in an Excel workbook:

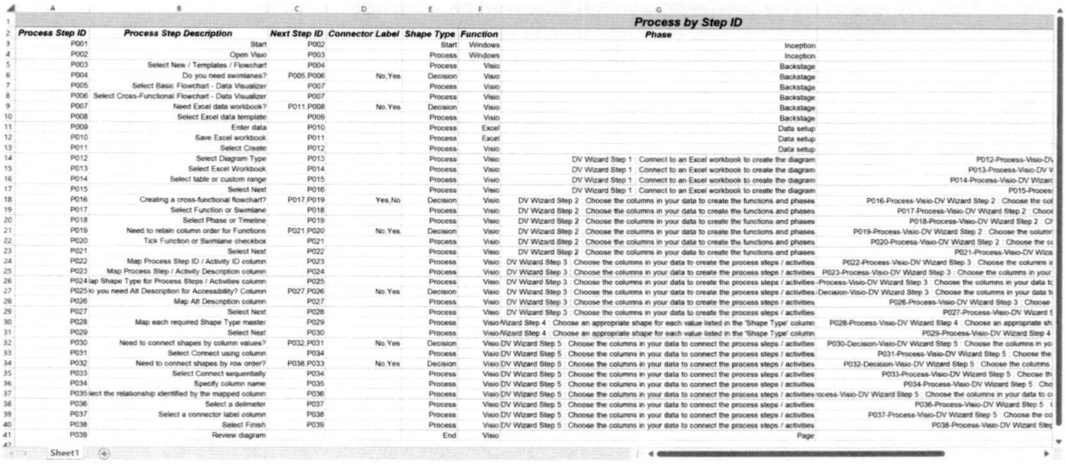

Process by Step ID

Process Step ID	Process Step Description	Next Step ID	Connector Label	Shape Type	Function	Phase	
P001	Start	P002		Start	Windows	Inception	
P002	Open Visio	P003		Process	Windows	Inception	
P003	Select New / Templates / Flowchart	P004		Process	Visio	Backstage	
P004	Do you need swimlanes?	P005,P006	No,Yes	Decision	Visio	Backstage	
P005	Select Basic Flowchart - Data Visualizer	P007		Process	Visio	Backstage	
P006	Select Cross-Functional Flowchart - Data Visualizer	P007		Process	Visio	Backstage	
P007	Need Excel data workbook?	P011,P008	No,Yes	Decision	Visio	Backstage	
P008	Select Excel data template	P009		Process	Visio	Backstage	
P009	Enter data	P010		Process	Excel	Data setup	
P010	Save Excel workbook	P011		Process	Excel	Data setup	
P011	Select Create	P012		Process	Visio	Data setup	
P012	Select Diagram Type	P013		Process	Visio	DV Wizard Step 1 : Connect to an Excel workbook to create the diagram	P012-Process-Visio-D\
P013	Select Excel Workbook	P014		Process	Visio	DV Wizard Step 1 : Connect to an Excel workbook to create the diagram	P013-Process-Visio-DV V
P014	Select table or custom range	P015		Process	Visio	DV Wizard Step 1 : Connect to an Excel workbook to create the diagram	P014-Process-Visio-DV Wizarc
P015	Select Next	P016		Process	Visio	DV Wizard Step 1 : Connect to an Excel workbook to create the diagram	P015-Proces:
P016	Creating a cross-functional flowchart?	P017,P019	Yes,No	Decision	Visio	DV Wizard Step 2 : Choose the columns in your data to create the functions and phases	P016-Process-Visio-DV Wizard Step 2 : Choose the col
P017	Select Function or Swimlane	P018		Process	Visio	DV Wizard Step 2 : Choose the columns in your data to create the functions and phases	P017-Process-Visio-DV Wizard Step 2 : Choo
P018	Select Phase or Timeline	P019		Process	Visio	DV Wizard Step 2 : Choose the columns in your data to create the functions and phases	P018-Process-Visio-DV Wizard Step 2 : Ch
P019	Need to retain column order for Functions	P021,P020	No,Yes	Decision	Visio	DV Wizard Step 2 : Choose the columns in your data to create the functions and phases	P019-Process-Visio-DV Wizard Step 2 : Choose the colum
P020	Tick Function or Swimlane checkbox	P021		Process	Visio	DV Wizard Step 2 : Choose the columns in your data to create the functions and phases	P020-Process-Visio-DV Wizard Step 2 : Choose the c
P021	Select Next	P022		Process	Visio	DV Wizard Step 2 : Choose the columns in your data to create the functions and phases	P021-Process-Visio-DV Wiza
P022	Map Process Step ID / Activity ID column	P023		Process	Visio	DV Wizard Step 3 : Choose the columns in your data to create the process steps / activities	P022-Process-Visio-DV Wizard Step 3 : Choose the columns i
P023	Map Process Step / Activity Description column	P024		Process	Visio	DV Wizard Step 3 : Choose the columns in your data to create the process steps / activities	P023-Process-Visio-DV Wizard Step 3 : Choose the columns in your
P024	lap Shape Type for Process Steps / Activities column	P025		Process	Visio	DV Wizard Step 3 : Choose the columns in your data to create the process steps / activities	-Process-Visio-DV Wizard Step 3 : Choose the columns in your data tc
P025	lo you need Alt Description for Accessibility? Column	P027,P026	No,Yes	Decision	Visio	DV Wizard Step 3 : Choose the columns in your data to create the process steps / activities	-Decision-Visio-DV Wizard Step 3 : Choose the columns in your data t
P026	Map Alt Description column	P027		Process	Visio	DV Wizard Step 3 : Choose the columns in your data to create the process steps / activities	P026-Process-Visio-DV Wizard Step 3 : Choose
P027	Select Next	P028		Process	Visio	DV Wizard Step 3 : Choose the columns in your data to create the process steps / activities	P027-Process-Visio-DV Wizard S
P028	Map each required Shape Type master	P029		Process	Visio	Wizard Step 4 : Choose an appropriate shape for each value listed in the 'Shape Type' column	P028-Process-Visio-DV Wizard Step 4 : Choose an appropriate sh
P029	Select Next	P030		Process	Visio	Wizard Step 4 : Choose an appropriate shape for each value listed in the 'Shape Type' column	P029-Process-Visio-DV Wizard Step 4
P030	Need to connect shapes by column values?	P032,P031	No,Yes	Decision	Visio	DV Wizard Step 5 : Choose the columns in your data to connect the process steps / activities	P030-Decision-Visio-DV Wizard Step 5 : Choose the columns in yo
P031	Select Connect using column	P034		Process	Visio	DV Wizard Step 5 : Choose the columns in your data to connect the process steps / activities	P031-Process-Visio-DV Wizard Step 5 : Choose the
P032	Need to connect shapes by row order?	P038,P033	No,Yes	Decision	Visio	DV Wizard Step 5 : Choose the columns in your data to connect the process steps / activities	P032-Decision-Visio-DV Wizard Step 5 : Choose the columns
P033	Select Connect sequentially	P034		Process	Visio	DV Wizard Step 5 : Choose the columns in your data to connect the process steps / activities	P033-Process-Visio-DV Wizard Step 5 : Choose th
P034	Specify column name	P035		Process	Visio	DV Wizard Step 5 : Choose the columns in your data to connect the process steps / activities	P034-Process-Visio-DV Wizard Step 5 : Cho
P035	lect the relationship identified by the mapped column	P036		Process	Visio	DV Wizard Step 5 : Choose the columns in your data to connect the process steps / activities	ocess-Visio-DV Wizard Step 5 : Choose the columns in your data to c
P036	Select a delimeter	P037		Process	Visio	DV Wizard Step 5 : Choose the columns in your data to connect the process steps / activities	P036-Process-Visio-DV Wizard Step 5 : (
P037	Select a connector label column	P038		Process	Visio	DV Wizard Step 5 : Choose the columns in your data to connect the process steps / activities	P037-Process-Visio-DV Wizard Step 5 : Choose the co
P038	Select Finish	P039		Process	Visio	DV Wizard Step 5 : Choose the columns in your data to connect the process steps / activities	P038-Process-Visio-DV Wizard Ste
P039	Review diagram			End	Visio	Page	

Figure 9.18 - The exported report in Excel

The **Excel** option always creates a table with column headers and a title row above it. This formatting was coded many years ago and only creates a named range, `VisRpt`, and does not create a more modern Excel table.

Optional Excel add-in to convert the report into a modern table

There is a free **Shape Report Converter** add-in for Excel available from the *Microsoft App Store*, which can be found in **Insert | Get Add-ins**.

Read more about this at `https://bvisual.net/products/visio-shape-report-converter/`, but it simply converts the Excel report named range, as seen in the previous screenshot, to the modern table shown here, which is suitable for better integration with other systems and for use with **Get & Transform Data (PowerQuery)**:

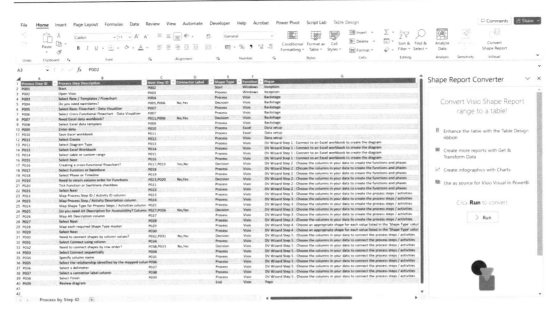

Figure 9.19 - The converted table in Excel

We can use the preceding Excel table as a source for PowerQuery and import it into a **List** in SharePoint or Teams, for example, or as a data source for Power BI, as seen in the next section.

Embedding processes in Microsoft Power BI for interaction

Power BI is a great app for analyzing or interacting with live data, and Microsoft provides **Visio Visual**, which can be added from the **Visualizations | Get More Visuals…** dialog. This gives us the ability to add pages from Visio documents into Power BI reports. This means that we can overlay live statistics from a process that might be in use, for example, the count of the number of help desk calls at particular parts of the flow. We have been using the process steps for Data Visualizer so far in this chapter, so we will use the Excel table exported from Visio in the previous section.

We can display the data in Power BI to add text labels to each flowchart step or to color the shapes by value in Visio Visual.

You can download a free guide to using Visio and Power BI together from `https://bvisual.net/resources/power-up-your-visio-diagrams/`, and we will learn some key techniques in this section.

Preparing a Visio diagram for Power BI

All we need is a unique identifier for each shape and a data source in Power BI that has that unique identifier too. Then we can map the dataset to the shapes automatically. The unique identifier of each shape could be the text label, but it can also be a **Shape Data** row value. The export to Excel that we did in the last section contains the **Process Step ID** column, which has unique values.

If the shapes have no suitable text or **Shape Data** values, then we would have to resort to manually mapping each shape to a row in a specific dataset in Power BI.

We can only embed one page in each Visio visual in Power BI, and since we are going to overlay each shape with text and color, we could have a completely grayscale page with empty rectangles if they have a **Shape Data** row with a suitable unique value.

Visio Visual will hide any *data graphics*, so we can forget everything we learned in the *Adding data graphics to highlight information* section in *Chapter 7* for pages that will be embedded in Power BI.

In this example, we have left the **Process Description** text on each shape, as in the next screenshot, but even that is not necessary because we have the **Process Step ID** value:

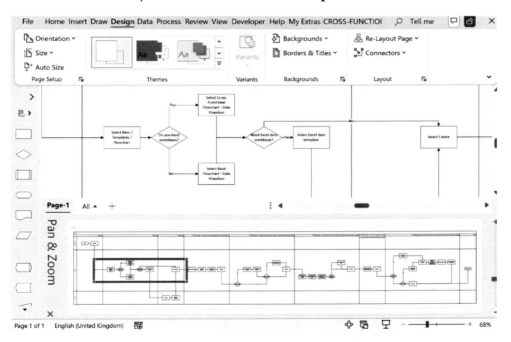

Figure 9.20 - Optionally grayscale the Visio page

In this case, we applied **No Theme** from the **Design | Themes** ribbon gallery to the page, but we could have alternatively applied a gray color to each layer.

> **Important note**
> There is a limit to the number of shapes on a page that can be handled by Visio Visual, but it is probably too high for most process diagrams to reach. However, the aforementioned guide has instructions on how to overcome this.

Preparing data for Power BI

We have prepared our Visio page for embedding in Power BI, so the next stage is preparing our data.

If we want to use the **Color by Value** feature, then the data values need to be numeric, unlike the data graphics in Visio, which could use numbers or text.

Our Excel table has three columns that we might wish to use for **Color by Value**, namely **Shape Type**, **Function**, and **Phase**. Unfortunately, they are all text values, so we need to create numeric alternatives for each column. This is where PowerQuery is so useful. In Excel, we can use **Data | Get & Transform Data | From Table/Range** to create a new query on our source table.

This is not a book on PowerQuery, but the next screenshot is the result of selecting the *Function* column in PowerQuery, then adding **Index Column** to create a unique number for each value:

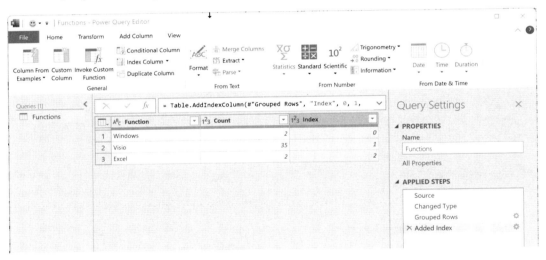

Figure 9.21 - Creating a new Group By query in Excel

This query can then be saved as a new query. The same can be done for **Phase** and **Shape Type**, and the next screenshot shows **Merge** of the new **ShapeTypes** query back to the original source table and joining on the **Shape Type** column:

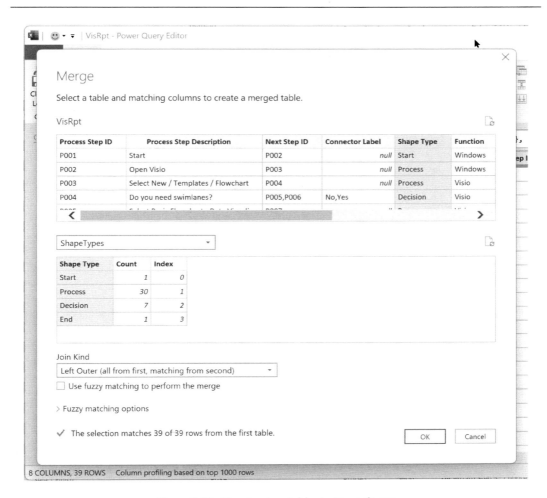

Figure 9.22 - Merging two tables in PowerQuery

Once the new query is joined in this way, it should be expanded, but only the **Index** column is required. In the following screenshot, the Functions table is expanded, the **Index** column is checked, and the **Use original column name as prefix** option is checked:

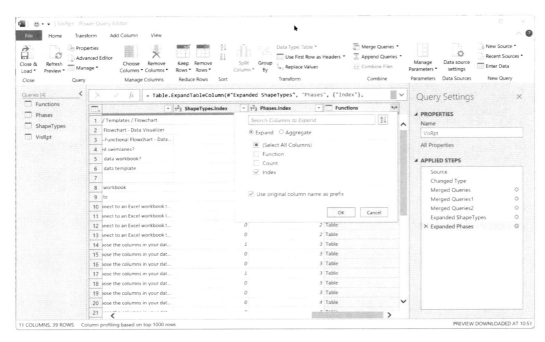

Figure 9.23 - Expanding the merged table

The following screenshot shows that a new query, DVProcess, has been created with merged **Index** values from the **Functions**, **Phases**, and **ShapeTypes** columns:

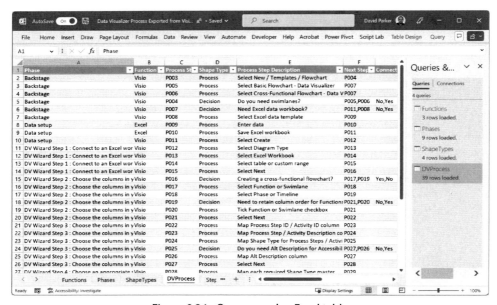

Figure 9.24 - Query saved as Excel table

There are three extra columns, **ShapeTypes.Index**, **Phases.Index**, and **Functions.Index** offscreen to the right of the preceding query. These provide us with the numerical values that we need to use **Color by Value** in Power BI Visio Visual.

The sample `Data Visualizer Process Exported from Visio.xlsx` file can be found in the *Chapter 9* folder on the GitHub site.

Embedding into Power BI

Now that we have prepared our data, we can open Power BI Desktop to design our report. We can choose **Get Data,** then **Import data from Excel** and select our workbook, and we will be presented with a choice of tables and queries. We should choose the query, in this case, `DVProcess`, and then click **Load** to import it into Power BI, as in the following screenshot:

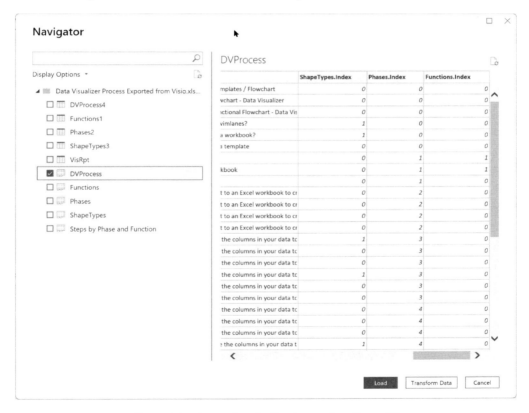

Figure 9.25 - Importing the Excel query into Power BI

We now have our source data in Power BI, and if we do not already have the Visio Visual, we need to get it with the **Get more visuals** command on the **...** button in the **Visualizations** panel. We can then click the **Visio** button that gets added to drop it onto the report tab, where we can move it and resize it, as in the next screenshot:

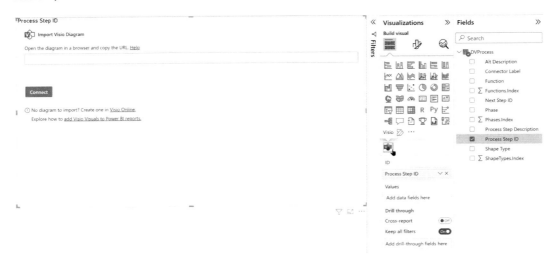

Figure 9.26 - Adding the Visio Visual to the Power BI tab

Then we need to get a suitably permissioned link to our Visio document. In the following screenshot, we have navigated to the Visio document in **OneDrive for Business**, and used the right-click menu **OneDrive | Share** dialog to get a read-only URL:

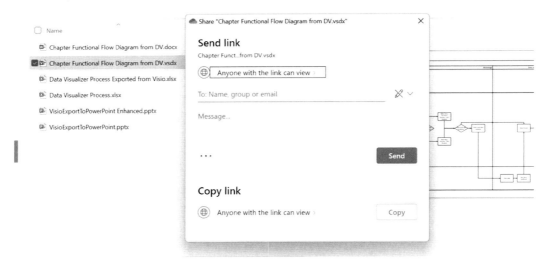

Figure 9.27 - Copying the URL for a Visio document

This URL is then pasted into the Visio Visual, the **Connect** button is clicked, and the `Process Step ID` key field is checked in the **Fields** panel, as in the following screenshot:

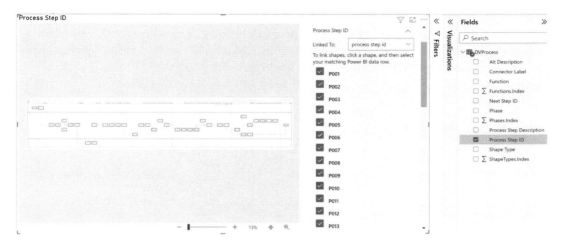

Figure 9.28 - Mapping the unique identifiers in Power BI

This is the main mapping between the data and the diagram, and the mapped **Process Step ID** values are shown automatically checked in the preceding screenshot.

Adding text to shapes

Now that we have mapped the data and diagram, we can choose any number of other fields to display as **Text** in and around each shape. The following screenshot shows the `Phase Abbrev` field (a custom column we created in PowerQuery to shorten the length of the text):

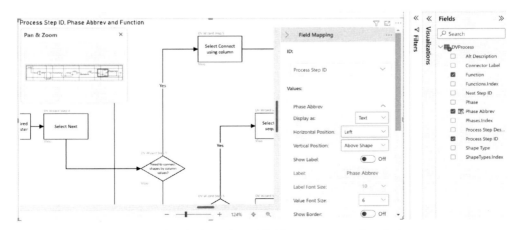

Figure 9.29 - Displaying selected fields as text around each shape

The preceding screenshot shows there are a number of settings that we can choose for each text label.

Coloring by value

Unlike displaying **Text**, we can only have one active **Colors** setting at a time. In this example, we are going to set ShapeTypes.Index as the value to color by, so we check the field in the **Fields** panel, then change **Display as** to **Colors** in the Visio Visual editing panel. In the following screenshot, ShapeTypes.Index is actually displayed as **Average of ShapeType…**. This is because we want the visual to zoom into the selected process step from a row we select in the **Table** visual that has been added below the Visio visual. We change the default aggregation for **ShapeTypes Index** by clicking the down arrow at the bottom of the **Visualizations** panel. We need to change to any aggregation except for **Don't summarize**, so **Average** has been chosen in this example:

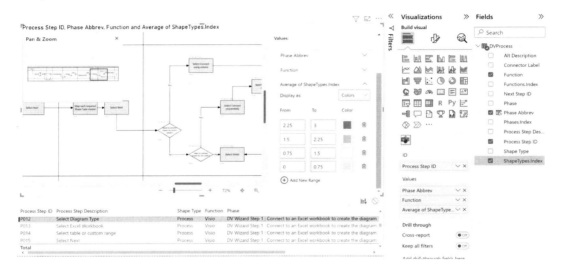

Figure 9.30 - Setting the Colors values

We have also renamed the Average of ShapeTypes.Index field for the visual as ShapeType Index for brevity. This option is also available on the context menu, shown as follows:

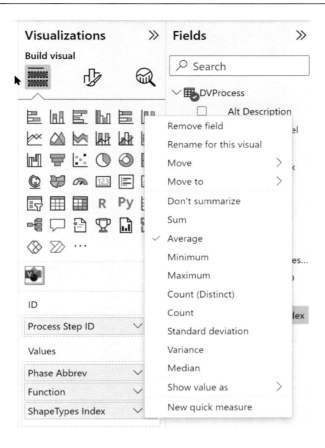

Figure 9.31 - Ensure that the aggregation is not Don't summarize

Viewing Visio in Power BI

So, now we can add a couple of **Slicer** visuals on the left for the **Function** and **Phase** values and a **Card** visual in the bottom -left corner to display the full text of the **Phase** value, as shown:

Figure 9.32 - Using the Power BI report

Now we can select a value in the **Function** or **Phase** slicer, for example, and just the steps with that value are colored, as shown in the following screenshot:

Figure 9.33: Checking a slider colors the shapes

The *Table* is also filtered by the *Slicer* visuals and displays the fields for the same process steps.

If we select a row in the *Table* visual, then the Visio Visual will zoom into the process step that it is bound to, as can be seen in the following screenshot:

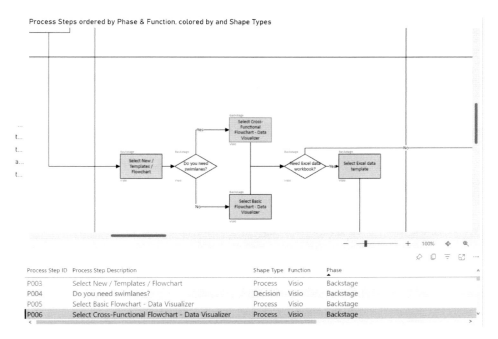

Figure 9.34 - Selecting an item zooms to the shape

So, now we have a fully interactive Power BI report that could be published and consumed by many colleagues throughout our organization.

Summary

In this chapter, we learned about some of the many ways that we can integrate our process flow diagrams with other Microsoft applications. All of this has been achieved with very little advanced knowledge of Visio and without any serious customizations. Visio is capable of so much more, and we will devote the last two chapters of this book to looking under the hood to see how it works. We can then explore ways that we can customize it for our own needs and circumstances.

10
Customizing Master Shapes and Templates

Microsoft Visio provides many master shapes and templates for creating process diagrams, but almost all of them can be improved by a little customization to suit an organization's particular requirements. These additional enhancements to master shapes and templates can be shared with others so that they can be made available to all, including **Visio for the web** users. **Visio** shapes get their smartness from a spreadsheet-like **ShapeSheet**, which contains formulas in each cell, just like **Excel**. These formulas control every shape property, from the size of a shape and the format of its lines and fills to the visibility of its parts. This chapter introduces the basics of custom shapes. The concepts are easy to comprehend for anyone who has dabbled with cell formulas in Excel. We will be covering the following topics:

- Understanding the importance of master shapes
- Reviewing existing selected process master shapes
- Adding Description shape data to existing master shapes
- Adding Duration to shape data
- Assign line weight, style, or color by Owner
- Matching the shape color with the swimlane color

Technical requirements

These are the Microsoft apps that will be utilized in this chapter. We should also have access to at least one of the Visio desktop editions:

- **Visio Plan 2**: Desktop subscription app
- **Visio Professional**: Windows one-time purchase only
- **Visio Standard**: Windows one-time purchase only

The customizations in this chapter can only be created with the desktop version of Visio, but the modified master shapes in the customized Visio documents can also be used in Visio for the web.

There are two files, `ButtonFace IDs.vsdx` and `Enhanced Basic Flowchart.vsdx`, available in this book's GitHub repository at `https://github.com/PacktPublishing/Visualize-complex-processes-with-Microsoft-Visio/tree/main/Chapter10`.

Understanding the importance of master shapes

Throughout this book, we have mainly been creating process flowchart diagrams via automation or by dragging and dropping master shapes from a stencil onto a page. We created connections between flowchart shapes with the connector tool or by dragging out the *Auto Connect* arrows from one shape to another. In each case, we have been creating instances of a master shape. So, what do we mean by a master shape, and why are they so important?

We have already learned how we can drag and drop shapes from stencils, but what we do not usually see is that every time we drag and drop a master shape from a stencil, Visio checks if we have used a master shape with the same name before. If we have not used it before, then Visio automatically creates a copy of the master shape and places it into the normally hidden **Document Stencil**, and then drops an instance of this copy onto the page. Then, whenever we drop another instance of the same master shape, Visio merely creates a reference to the copy of the master shape in the **Document Stencil** area.

Viewing the Document Stencil

In the following sequence of screenshots, the **Document Stencil** area is initially shown without any master shapes. However, later, the **Process** master shape is dragged and dropped three times from the **Basic Flowchart Shapes** stencil onto a page. By doing this, these shapes become instances of the master shape in the **Document Stencil** area:

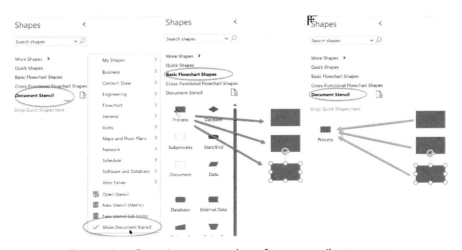

Figure 10.1 – Dragging a master shape from a stencil onto a page

The **Document Stencil** can be opened from the **More Shapes** menu options on the **Shapes** panel, or we can open the **Drawing Explorer** window from the **Developer** ribbon (see *Figure 10.2*). The **Developer** tab is visible when **File | Options | Advanced | General | Run in developer mode** is ticked, or the **Developer** tab is ticked under **Customize Ribbon | Main Tabs**.

Understanding the Drawing Explorer window

The **Drawing Explorer** window is a tree view, and we can expand the **Shapes** branch under each page in the **Foreground Pages** branch to see a list of each shape. Selecting a shape node in the explorer will select the shape on the page, and even turn to that page if it is not already active. Each shape node has a right-click context menu that allows us to open the **Shape Data** window, then the **Layer** dialog, so that we can delete the shape and open the **ShapeSheet** window:

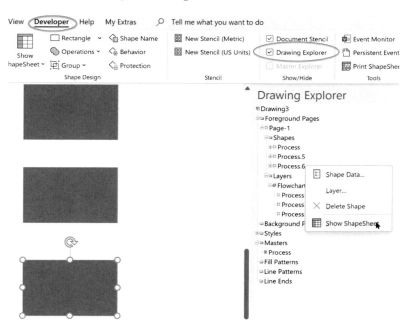

Figure 10.2 – Drawing Explorer opened from the Developer ribbon

Notice that the flowchart shapes are pre-assigned to the **Flowchart** layer, so we can see each one under this layer's branch too.

Important Note

The **Drawing Explorer** window will list all of the masters in the document, but the **Document Stencil** area will only show those that are not hidden. Visio automatically hides some types of masters, such as **Data Graphics**.

Shape instances inherit values from a master shape

If we connect these **Process** shapes together, as in the following screenshot, then Visio will automictically create a **Dynamic connector** master in the document or use the existing one if it exists already:

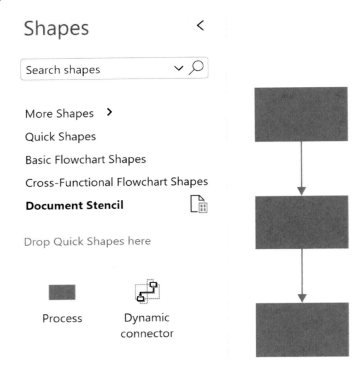

Figure 10.3 – The Dynamic connector master shape

Of course, each shape instance needs to keep a record of its page and position on the page, as well as other localized data such as the text, size, rotation angle, fill and line patterns, and colors. It will also keep a copy of the data values that we enter into the **Shape Data** window. However, many other properties are merely inherited from the master shape in the **Document Stencil** area. This keeps the size of the file small and faster to work with.

This also means that the Visio document can be passed around, and any existing shapes can be edited and duplicated without needing the source stencil present.

We can also make some edits to the master shape in the **Document Stencil** area – they will be automatically inherited by all of its instances on every page in the document. The master edit window can be opened by choosing the **Edit Master Shape...** option in the right-click menu of the master in the **Document Stencil** area:

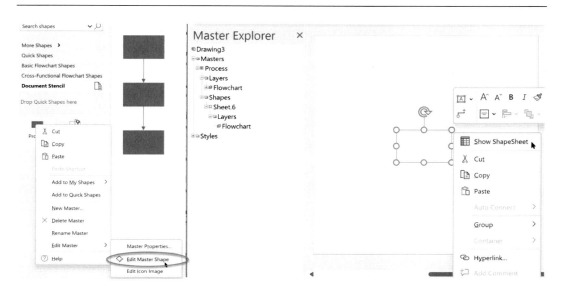

Figure 10.4 – The Edit Master Shape window

If we make edits and then close the **Master Edit** window, and then make some changes to the fill color, as shown in the following screenshot, then we will be prompted to update all of its instances. If we click **Yes**, then all of the instances will also be changed:

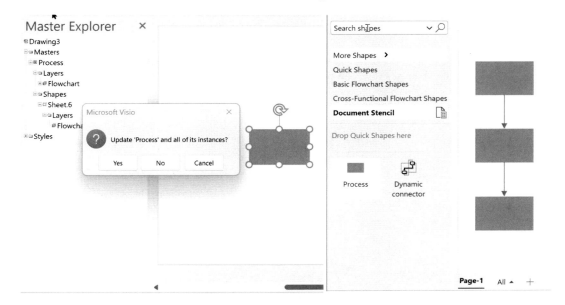

Figure 10.5 – The Master Edit window

However, if we do edit the master shape in the **Document Stencil** area, Visio will consider that this master shape is not the same as the original master shape on the source stencil unless we make a small edit to tell it otherwise. If we do not make this change, then Visio will create another copy of the master shape from the source stencil and new instances will reference it rather than our revised master shape:

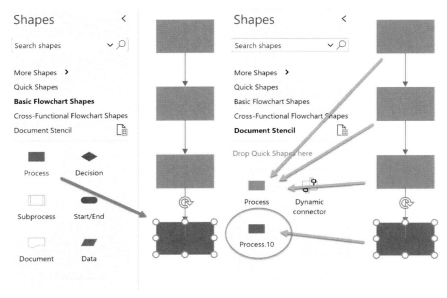

Figure 10.6 – Accidently creating a duplicate master shape

To fix the unnecessary duplication, we need to tick the **Match master by name on drop** option in the **Master Properties** dialog, which can be opened from the right-click menu of the master shape, as shown here:

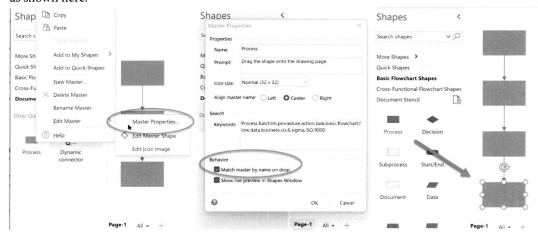

Figure 10.7 – Avoiding duplicate master shapes

Now, Visio will check the master name of the shape being dragged from a stencil. If it finds that there is one with this name already, then it will use it, and not create a duplicate master shape.

> **Important Note**
> The **Match master by name on drop** setting works most of the time, but it can fail if the two master shapes are radically different. This will mean that a duplicate master shape will be created, and then we must use **Home | Editing | Change Shape** to correct this.

Introducing the ShapeSheet

The preceding example is trivial because we only changed the color fill, but we may want to make more significant customizations. To do that, we need to know how Visio shapes become so smart. The secret is the *ShapeSheet*, which is similar to an Excel worksheet, where we have cells where we can enter formulas. Of course, Visio is more graphical than Excel, so it has many functions for graphics, whereas Excel has functions in many categories, including financial, statistical, and engineering functions.

You can learn more about the ShapeSheet at `https://learn.microsoft.com/office/client-developer/visio/concepts-visio-shapesheet` and formulas at `https://learn.microsoft.com/office/client-developer/visio/about-formulas`.

One of the effects of switching on **Developer Mode** was the addition of a **Show ShapeSheet** option on the right mouse menu of each shape and page, but we can also open the *ShapeSheet* from the **Developer | Shape Design | Show ShapeSheet** ribbon button. The *ShapeSheet* has a choice of two views, called **Formulas** and **Values**, which can be toggled using the **Shape Design | View** ribbon buttons, or from the right mouse menu in *ShapeSheet*. Each page and the document itself are special types of shapes and also have a *ShapeSheet*, which can also be opened similarly.

The following screenshot shows the formulas of a **Process** shape:

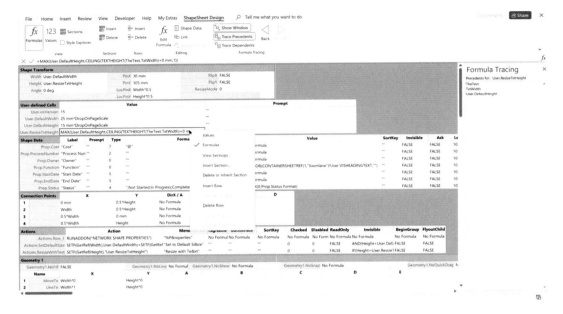

Figure 10.8 – The ShapeSheet of a Process shape

This may seem a little overwhelming at first, but we will only be looking at a few sections. We can switch off the visibility of some sections using the **View Sections** dialog, which can be opened from the **Sections** button in the ribbon, or by using the **View Sections…** option in the right-click menu:

Figure 10.9 – The View Sections dialog for the ShapeSheet

We would not normally want to edit the *ShapeSheet* of an instance of a master shape because it would only affect that one shape. It is better to edit the master shape itself; then, the changes will be inherited by all of the instance shapes.

Reviewing existing selected process master shapes

If we click the **Edit Master Shape ...** option in the right-click menu of the **Process** master in our **Document Stencil** area, we will see that the **Shape Data** section looks like this:

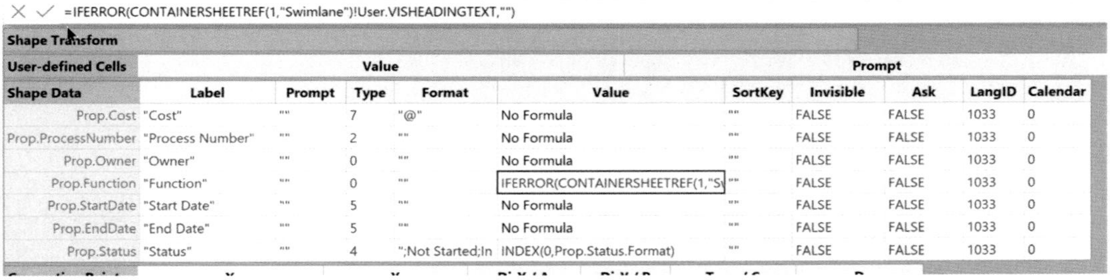
=IFERROR(CONTAINERSHEETREF(1,"Swimlane")!User.VISHEADINGTEXT,"")

Shape Transform

User-defined Cells	Value	Prompt

Shape Data	Label	Prompt	Type	Format	Value	SortKey	Invisible	Ask	LangID	Calendar
Prop.Cost	"Cost"	""	7	"@"	No Formula	""	FALSE	FALSE	1033	0
Prop.ProcessNumber	"Process Number"	""	2	""	No Formula	""	FALSE	FALSE	1033	0
Prop.Owner	"Owner"	""	0	""	No Formula	""	FALSE	FALSE	1033	0
Prop.Function	"Function"	""	0	""	IFERROR(CONTAINERSHEETREF(1,"S	""	FALSE	FALSE	1033	0
Prop.StartDate	"Start Date"	""	5	""	No Formula	""	FALSE	FALSE	1033	0
Prop.EndDate	"End Date"	""	5	""	No Formula	""	FALSE	FALSE	1033	0
Prop.Status	"Status"	""	4	";Not Started;In	INDEX(0,Prop.Status.Format)	""	FALSE	FALSE	1033	0

Figure 10.10 – The Shape Data section of a Process shape

The first thing we should notice is that the formulas are all *blue* text, whereas they were *black* in *Figure 10.10*. This is because inherited formulas and values are colored *black* but those that are not inherited are colored *blue*.

Hopefully, you have noticed that this section defines what is displayed in the **Shape Data** window. This is an optional section of the *ShapeSheet*, which means that it does not exist on all shapes, unlike some other sections that need to exist for Visio to work and cannot be deleted. The **Shape Data** section used to be called *Custom Properties* originally (and referred to as `Prop` in formulas) and can have many rows, which can be named for ease of reference.

See `https://learn.microsoft.com/office/client-developer/visio/shape-data-row-shape-data-section` for more information about the **Shape Data** section. The column headings are as follows:

- **Row name**: The unique name of the row in this section
- **Label**: The text that appears as the label in the **Shape Data** window
- **Prompt**: An optional tooltip
- **Type**: A number from `0` to `7` to specify the type of data in this row (see below)
- **Format**: A display format for the value, or a semi-colon-separated list of text values if **Type** is `1` or `4`
- **Value**: The entered value or a formula

- **SortKey**: Optional alpha-numeric text to sort by

- **Invisible**: Specifies if the row should be invisible

- **Ask**: Specifies if the row should be prompted for whenever a new shape instance is created

- **LangID**: The language identifier – for example, *US English* is 1033 and *UK English* is 2057

- **Calendar**: The number of the calendar locale – for example, *Western* is 0 and is used for dates

Types of Shape Data

There is only a small list of **Shape Data** types to choose from (see https://learn.microsoft.com/office/client-developer/visio/type-cell-shape-data-section), but here is a summary:

- 0: String or text. Optionally, you can format the display with the **Format** cell.

- 1: A fixed list. Enter the list as semi-colon-separated text in the **Format** cell. Users do need to choose an entry in the list.

- 2: Number. Optionally, you can format the display with the **Format** cell.

- 3: TRUE or FALSE.

- 4: A variable list. Here, you must enter the initial list as semi-colon-separated text in the **Format** column. Users do not need to choose from the list.

- 5: Date or time. There is a calendar popup but unfortunately, there is no clock to set the time. Use the **Format** column to set how the date and/or time is displayed. The earliest date possible is 1st Jan 1900.

- 6: Duration. This is stored as days and parts of a day but can be optionally displayed as elapsed weeks, days, hours, months, minutes, or seconds with the **Format** cell.

- 7: Currency. Optionally, you can format the display with the **Format** cell.

See https://learn.microsoft.com/office/client-developer/visio/about-date-time-and-duration-values for more information about date, time, and duration values.

We will now learn about a few techniques we can use to enhance our **Process** master shape, and then apply the same changes to the other flowchart shapes.

Adding description shape data to existing master shapes

The flowchart shapes are normally labeled with a terse description of the action that is needed, but we do not have a built-in **Shape Data** row to enter a longer description. There is a **ScreenTip** available on the **Insert** | **Text** ribbon group, which can be used to add multi-line text to each shape that appears when we hover the mouse over it. However, this text does not appear in a **Shape Data** row, so we cannot enter this text easily in the **Shape Data** window, nor can we easily extract it with reports or display it in Data Graphics.

Fortunately, we can create a new **Shape Data** row – let's call it `Description` – by using the **ShapeSheet Design | Rows | Insert** ribbon command, or the right-click menu's **Insert Row** command within the **Shape Data** section, as shown in the following screenshot:

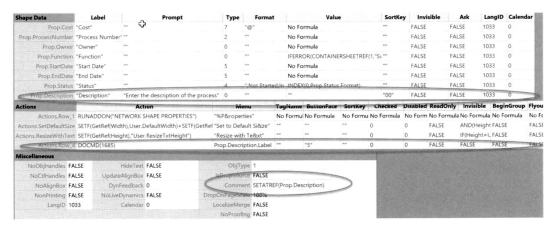

Figure 10.11 – Adding a Description Shape Data row

Notice that we have added `"Description"` as the **Label**, a longer **Prompt**, and `"00"` in the **SortKey** cell. The latter will ensure that the **Description** row is shown at the top of the **Shape Data** window.

> **Important note**
>
> Be careful when copying and pasting code from the internet because it can use the wrong characters. For example, opening slanting quote. and Closing slanting quote should be replaced with the " character.

We can also insert a new row into the **Actions** section, which we don't need to name, and enter a reference to **Label** in the **Menu** cell with `=Prop.Description.Label`.

Then, we can add a call to open the **ScreenTip** dialog with a formula that calls one of the **Visio** `visUICmds` (see `https://learn.microsoft.com/office/vba/api/visio.visuicmds` for more information) - for example, `=DOCMD(1685)`.

You can learn more about the **Actions** section at `https://learn.microsoft.com/office/client-developer/visio/actions-section`.

Then, we need to tie our `Description` **Shape Data** row with the **ScreenTip** dialog, which used to be called *Comments*, so we must add `=SETATREF(Prop.Description)` in the **Comment** cell of the **Miscellaneous** section.

This ensures that any text entered into the **ScreenTip** dialog is synchronized with any text that is entered into the **Description Shape Data** row, as shown here:

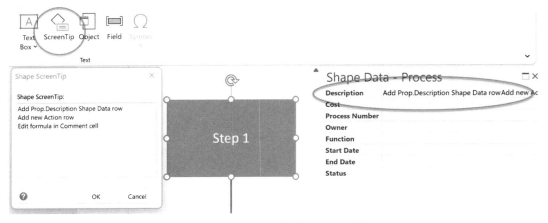

Figure 10.12 – Editing the ScreenTip dialog

Although the **Shape Data** rows only display a single line of text, you can paste in many lines from, say, Notepad. You can store approximately 64k characters in a **Shape Data | Value** cell.

The following screenshots show how the text in the **Comment** cell is shown when the mouse cursor is kept still over the shape for a short time. It also shows the right-click menu command, with an icon, for opening the **ScreenTip** dialog:

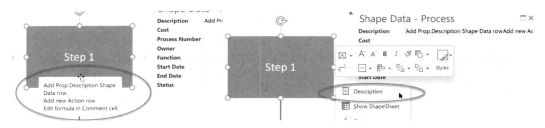

Figure 10.13 – Displaying the ScreenTip dialog and right mouse action

Shape Data rows do not always have to be editable, and we have the choice to hide them by setting the **Invisible** cell to TRUE or a formula that evaluates to TRUE. We can also keep them visible but prevent them from being edited, as we will now learn.

Adding Duration to shape data

All of the flowchart shapes have **Start Date** and **End Date Shape Data** rows, and we can add another row, **Duration**, to calculate the number of days between the two. We can use the **Define Shape Data** dialog to add, delete, or edit rows, but we cannot use it for entering formulas in the **Value** cell. The following screenshot shows the **Define Shape Data...** command, which is available from the right-click menu of the **Shape Data** window header:

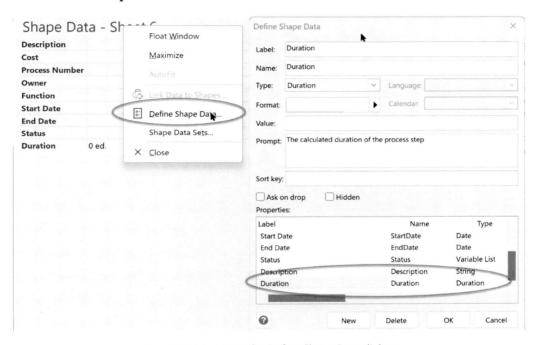

Figure 10.14 – Using the Define Shape Data dialog

So, we need to go back into the *ShapeSheet* to enter a formula for the **Value** cell:

Figure 10.15 – Entering a formula in the ShapeSheet

In this case, we protect the value by enclosing the calculation with the GUARD (...) function, as shown here:

```
=GUARD(Prop.EndDate-Prop.StartDate)
```

The **Define Shape Data** dialog can be used to enter the formula into the **Format** cell, as shown here:

Figure 10.16 – Selecting a format for the Duration type

Similarly, we can apply a format to the **Start Date** and **End Date** rows, as follows:

```
="{{d-MMM-yy}}"
```

With that, the **Duration** value has been calculated, and the user cannot accidentally edit the value, as shown here:

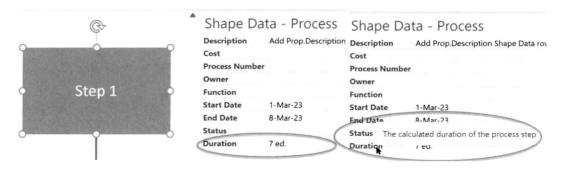

Figure 10.17 – Displaying calculated values

Now, we will look at some ways that the appearance of lines can automatically reflect data values.

Assigning line weight, style, or color by Owner

Each of the flowchart shapes has an *Owner* **Shape Data** row, which can be any entered value, but often, there is a list of potential owners that could be selected from a list. So, we can change the **Type** to 1, which is a fixed list. Then, we need to enter a semi-colon-separated list and start it with a semi-colon so that the first option is empty, which means none:

```
=";HR;IT;Facilities"
```

Whenever a value is selected from the fixed list, a formula is entered into the form by Visio, with the index number of the selected option in the list:

```
=INDEX(1,Prop.Owner.Format)
```

However, we want to use the index number in other formulas, so we will create a new row in the **User-defined Cells** section, which we have named `OwnerIndex`, with the following formula in the **Value** cell:

```
=LOOKUP(Prop.Owner,Prop.Owner.Format)
```

This will return the index number, which we can then use in the **Line Format** section, as shown here:

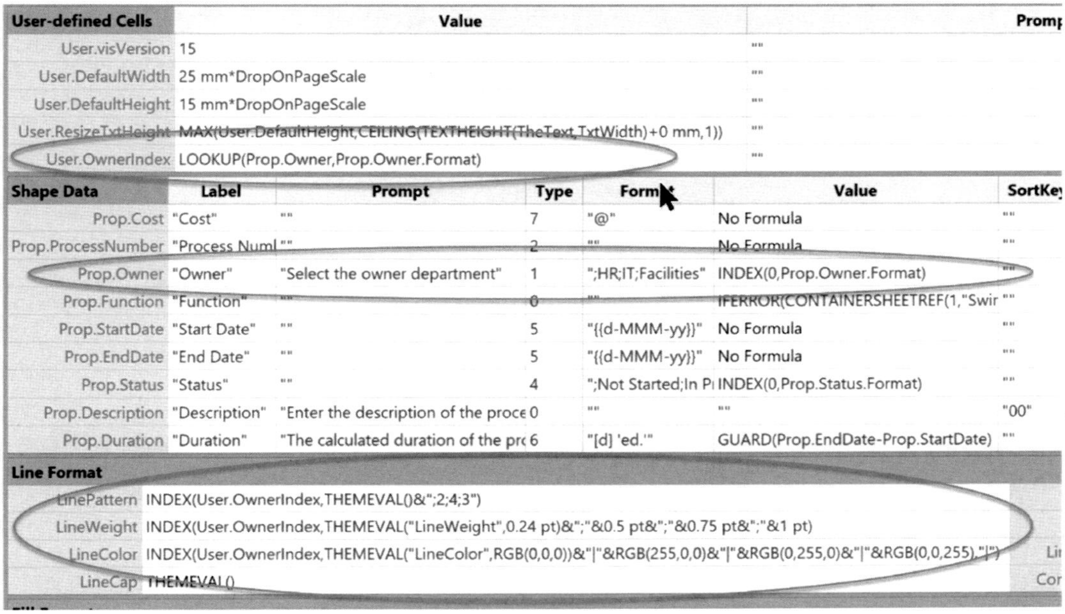

User-defined Cells		Value			Promp
User.visVersion	15			""	
User.DefaultWidth	25 mm*DropOnPageScale			""	
User.DefaultHeight	15 mm*DropOnPageScale			""	
User.ResizeTxtHeight	MAX(User.DefaultHeight,CEILING(TEXTHEIGHT(TheText,TxtWidth)+0 mm,1))			""	
User.OwnerIndex	LOOKUP(Prop.Owner,Prop.Owner.Format)			""	

Shape Data	Label	Prompt	Type	Format	Value	SortKey
Prop.Cost	"Cost"	""	7	"@"	No Formula	""
Prop.ProcessNumber	"Process Numl"	""	2	""	No Formula	""
Prop.Owner	"Owner"	"Select the owner department"	1	";HR;IT;Facilities"	INDEX(0,Prop.Owner.Format)	""
Prop.Function	"Function"	""	0	""	IFERROR(CONTAINERSHEETREF(1,"Swir	""
Prop.StartDate	"Start Date"	""	5	"{{d-MMM-yy}}"	No Formula	""
Prop.EndDate	"End Date"	""	5	"{{d-MMM-yy}}"	No Formula	""
Prop.Status	"Status"	""	4	";Not Started;In Pi	INDEX(0,Prop.Status.Format)	""
Prop.Description	"Description"	"Enter the description of the proce	0	""	""	"00"
Prop.Duration	"Duration"	"The calculated duration of the prc	6	"[d] 'ed.'"	GUARD(Prop.EndDate-Prop.StartDate)	""

Line Format	
LinePattern	INDEX(User.OwnerIndex,THEMEVAL()&";2;4;3")
LineWeight	INDEX(User.OwnerIndex,THEMEVAL("LineWeight",0.24 pt)&";"&0.5 pt&";"&0.75 pt&";"&1 pt)
LineColor	INDEX(User.OwnerIndex,THEMEVAL("LineColor",RGB(0,0,0))&"|"&RGB(255,0,0)&"|"&RGB(0,255,0)&"|"&RGB(0,0,255),"|")
LineCap	THEMEVAL()

Figure 10.18 – Changing the line format with the Owner selection

The **User-defined Cells** section is another section where we can add rows, but it does not have any visibility in the normal UI, so it is used for storing hidden values and calculations. See `https://learn.microsoft.com/office/client-developer/visio/user-defined-cells-section` for more information.

The **Line Format** section is mandatory, and we cannot add or delete any rows, but we can edit the formulas, which we have done as follows:

- **LinePattern**

  `=INDEX(User.OwnerIndex,THEMEVAL()&";2;4;3")`

- **LineWeight**

  `=INDEX(User.OwnerIndex,THEMEVAL("LineWeight",0.24 pt)&";"&0.5 pt&";"&0.75 pt&";"&1 pt)`

- **LineColor**

  `=INDEX(User.OwnerIndex,THEMEVAL("LineColor",RGB(0,0,0))&"|"&RGB(255,0,0)&"|"&RGB(0,255,0)&"|"&RGB(0,0,255),"|")`

These formulas still allow the user to change them in the UI, but we can prevent that by surrounding them with GUARD (…), just like we did for the `Prop.Duration` value. The first two formulas use the `User.OwnerIndex` value to return a value from a semi-colon-separated list. All line pattern values are numbers that can be read from the **Dash type** drop-down menu on the **Format Shape** panel. The default list separator is a semi-colon, but some languages use a semi-colon as a separator for RGB values. So, we have used a | character as the separator for **LineColor**, which means that we have to add a third argument to the INDEX (…) function.

The **Process** shape now has a different line format for each *Owner* option, as follows:

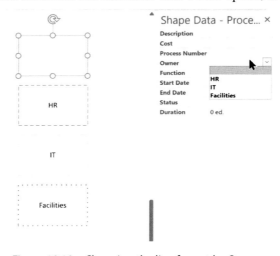

Figure 10.19 – Changing the line format by Owner

Another option would be to set the fill color of the **Process** shape, but we could also match the shape's color with the swimlane that it is within.

Matching the shape color with the swimlane color

If we look back at the **Shape Data** section in the *ShapeSheet* for the **Process** shape, we will see the following formula for the **Value** cell in the **Prop.Function** row:

```
=IFERROR(CONTAINERSHEETREF(1,"Swimlane")!User.VISHEADINGTEXT,"")
```

This is the formula that displays the header text of the *Swimlane* shape that the process is within. It does this by returning the value that is in the `User.visHeadingText` cell of the first shape with the `"Swimlane"` category that it is a member of. If it is not within a *Swimlane* shape, then it just displays an empty string.

Now that we know this, we can write a similar formula to get the fill color of the *Swimlane* shape, or just use the color of the current theme if it is not contained:

```
=IFERROR(CONTAINERSHEETREF(1,"Swimlane")!FillForegnd,THEMEVAL())
```

Now, we can put this into the **FillForegnd** cell in the **Fill Format** section of the *Process* master shape, as follows:

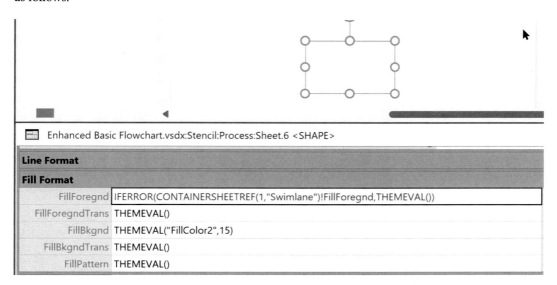

Figure 10.20 – Modifying the FillForegnd formula

Once we have saved the master shape, we can change the fill color of the *Swimlane* shapes, and any **Process** shapes will automatically adopt the color of the *Swimlane* shape when we move them from one to the other:

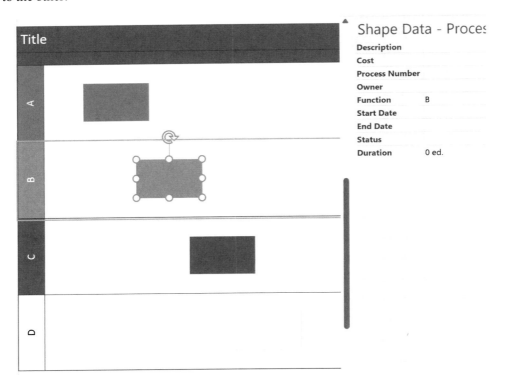

Figure 10.21 – Process shapes matching their Swimlane color

We have just seen how the **Process** shape knows which *Swimlane* it lies within, and then uses this to display the *Swimlane* header text and adopt the same color. The *Separator* (*Phase*) shapes are also containers perpendicular to the *Swimlane* shapes. We will learn how we can reference them in the next chapter.

Summary

In this chapter, we learned about some of the ways we can add smartness to Visio shapes by looking at some formulas that can be entered into the cells of a **ShapeSheet**. We saw how this is similar to entering formulas in Excel and learned how most shapes on a page inherit their behavior from the master shape that is kept in the normally hidden **Document Stencil** area.

In this book's next and final chapter, we will continue to explore other enhancements that we can make to the flowchart shapes so that we can provide custom templates that improve our efficiency and quality.

11

Improving the Provided Flowchart Shapes

In the previous chapter, we learned how Visio shapes get their smartness from the formulas entered in the ShapeSheet, and how we can customize master shapes to provide more functionality. In this chapter, we will continue with more customizations that can improve productivity and accessibility too.

We will learn how to display both the function and phase of shapes within cross-functional flowcharts and the label of the built-in container shapes. We will see how to utilize one of the desktop Visio add-ons to enhance callout shapes. Finally, we will look at ensuring that our diagrams are accessible to all.

In this chapter, we will cover these key topics:

- Adding the phase of swimlane to process shapes
- Inheriting the labels of built-in containers
- Automatically highlighting unglued connectors
- Adding configure options to callouts
- Maintaining callout associations on hidden layers
- Providing meaningful alternate text
- Automatically setting high contrast shape text
- Sharing custom templates

Technical requirements

These are the Microsoft apps that are utilized in this chapter, and we should have access to at least one of the Visio desktop editions:

- **Visio Plan 2**: Desktop subscription app
- **Visio Professional**: Windows one-time purchase
- **Visio Standard**: Windows one-time purchase

The customizations in this chapter can only be created with desktop Visio, but the modified Visio documents can be used in Visio for the web.

There are two files, `Accessibility in Visio Diagrams Enhanced.vsdx` and `Enhanced Cross-Functional Flowchart.vsdx`, available in the **GitHub** repository at `https://github.com/PacktPublishing/Visualize-complex-processes-with-Microsoft-Visio/tree/main/Chapter11`.

Adding the phase of swimlane to process shapes

We learned about the formula in the **Value** cell of the `Prop.Function` row, which displays the label text of the swimlane that the flowchart shapes are within. The formula is as follows:

```
=IFERROR(CONTAINERSHEETREF(1,"Swimlane")!User.VISHEADINGTEXT,"")
```

The **Swimlane** shape is actually a group shape with two sub-shapes, one of which is the colored rectangle shape with the label text in it. We are using the **Horizontal Cross-Functional Flowchart** sample in this section, which can be created from the **New | Templates | Flowchart | Cross-Functional Flowchart** template:

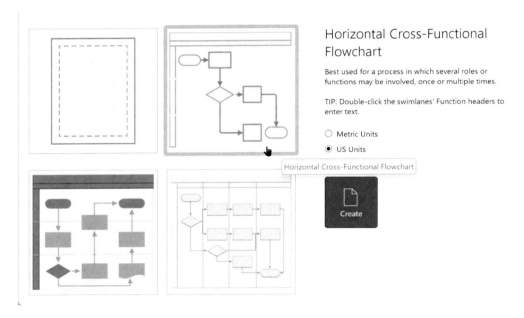

Figure 11.1 – Blank and sample diagrams

When we type the text on one of these **Swimlane** shapes, we add text into this sub-shape, not onto the group shape. In the following screenshot, we have the **Drawing Explorer** window open and we have expanded the tree view of **Swimlane.9**, which has two sub-shapes, **Sheet.10** and **Sheet.11**:

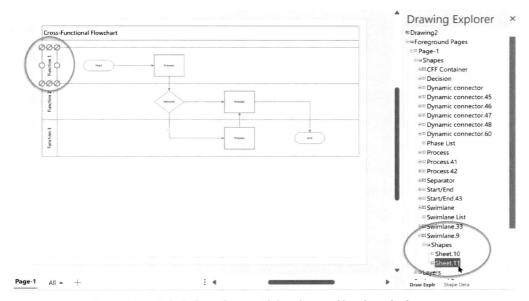

Figure 11.2 – A Swimlane shape with heading and border sub-shapes

---

Important note

Visio creates a unique sequential ID for every shape on the page that it is created in. This ID cannot be edited, and we can always reference a shape using the Sheet.xx form, where xx is this unique ID. Visio also automatically names every instance of a master shape created on a page with <master name>.xx, apart from the first instance, which is just the master name. This name can be edited, but the new name must be unique on the page.

The formula in the function **Shape Data** row of each flowchart shape works because there is a User.visHeadingText cell in the **Swimlane** shape that displays the text of the sub-shape with the following formula:

```
=SHAPETEXT(Sheet.xx!TheText)
```

The following screenshot of the **Swimlane** shape's ShapeSheet, **Sheet.9**, has the **Formula Tracing** window open too, which shows that the User.visHeadingText row in the **Value** cell is referenced by formulas in Prop.Function in the **Value** cells in the **Start/End** and **Process** shapes:

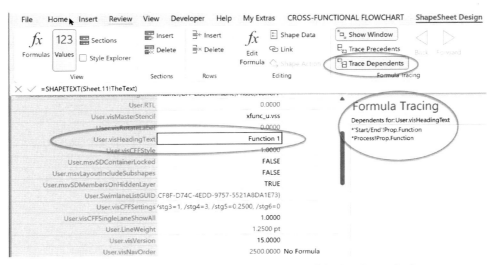

Figure 11.3 – A swimlane cell referencing the text of the heading sub-shape

The **ShapeSheet Design** tab is only visible when a ShapeSheet is selected, and the **Formula Tracing** window can be opened with the **ShapeSheet Design | Formula Tracing | Show Window** button.

> **Important note**
> Visio internally uses some special **User-defined Cells**, whose names mostly start with either `vis` or `msv`, although not exclusively. There is no definitive list of these reserved names, but whenever you see one, be aware that their values will change the behavior of the shape.

The swimlane shapes are not the only container shapes of which the **Process** shape and other flowchart shapes are members. The cross-functional flowcharts all contain at least one **Separator** shape that straddles all of the **Swimlane** shapes, which can be seen if the **CROSS-FUNCTIONAL FLOWCHART | Design | Show Separators** option is checked. These **Separator** shapes are very similar to the **Swimlane** shapes and contain border and heading sub-shapes, too, as shown in the next screenshot:

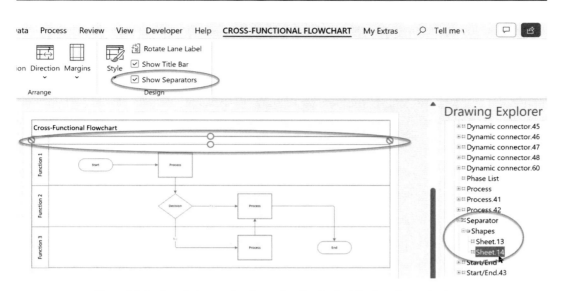

Figure 11.4 – A swimlane cell referencing the text of the heading sub-shape

We can add text to this default **Separator** shape, say `Phase Z`, and we can add more **Separator** shapes, as in the following screenshot, but the **Process** shapes do not display the label text of the **Separator** shape that they are within:

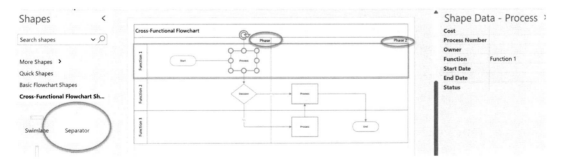

Figure 11.5 – A swimlane cell referencing the text of the heading sub-shape

However, we can add this functionality!

Adding User.visHeadingText to the Separator shapes

We just need to open the ShapeSheet of the **Separator** master shape in the document stencil with the **Edit Master Shape…** command from the right-click menu. Then we add a row, `visHeadingText`, into the **User-defined Cells** section.

However, we should ensure that there is a row named `visNavOrder` first. We do not need to add any formula because Visio will automatically add this row and a value itself, but experience says that we should add it first so Visio does not need to, and possibly mess up our values!

Then we need to identify which of the two sub-shapes contain the text that is typed in. This is best done with the **Developer | Show/Hide | Master Explorer** window open. Simply expand the branches in the tree view, and click on the shape names to see which one references the **Phase** text. It is **Sheet.6** in the following screenshot:

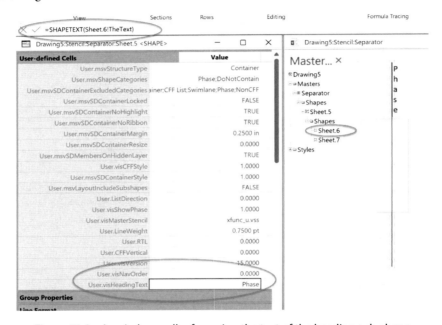

Figure 11.6 – A swimlane cell referencing the text of the heading sub-shape

Then we can enter the following formula into the new User.`visHeadingText` row in the **Value** cell:

```
=SHAPETEXT(Sheet.6!TheText)
```

This will surface the label text to the top shape of the group shape so that we can reference it from other shapes. We do not need to worry about any automatic shape renumbering that Visio will do when the phase shape instances are created because the formula will automatically be updated to use the `Sheet.x` identifier of the new shape.

Important note

We must always ensure that the **Match master by name on drop** option is checked, as previously stated in *Chapter 10*, so that we do not accidentally create duplicate masters.

We can now close and save the **Separator** master shape and turn our attention to the **Process** master shape.

Adding Phase to the flowchart shapes

We can now add a row named Phase to the **Shape Data** section, with **Type** = 0, and **Label** = Phase, as shown in the following screenshot:

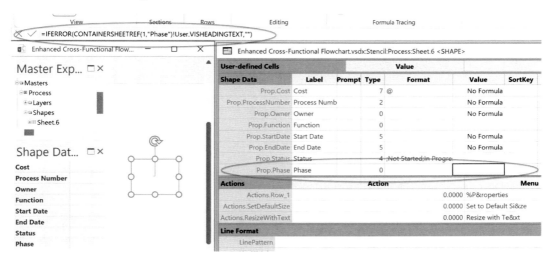

Figure 11.7 – A swimlane cell referencing the text of the heading sub-shape

Then we just need to add the following formula into the **Value** cell:

```
=IFERROR(CONTAINERSHEETREF(1,"Phase")!User.VISHEADINGTEXT,"")
```

This formula will display the text in the User.visHeadingText cell of the first container with the "Phase" category that it is a member of.

If we do not want the user to accidentally edit this value, then we can surround the formula with the GUARD() function, as shown here:

```
=GUARD(IFERROR(CONTAINERSHEETREF(1,"Phase")!User.VISHEADINGTEXT,""))
```

Viewing the Phase text in the Process shape

Now that we have made these enhancements, we can see every **Process** shape will display the **Phase** shape (the **Separator** shape) that it is within, in addition to the **Function** shape (the **Swimlane** shape), as shown in the following screenshot:

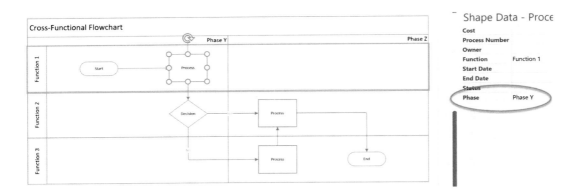

Figure 11.8 – Viewing Phase in a Process shape

We can now include **Phase** as a column in any export that we may want to do using **shape reports** or with custom code.

Now, we just need to add the `Phase` row to the **Shape Data** section of all of the other flowchart shapes!

We have seen how we can automatically propagate the label text into the `Function` and `Phase` rows in **Shape Data** from the **Swimlane** and **Separator** shapes that they are within, but what about the built-in containers that can be added from the **Insert** | **Diagram Parts** | **Container** gallery?

Inheriting the labels of built-in containers

These container shapes displayed in the gallery are just more master shapes from a built-in stencil. We can enhance them by adding similar properties to the **Swimlane** shapes. The following diagram has had the names of each one added:

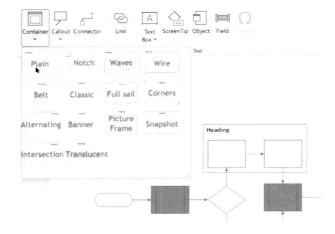

Figure 11.9 – The built-in container shapes

We can enhance as many of these as we want to, but first, we must copy the master from the built-in stencil to **Document Stencil**. To do this, we just need to add each one to a page in our document and then delete the copy on the page. This will leave the master in **Document Stencil**, as shown in the following screenshot:

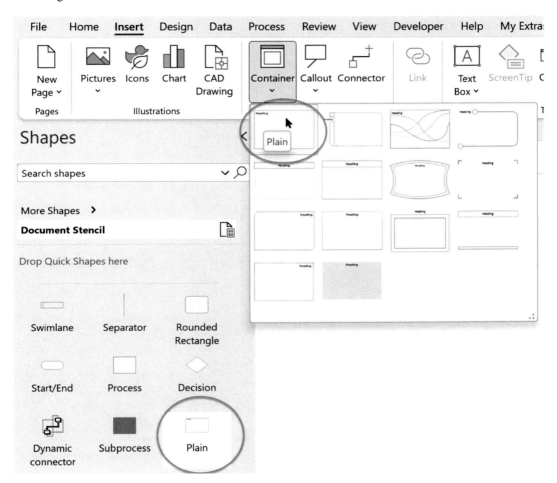

Figure 11.10 – Creating a copy of a built-in container master shape

Then we can edit this local copy of the master shape and add the `User.visNavOrder` and `User.visHeadingText` rows, as we did in the previous section for the **Separator** shape. Again, check which of the sub-shapes contain the text by using the **Master Explorer** window, as shown in the next screenshot:

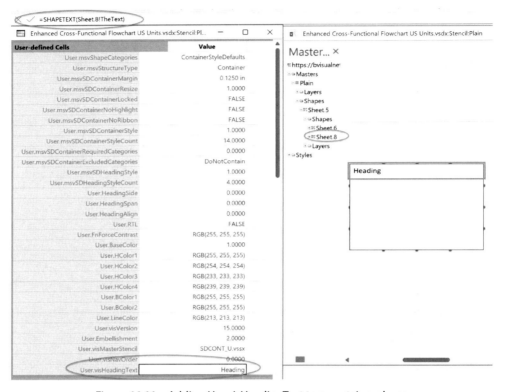

Figure 11.11 – Adding Uer.visHeadingText to a container shape

Now we have a choice to make about the category of the container shapes. We could edit the value in the `User.msvShapeCategories` row in the **Value** cell, or we could add another category with a semi-colon list separator. In this example, we have left the formula as follows:

```
="ContainerStyleDefaults"
```

> **Important note**
>
> Do not add **Swimlane** as a category for these containers because it is reserved for use by the Visio engine and can cause undesirable side effects.

We can now add another **Shape Data** row to our **Process** shape, which will inherit the label of any enhanced container that it is within:

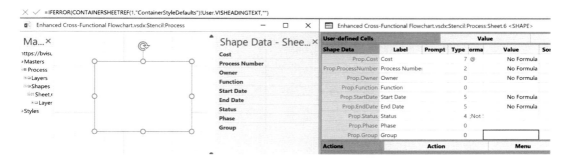

Figure 11.12 – Adding a Prop.Group row to the Shape Data section

This time, the formula for the **Value** cell in the Prop.Group row is as follows:

```
=IFERROR(CONTAINERSHEETREF(1,"ContainerStyleDefaults")!User.
VISHEADINGTEXT,"")
```

Now we can band our **Process** shapes together in a container and inherit the label in a **Shape Data** row, as shown in the following diagram:

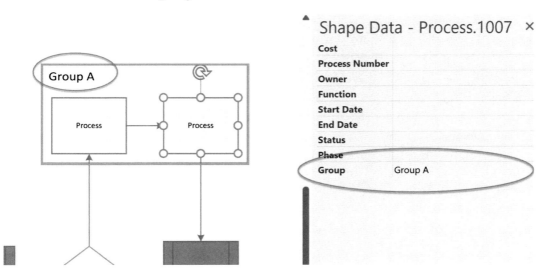

Figure 11.13 – Inheriting the label of a container shape

Moreover, we can use these container shapes within a cross-functional flowchart, where they can even span swimlanes or separators, as in the following screenshot:

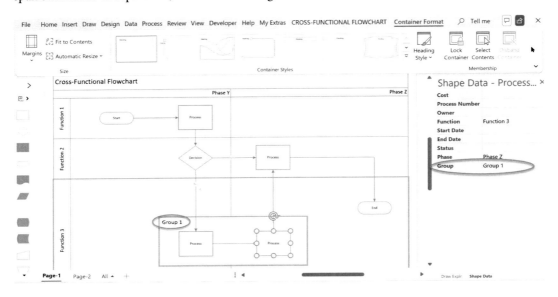

Figure 11.14 – Inheriting the label of a container shape in a cross-functional flowchart

Note that these containers have an extra ribbon tab, **Container Format**, which we can use to modify **Size**, **Container Styles**, or **Membership**.

So, our enhanced container shapes will be used from the standard ribbon now instead of the original ones supplied by Microsoft.

Important note

When we have created our enhanced masters in **Document Stencil**, we must not use **Remove unused master shapes** on the **Files Size Reduction** tab of the **Remove Hidden Information** dialog opened with the **File | Info | Check for Issues** button because it will delete our custom masters.

Now that we have an extra way of banding the **Process** shapes together, we will look at how to make connectivity errors obvious.

Automatically highlighting unglued connectors

The **Dynamic connector** master can be enhanced to be displayed as a red dashed line, for example, if it is not connected at both ends.

Again, we must edit the **Dynamic connector** master in local **Document Stencil** and consider the `LinePattern` and `LineColor` cells in the **Line Format** section and the `BegTrigger` and `EndTrigger` cells in the **Glue Info** section, as in the following screenshot:

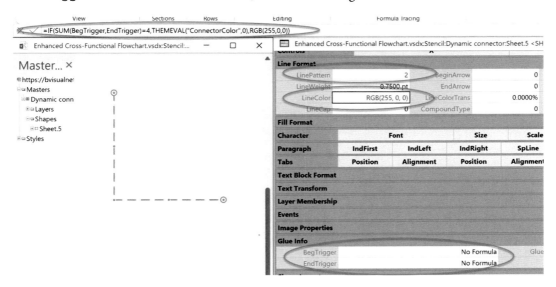

Figure 11.15 – Show unconnected lines with a red dash

It is possible to check whether the connector is connected at both ends by checking that the formulas that will be automatically assigned by Visio to the `BegTrigger` and `EndTrigger` cells each evaluate to 2.

The default formula for the `LinePattern` cell is as follows:

```
=THEMEVAL("ConnectorPattern")
```

Visio has an *ID* number for each of the built-in patterns, which you can see on the **Format Shape** panel. So, if we want it to be dashed, which is *ID* = 2, we can enter the following formula into the `LinePattern` cell:

```
=IF(SUM(BegTrigger,EndTrigger)=4,THEMEVAL("ConnectorPattern"),2)
```

Similarly, the default formula for the `LineColor` cell is as follows:

```
=THEMEVAL("ConnectorColor",0)
```

There are also *ID* numbers for the first 24 colors in a Visio document; for example, red is 2, but we can also use the RGB (...) formulas. Therefore, we can make the lines turn red if they are not connected with the following formula in the `LineColor` cell:

```
=IF(SUM(BegTrigger,EndTrigger)=4,THEMEVAL("ConnectorColor",0),
RGB(255,0,0))
```

Then, when we have saved the **Dynamic connector** master, we can see if any connectors are not connected at each end, as shown in the following screenshot:

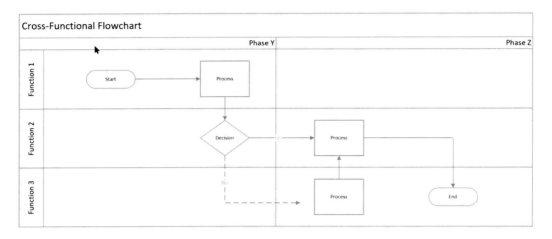

Figure 11.16 – Easily spotting unconnected connectors

This small change makes it easier to spot issues.

Adding configuration options to callouts

Desktop Visio also has a number of built-in callout shapes, as shown in the following screenshot, with their master names overlaid:

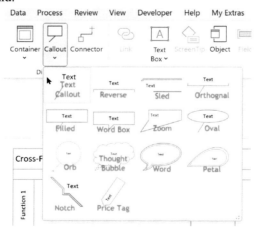

Figure 11.17 – The built-in callouts

There is also a **More Shapes | Visio Extras | Callouts** stencil that has three interesting master shapes at the very bottom. These three master shapes are called **Custom callout 1**, **Custom callout 2**, and **Custom callout 3**, and use a Visio add-on called **cc** that will open the **Configure callout** dialog , where you can choose which of the **Shape Data** rows to display from the associated shape:

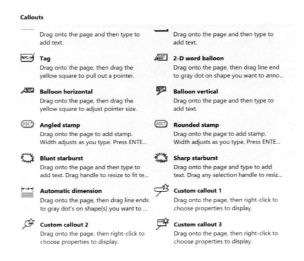

Figure 11.18 – The Callouts stencil

We can enhance the built-in callouts in a similar way to how we enhanced the built-in containers. We just need to bring a copy of the master into our document and then edit the master shape, as shown in the following screenshot:

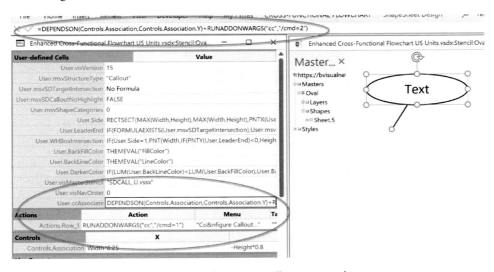

Figure 11.19 – Enhancing a callout master shape

In this case, we should add a `visNavOrder` row into the **User-defined Cells** section, then add one named `ccAssociate` and then add the following formula to its **Value** cell:

```
=DEPENDSON(Controls.Association,Controls.
Association.Y)+RUNADDONWARGS("cc","/cmd=2")
```

We can then insert an **Actions** section and add a row with the following formula in the **Action** cell:

```
=RUNADDONWARGS("cc","/cmd=1")
```

Then add the following formula into the **Menu** cell:

```
="Co&nfigure Callout..."
```

This will provide us with a right-click menu command to open the **Configure callout** dialog, as shown in the following screenshot:

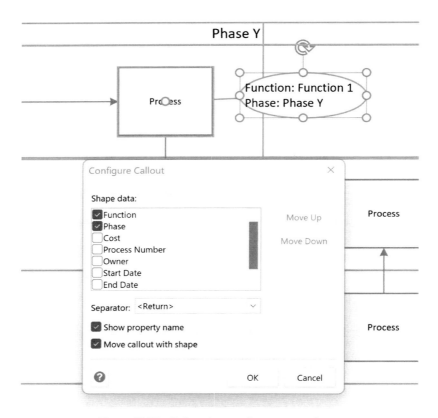

Figure 11.20 – Enhancing a callout master shape

The dialog will also pop up whenever we associate the **callout** shape with another shape by dragging the yellow control point onto it.

Maintaining callout associations on hidden layers

We should take the opportunity to fix an issue with the built-in callout shapes. They will lose their association with other shapes if their layer is made invisible. To prevent this, we can add a missing **User-defined Cells** row called msvSDMembersOnHiddenLayer, as shown in the following screenshot:

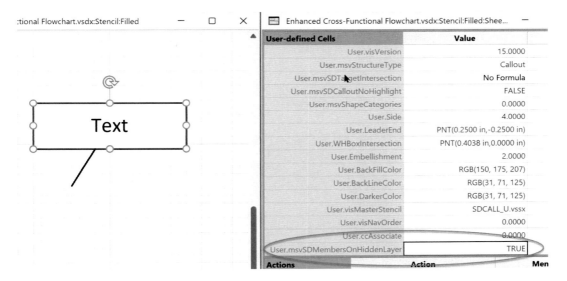

Figure 11.21 – Preventing disassociation if a layer is made invisible

We just need to enter TRUE into the **Value** cell. This will ensure that the callout stays associated even if the layer is made invisible.

We can control the appearance of flowchart diagrams by changing the visibility of notes and callouts and printing or viewing flowcharts with the **Layer Properties** dialog opened from **Home | Editing | Layers**.

Making diagrams accessible

Our process flowcharts should be accessible to all, and there are a few ways that we can try to achieve this in the web or the desktop version. Desktop Visio has an **Accessibility** panel that is opened from the **Review | Accessibility | Check Accessibility** button. This will list some of the errors for missing **alternative text** (**alt text**), but it does not address poor contrast between the text and its background, nor does it assess the logical order of tabbing around the pages. So, we may need to do this manually or come up with ways to fix these issues automatically.

The following flowchart describes the steps required if we start with Visio for the web or desktop Visio:

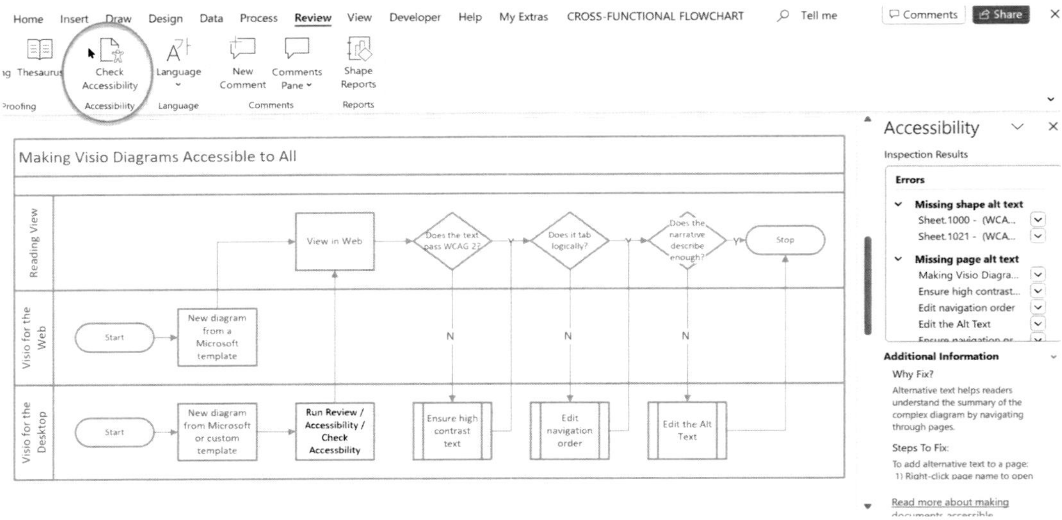

Figure 11.22 – Making diagrams accessible

The *Web Content Accessibility Guidelines* (see `https://www.w3.org/TR/WCAG`) should be viewed to understand what we should need to consider. In particular, we will go through the following:

- The contrast between any text and its background to improve legibility
- The tab order of shapes on the page to provide meaningful navigation
- The alternative narrated text when a shape is focused on

There is also a **Check Accessibility** button on the **Shape** tab in Visio for the web, which opens a similar panel, but also directs us to edit in desktop Visio to fix most issues.

Automatically setting high-contrast shape text

The best contrast between the text and the background is achieved with black text with a white background, but this is not always the most engaging or informative presentation, so we may want to use some color. Some built-in themes do provide a suitable contrast between the text and the shape background, but some do not. Also, we may want to use color to highlight different **Shape Data** values or other information. If we use dark background colors on the shapes, we will need to change the text color to white to ensure better contrast. We should use a solid fill color in our shapes because patterned backgrounds make it more difficult to read the text. We could manually change the text color from black to white, but it is more efficient to automate this transition.

The following flowchart describes the process for these design decisions:

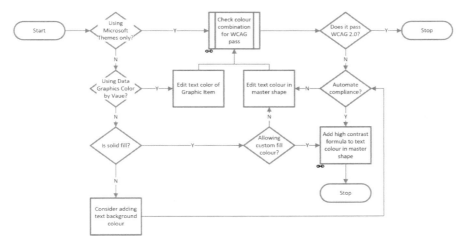

Figure 11.23 – Deciding on high-contrast text

The website at `https://contrast-ratio.com` can be used to manually check when text should be changed from black to white, but we can ensure that the text color automatically changes between black and white with some changes to the ShapeSheet of our **Process** shape and other master shapes.

The following screenshot highlights the changes made to the ShapeSheet and the formula for the new `User.fnHighContrast` cell is so long that it is best entered using the **ShapeSheet Design | Editing | Edit Formula** dialog:

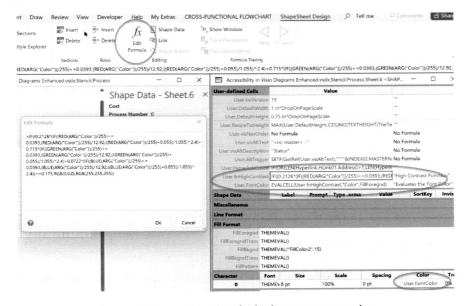

Figure 11.24 – Automating the high-contrast text color

This formula for the new **User-defined Cells** row named `fnHighContrast` can be entered into the **Edit Formula** dialog with multiple lines because Visio will automatically remove them when we close it:

```
=IF(
(
  0.2126*(IF((RED(ARG("Color")))/255)<=0.0393,
  (RED(ARG("Color")))/255)/12.92,
  ((RED(ARG("Color")))/255)+0.055)/1.055)^2.4)
  +0.715*(IF((GREEN(ARG("Color")))/255)<=0.0393,
  (GREEN(ARG("Color")))/255)/12.92,
  ((GREEN(ARG("Color")))/255)+0.055)/1.055)^2.4)
  +0.0722*(IF((BLUE(ARG("Color")))/255)<=0.0393,
  (BLUE(ARG("Color")))/255)/12.92,
  ((BLUE(ARG("Color")))/255)+0.055)/1.055)^2.4)
)
>=0.175,RGB(0,0,0),RGB(255,255,255))
```

The preceding formula is called by a formula in another new **User-defined Cells** row named `FontColour` with the following formula:

```
=EVALCELL(User.fnHighContrast,"Color",FillForegnd)
```

So, this formula passes the color in the **FillForend** cell and evaluates the red, green, and blue components of the color to return either black or white color.

The **Color** cell in the **Character** section is then updated with reference to this color with the following formula:

```
=User.FontColour
```

The following screenshots show how the text color changes automatically from black to white when the background fill color is darkened:

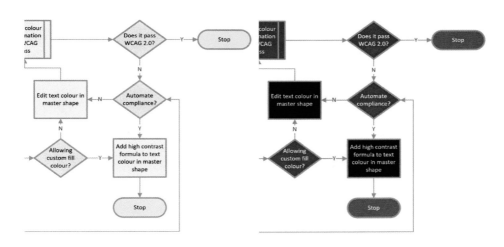

Figure 11.25 – Text color changes automatically with background color changes

Setting the tab order

We briefly mentioned navigation order in *Chapter 3*, and how we can open the **Diagram Navigator** panel from **View** | **Show** | **Task Panes** | **Navigation**, as shown in the following screenshot:

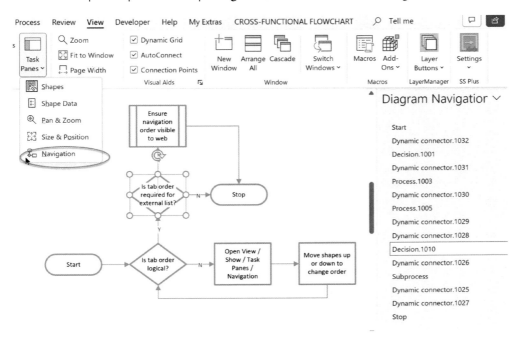

Figure 11.26 – Editing the tab order of pages

Unfortunately, there is no easy way of automatically re-ordering the tab order. It is initially in the order that the shapes are dropped on the page, but that may not be the most logical order to tab around the page. Moreover, the same shape cannot be in two positions in the order, so we have to choose which direction to initially leave a decision diamond. All we need to do is select a shape in the **Diagram Navigation** panel and move it vertically to a new position.

One enhancement we can do in the ShapeSheet is to add an invisible **Shape Data** row to expose the **Navigation Order** value for *Data Graphics* or reports:

Shape Data	Label	Prompt	Type	orma	Value	iortKe	Invisibl
Prop.Cost	"Cost"	""	7	"@"	No Formula	""	FALSE
Prop.ProcessNumber	"Process Numbe	""	2	""	GUARD(User.visNavOrder)	""	FALSE
Prop.Owner	"Owner"	""	0	""	No Formula	""	FALSE
Prop.Function	"Function"	""	0	""	IFERROR(CONTAINERSHEETREF	""	FALSE
Prop.StartDate	"Start Date"	""	5	""	No Formula	""	FALSE
Prop.EndDate	"End Date"	""	5	""	No Formula	""	FALSE
Prop.Status	"Status"	""	4	""	";Not INDEX(0,Prop.Status.Format)	""	FALSE
Prop.visNavOrder	"Navigation Ord	"Read-only	2	"0"	GUARD(User.visNavOrder)	""	TRUE

Figure 11.27 – Editing the tab order of pages

The =GUARD(User.visNavOrder) formula in the **Value** cell can only be entered if we have previously added the visNavOrder row in the **User-defined Cells** section.

This new **Shape Data** row has also been named visNavOrder in the preceding screenshot, and given a **Type** cell value of 2 (numeric), with a **Format** cell value of "0", and an **Invisible** cell value of TRUE.

Providing meaningful alternate text

When a screen reader is used and a shape is focused, it narrates the **Alt Text Title**, and some will then proceed to narrate the **Description** field text if the user pauses long enough. This can really help visually impaired users understand a diagram. Therefore, we should take some effort to provide meaningful alt text for each of our significant shapes and pages. This can be done manually with the third tab of the **Format Shape** panel. Unfortunately, this tab currently looks like a **Size & Position** icon and even the tooltip says it is, but it is the **Alt Text** panel, as shown in the following screenshot:

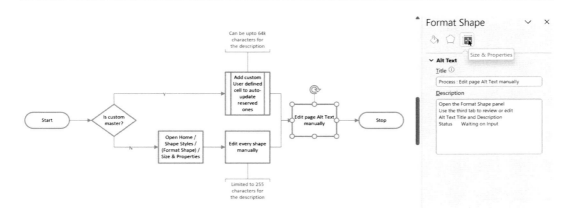

Figure 11.28 – Viewing or editing alt text

This panel can be opened from the right-click menu of a shape, and there is also an **Alt Text** tab on the **Page Setup** dialog.

> **Important note**
> The built-in Windows narrator settings can be opened by pressing the Windows logo key + *Ctrl* + *N*.

There is a way to automate the **Alt Text** panel **Title** and **Description** fields from **Shape Data** and other properties of a shape. This is done with another enhancement to the ShapeSheet of the master shape, where we need to add three new rows, `visAltText`, `visAltDescription`, and `AltTrigger`, as shown as follows:

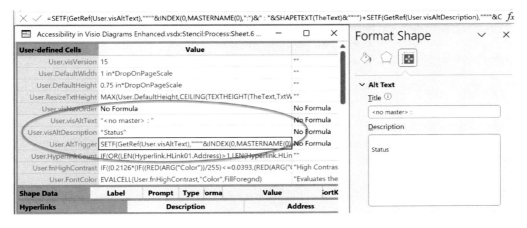

Figure 11.29 – Formula to automatically update alt text

User.visAltText is a reserved name and is displayed in the **Title** textbox on the **Alt Text** panel. User.visAltDescription is also a reserved name and is displayed in the **Description** multi-line textbox on the **Alt Text** panel. Visio will automatically add them to the shape instance if we use the **Alt Text** panel manually to enter text, so we will get control of them by inserting them into the master shape.

The AltTrigger row could be named differently, but it is handy to distinctively name rows that push data into other cells. It has a formula with two SETF(...) functions that copy the values from other cells or functions to another:

```
=SETF(GetRef(User.visAltText),
""""&INDEX(0,MASTERNAME(0),":")&"  :  "&SHAPETEXT(TheText)&"""")+
SETF(GetRef(User.visAltDescription),
""""&Comment&CHAR(13)&CHAR(10)&
Prop.Status.Label&CHAR(9)&Prop.Status&"""")
```

The first SETF(...) function pushes the first part of the value returned by the MasterName(0) function, and the shape text, separated with a colon, into the User.visAltText cell.

The second SETF(...) function pushes the **ScreenTip** text along with the label and then a tab (Char(9)) and a Status value, separated with a newline (Char(13)&Char(10)), into the User.visAltDescription cell.

Sharing custom templates

We have now learned how to enhance the existing master shapes in Visio to add extra functionality and accessibility. Of course, we need to apply these enhancements to all of the master shapes in **Document Stencil**, which we can then hide and leave the **Basic Flowchart Shapes** and **Cross-Functional Flowchart Shapes** stencils visible and docked. We can then save our custom Visio document as a template, and give it to others to add to their Custom Office Templates folder, for example. They can then create new Visio diagrams from this template and will have all the enhanced features. These features, apart from the **Configure Callout** dialog, will also work in Visio for the web because they are just ShapeSheet functions.

Alternatively, the custom template can be added as a content type in SharePoint, which is beyond the scope of this book, or it can be added to the list of templates in **Teams** and **SharePoint** as described in *Chapter 8*.

However, in desktop Visio, we can also use the **File Locations** dialog opened from **File | Options | Advanced | General | File Locations**, as shown in the following screenshot:

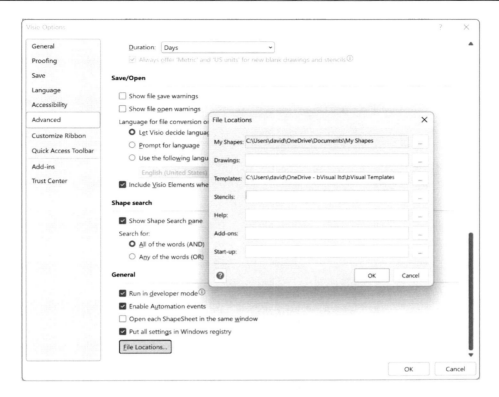

Figure 11.30 – Editing File Locations in desktop Visio

This will have the **My Shapes** option pre-filled during the installation of Visio, and this is a quick location to store any custom stencils in. Optionally, custom stencils can be located in a path entered into the **Stencils** text box. In this example, we have saved our custom template, with a `.vstx` extension, into a SharePoint document library, **Process Templates**, within another, **bVisual Templates**:

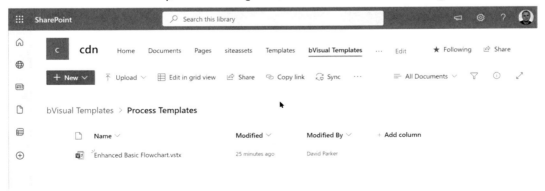

Figure 11.31 – Store custom templates in a sub-folder

The parent folder has been saved as a desktop shortcut to **OneDrive**, with the drop-down menu from the three dots circled above, and this path was entered in the **File Locations** dialog in *Figure 11.30*. Notice that the sub-folders, or SharePoint document libraries, appear as folder icons in the **Templates** tab of **File | New** in the desktop Visio **user interface** (**UI**):

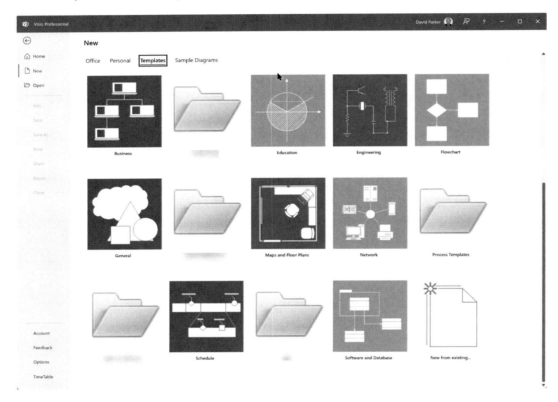

Figure 11.32 – Custom template folders in desktop Visio

This technique does not require the Visio template to be in SharePoint, but it is a useful way to make the file available within your organization. We can also use a network-share folder, but it is good practice to point the file location to a folder with the templates in sub-folders. If we do not do this, then the custom templates will appear directly on the **Templates** tab in the Visio UI.

We can make a more professional-looking custom template by entering a value in the **Title** field and text in the **Comments** field in the **File | Info | Properties** dialog:

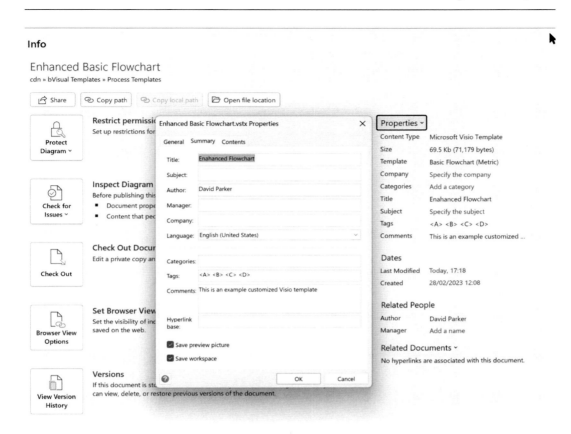

Figure 11.33 – Template title and comments in desktop Visio

We can also provide a custom thumbnail for the template to display in the Visio UI.

Open the ShapeSheet of the **Document** option using the **Developer | Shape Design | Show ShapeSheet** drop-down menu, as shown in the following screenshot:

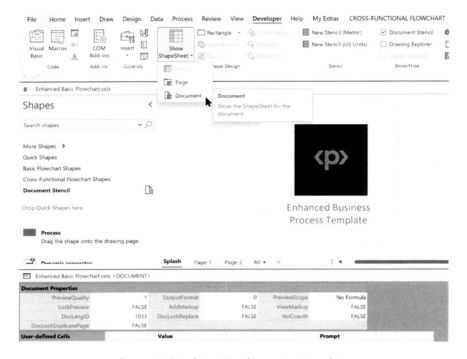

Figure 11.34 – Preparing the custom template

These are the steps to save the custom template with a custom thumbnail image:

1. Insert a new page and move it to the first position.

2. Make the page square.

3. Add image and text to create the thumbnail.

4. Change the **PreviewQuality** value to 1 (*detailed*).

5. Change the **LockPreview** value to False.

6. Close the **Document Stencil** dialog.

7. Save the template.

8. Change the **LockPreview** value to True.

9. Optionally delete the first page.

10. Save the template again.

11. Close the template.

Once this is done, you will see the template thumbnail, title, and comments in the custom folder in desktop Visio, as shown here:

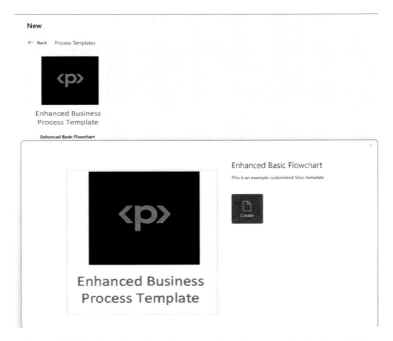

Figure 11.35 – Creating New from a custom template in desktop Visio

There is another way to install custom templates, and stencils, to make them appear in the desktop Visio UI, but that requires creating an installation package. This method is beyond the scope of this book.

Summary

We are at the end of this book now, and we have learned how to create process flow diagrams with both the web and desktop editions of Visio. We have learned how we can create flowcharts automatically from an Excel table, and we can save diagrams back into an Excel table. We have seen how we can create a **Power Automate Flow** from a BPMN diagram, and how we can export to Word, PowerPoint, and Excel. We have learned how can enhance existing master shapes and distribute them to others in a custom template. We have done all of this without using any **Visual Basic for Applications** (**VBA**), built into desktop Visio, or any external programming application such as C# or vb.net. We have just scratched the surface of the smartness that Visio is capable of, but this book has to finish somewhere!

Author's note

I started using Visio in my consulting work in the mid-1990s because of its flexibility to be adapted for almost any data visualizing requirement. I am still learning more as it is improved and extended beyond Windows devices.

If you would like to learn more tips and tricks to enhance Visio, please check out my other books for Packt and read my articles at `blog.bvisual.net`.

David Parker, MVP, April 2023

Index